LIBRARY
NEWPORT
R.I.

Anonymous Gift

Also by Jack Holland

FICTION

The Prisoner's Wife

Druid Time

The Fire Queen

Walking Corpses

NONFICTION

Too Long a Sacrifice:
Life and Death in Northern Ireland
Since 1969

The American Connection:
U.S. Guns, Money, and Influence
in Northern Ireland

INLA:
Deadly Divisions *(with Henry McDonald)*

Phoenix: Policing the Shadows:
The Secret War Against Terrorism
in Northern Ireland
(with Susan Phoenix)

POETRY

Sean Juan, Cantos I and II

HOPE AGAINST HISTORY

JACK HOLLAND

HOPE AGAINST HISTORY

THE COURSE OF CONFLICT IN

NORTHERN IRELAND

A JOHN MACRAE BOOK

HENRY HOLT AND COMPANY • NEW YORK

Henry Holt and Company, LLC
Publishers since 1866
115 West 18th Street
New York, New York 10011

Henry Holt® is a registered trademark of
Henry Holt and Company, LLC.

Copyright © 1999 by Jack Holland

All rights reserved.
Published in Canada by Fitzhenry & Whiteside Ltd.,
195 Allstate Parkway, Markham, Ontario L3R 4T8.

Library of Congress Cataloging-in-Publication Data
Holland, Jack, 1947–
Hope against history : the course of conflict
in Northern Ireland / Jack Holland.—1st ed.
p. cm.
"A John Macrae book."
Includes index.
ISBN 0-8050-6087-1 (acid-free paper)
1. Northern Ireland—History. 2. Social conflict—
Northern Ireland—History. I. Title.
DA990.U46H63 1999
941.6—dc21 99-20540
CIP

Henry Holt books are available for special promotions
and premiums. For details contact: Director, Special Markets.

First Edition August 1999

Designed by Victoria Hartman

Printed in the United States of America
All first editions are printed on acid-free paper. ∞

1 3 5 7 9 10 8 6 4 2

DA
990
.U46
H63
1999

JUL 29 1999 B

113255

In memory of Martha Holland
(1910–1998)
and Margaret McNicholl
(1947–1998)

Too late for tears: thinking.
—John Berryman, *Dream Songs*

CONTENTS

ACKNOWLEDGMENTS

Much of the material that went into the making of this book was gathered over the course of many years of reporting on and writing about Northern Ireland. To all those who spoke to me, gave of their time, and shared their information, I record my gratitude, though most cannot be named.

I would like to thank David McKittrick for permission to use our unpublished history of the UDA, *The Assassins*. My thanks are due to "Joseph," who has proven to be an invaluable guide to the paramilitary underworld. My thanks, too, to Dr. Susan Phoenix for her generous assistance. And once again I, like so many others who have written about Northern Ireland, must say thank you to Yvonne Murphy at the Linen Hall Library, Belfast, for her unstinting efforts to uncover needed matter.

On a more personal note, I would like to thank Marcia Rock for her helpful criticism of the manuscript. To my wife, Dr. Mary Hudson, I can only repeat what I have said before in so many acknowledgments, that without her it would not have been possible.

PROLOGUE: AN IRISH RIP VAN WINKLE GOES TO WASHINGTON

IF AN IRISH Rip Van Winkle had been roused from his slumbers after twenty years and transported to Washington, D.C., on the evening of Saint Patrick's Day 1995, he would have scarcely believed what he saw.

Unusually warm weather had brought the daffodils out in bloom, and the capital was bathed in the russet colors of sunset. Spring had come early, and the clement weather had already encouraged a few people to cast off their jackets as they strolled along the city's wide boulevards. But it would not have been the weather that arrested the attention of the visitor transported from Ireland's recent troubled past.

President Bill Clinton, in his third year in office, was holding an Irish party to celebrate the feast day of Ireland's patron saint and its national holiday. In the small theater in the East Wing of the White House, under three ornate chandeliers, the Irish tenor Frank Patterson sang the sentimental Irish parlor song "The Rose of Tralee." The party had become a tradition since the days of Ronald Reagan. Clinton, however, had taken the occasion beyond the level of a sentimental get-together and celebration of shamrockery, though it retained something of those elements.

Even before he became president, the former governor of Arkansas had committed himself to putting the Ulster question on his administration's agenda. Most other presidents before him had preferred to avoid the issue. It was seen as a political quagmire in which the United States should not become stuck. As one U.S. senator said in 1978, "It's too hard to tell the good guys from the bad guys." Even Presidents Jimmy Carter and Ronald Reagan, who had addressed the problem, had done so intermittently and certainly did not allow it to assume anything like the importance it was to acquire during Clinton's first term in office. Certainly, for Clinton, there was a political calculation involved. He was anxious to solidify support among the so-called Reagan Democrats—conservative, mostly Catholic, Irish-American Democrats who had been appalled at what they viewed as the ultraliberal agenda of their party in the 1980s. Ireland was an issue that would strike a chord with them. But the president's Irish agenda was driven primarily by his own interest in the situation: He had been in England almost thirty years earlier when the first Northern Ireland civil rights demonstrators were marching in Belfast and Derry to protest discrimination against Catholics in housing and jobs.

Facing the low stage on which Patterson sang, a hushed crowd listened intently. But they were not the usual gathering of prominent Irish and Irish-American politicians, businessmen, and entertainers who are invited for the Saint Patrick's Day shenanigans in Washington—far from it. This was a historical occasion, one that would make our Rip Van Winkle from across the ocean rub his eyes in disbelief, perhaps thinking he had been placed under a charm.

Directly behind the table where the president and Mrs. Clinton sat next to Paul Newman and his wife, Joanne Woodward, sat a tall, lean, bearded man with his hands folded in front of him. The Irish Rip Van Winkle would have recognized him as Gerry Adams, president of Sinn Fein, the political arm of the outlawed Provisional Irish Republican Army. Twenty years before, when Rip Van Winkle went to sleep, Mr. Adams was locked up in Long Kesh Prison near Belfast, jailed as a leading member of the Belfast Provisionals. Since the early 1970s, Adams had been a key figure in the campaign of the Belfast PIRA, an organization dedicated to driving the British government out of Northern Ireland and uniting the country as one socialist republic. Now the picture of the bearded, beady-eyed intellectual, he had risen through the IRA ranks to a national leadership position and had taken command of its political structure, Sinn Fein, as well.

In those guerrilla days, Adams looked for support to the Sandinistas, the PLO, and the ANC, and was more accustomed to ballads of revolution and rebellion than parlor songs served up at Saint Patrick's Day galas in America, a country from which he had been barred for decades on the grounds that he was associated with terrorism. But thanks to Bill Clinton, in January 1994, Adams had been granted the first of several visas to visit New York City, which he did for three days. Throughout that brief period he received an enthusiastic welcome from the Irish-American honchos of the corporate world, among others, who made it clear that their support was ready for a genuine peace move; it depended on a vital decision from the Provisional IRA to end its twenty-five-year campaign of violence.

Adams's reception in the United States helped convince him that the time had come to press for a more peaceful approach to resolving the Ulster crisis than the one with which he and his organization had been traditionally associated. What Adams did not tell his Irish-American backers was that the Provisionals were in desperate straits, their campaign increasingly frustrated by the success of the undercover counterterror strategy of the security forces. They were looking for a way out, one that would allow them a graceful exit without being forced to admit defeat. This could not be achieved without compromise, of course, and if it meant joining in a singalong to Frank Patterson's rendition of "God Bless America," so be it. The former guerrilla chief could get dewy-eyed about it with the most patriotic American.

The day before Saint Patrick's Day, Adams had shaken the hand of President Clinton at a lunch with Newt Gingrich, the Speaker of the House. He was to do so again that evening. On neither occasion were photographers present to record the historic conjunction of violent Irish republicanism and the political establishment of the most powerful nation on earth.

Adams's visit of March 1995 was his fourth to the United States. Not only had the visa ban been lifted, but the authorities now allowed him and his colleagues in Sinn Fein to fund-raise in America—a change that would have been unimaginable twenty years earlier when the energy of federal government agencies was devoted to blocking money and arms being sent from PIRA's U.S. support network to the gunmen and bombers ambushing troops and police in the lanes and backstreets of Ulster.

Not far from where Mr. Adams stood listening to Patterson sing "The Rose of Tralee," our freshly awakened visitor from the past might have picked out a pallid, round-faced young man staring straight in front of him. Gary McMichael was the head of the Ulster Democratic Party, the political wing of the Ulster Defense Association, at one time the largest paramilitary group in Ulster dedicated to keeping it British. He did not look at Adams, nor did Adams look at him. Indeed, they studiously avoided eye contact. Twenty years ago the UDP did not exist, but the UDA did and was engaged in a vicious sectarian war directed mainly at Northern Ireland's Catholic population, which left hundreds of them dead. The UDA killed in the belief that such terror would frighten Catholics into abandoning their support for the Provisional IRA and its goals. If Rip Van Winkle did not recognize Gary McMichael at first glance, he would have noted, if he was an astute observer, a certain familiarity about the young man's appearance. Gerry Adams certainly would have. Mr. Adams's colleagues in the Provisional IRA had murdered Gary's father, John, a leading member of the UDA, in December 1987.

At a table not far from McMichael sat Joe English, a short bullterrier of a man with clipped spiky hair. When Rip Van Winkle had fallen asleep, English was no more than a local activist in the UDA's ruthless north Belfast death squads, which helped make that part of the capital city of Northern Ireland perhaps the most dangerous place in the country. By the early 1990s he had become the chairman of the organization. Under his leadership there was an upsurge in UDA violence against Catholics, which had prompted one leading Belfast IRA man to lament, "We were being slaughtered." Roughly speaking, for every British soldier the IRA killed between 1992 and 1994, the UDA killed eight Catholics. But violence seemed far from English's mind that evening as he sipped his Irish whiskey, seemingly enraptured by the Victorian melody that held the guests in the East Wing in its thrall.

Our Irish Rip Van Winkle would have begun scratching his head at this point, looking around for explanations as to how such dedicated enemies in an ancient war had found themselves in Washington as guests of an American president at that most green of occasions. Searching for answers, he might have approached the squat, bespectacled, middle-aged man who sat not far from the Clintons. John Hume, the leader of Ulster's largest nationalist party, the Social Democratic and Labor Party, had the agitated look of a man in a hurry, a slightly disheveled, untidy appearance that reminded one of the schoolteacher he was before becoming involved in the Northern Ireland civil rights movement thirty years earlier. Since those days of street protests and riots, which first drew the world's attention to the Ulster situation, the former teacher of French had earned a reputation as a fearless defender of basic democratic rights for Northern Ireland's Catholic minority and as an opponent of the paramilitary organizations like the UDA and the Provisional IRA. Once upon a time, McMichael's colleagues in the UDA had slashed to death Senator Paddy Wilson, one of Hume's fellow SDLP members, leaving his body and that of Irene Andrews, a woman friend, mutilated with knife wounds. One of the killers involved had described to a reporter how thrusting a knife into her breasts was like stabbing a pillow.

The Provisional IRA had also targeted SDLP party members, whom it regarded as collaborators, ready to compromise with the British government in its attempts to stabilize Ulster. Hume's home in Derry had been attacked more than once. In 1976 an enraged mob of Provisional IRA supporters had driven Gerry Fitt, Hume's predecessor as the leader of the SDLP, from his house in north Belfast. As of 1995 things had changed, "changed utterly." Hume had formed a close liaison with Adams. Later, in Washington, he would be seen sharing a drink with John White, one of the UDA men who had been convicted of the murder of Wilson and Andrews.

In certain periods during the decades of violence, Hume had been more welcome in Washington than in parts of Northern Ireland. He had built up a solid following on the Hill, with contacts among all the leading politicians, including the president himself. Thanks to this, he was able to construct a powerful and influential Irish-American lobby to bring pressure to bear on the British government to throw its support behind a daring new peace strategy that he had helped initiate three years before when he opened secret talks with the Provisional IRA. Without him, that Saint Patrick's Day evening in Washington in 1995 would never have taken place.

Giving vital support to Hume's efforts was another important guest: John Bruton, the Irish prime minister. For years one Irish government after another had condemned and imprisoned IRA members, and had campaigned in the United States to try to persuade Irish Americans to stop sending money and arms to republican organizations in Ireland. But Hume had convinced Bruton's predecessor, Albert Reynolds, that the Provisionals were changing and that their leaders were genuinely seeking a way out of the bloody morass they called the armed struggle where they had been stuck for decades, slugging it out with the forces of law and order in a dirty little war of attrition. The Irish government was convinced. Reynolds swung his support behind Hume's efforts. For the first time in over seventy years, all strands of Irish nationalism—the militant republicans, the moderates in Ulster, the government in Dublin, and the powerful Irish-American lobby in the United States—were united. The fruit of this unity was christened the Pan-Nationalist Front—a front that for years had been Adams's goal. But it was not viewed with sympathy by everyone in Ireland.

If the Irish Rip Van Winkle had looked around him carefully, he would have noticed several absences. There was no representative of the Ulster Unionists in attendance. The largest party in Northern Ireland, representing the aspirations of the Protestant majority, had stayed away, using the excuse that invitations to the affair had been sent out too late for it to respond. Most knew, though, that the Unionists were deeply unhappy at the spectacle of the apotheosis of Gerry Adams, whom they regarded as a cunning terrorist who had simply changed tactics temporarily. Though they welcomed the cessation of violence, they remained convinced that the Provisionals and their allies were as dangerous as ever—if not more so now that they had the approval and support of the Irish and U.S. political establishments.

Nor was there anyone present from Her Majesty's government. The Conservative Party government under Prime Minister John Major had fought bitterly to keep Adams out of the United States in the first place and had suffered a resounding diplomatic defeat. Clinton had telephoned Major after making his decision to grant the first Adams visa waiver in 1994 to explain why he had broken with precedent. Major did not return the call for three days. It took a while getting used to the fact that in the post–Cold War world, Britain's influence in Washington was on the wane. For decades its massive diplomatic establishment in Washington had been a formative influence on shaping U.S. policy toward Ireland and the crisis in Ulster. Their line had been consistent and simple: Ulster was Britain's business, and the United States should concentrate on what the British government saw as the federal government's only role—blocking illegal arms shipments to the Provisionals and curtailing Irish-American fundraising efforts on their behalf. But by Saint Patrick's Day 1995, all the roles had changed.

Six months before, on August 31, 1994, the Provisional IRA had declared a "cessation of military operations"—its first long-term halt in twenty years in its campaign of political violence and terror. Six weeks later, on October 13, the loyalist paramilitary groups, the UDA, and the smaller Ulster Volunteer Force and Red Hand Commandos followed suit. For the first time in the history of the Ulster crisis, all its chief paramilitary antagonists had stopped killing.

The Irish government moved fast, inviting Adams to Dublin. Prime Minister Albert Reynolds met with Hume and the Sinn Fein leader on the steps of Leinster House—the seat of the Irish parliament, the Dail—with a historic handshake that many hoped presaged a future of peace and political progress. Before long, Adams and other party members traveled to New York to meet with American supporters. They were followed that October by loyalist paramilitary representatives, speaking for the first time in New York to Irish Americans, whom they had traditionally viewed as the hopelessly naive backers of their hated enemy, the Provisional IRA.

Even a year or two earlier, such developments would have been unthinkable. In 1992 a leading historian of the Troubles had deemed the Ulster crisis "intractable," a problem without a solution. A feeling of inertia had set in long ago that a former British cabinet minister had characterized, when he summed up Britain's policy, as reducing the Ulster troubles to an "acceptable level of violence." But as the loyalists' cease-fire followed that of the republicans', euphoria replaced resignation and despair, the characteristic emotions generated by the Ulster crisis.

The euphoria was evident that night in the East Wing as the sunset turned vermilion and Frank Patterson burst into "The Town I Love So Well," a song about Derry city, Northern Ireland's second largest, which Protestants refer to as Londonderry. For hundreds of years the seventeenth-century walled city has been a symbol of Protestant colonial might and determination in Ireland, since it withstood the long siege of the Catholic King James in his struggle to defeat the Protestant William of Orange for the English throne in 1689. "The Town I Love So Well," written by Derry songwriter and entertainer Phil Coulter, has become almost as well known as that other song inspired by Derry, "Danny Boy," known formally as "The Londonderry Air."

Coulter's song describes the destruction of Derry during the years of political violence, years of "armored cars and bombed-out bars," of shootings, car bombings, ambush and assassination, riots, raids, and arrests—

years symbolized by barbed wire and the crumpled bodies of the thirteen unarmed demonstrators gunned down by British troops on January 30, 1972, in a massacre known forever as Bloody Sunday.

Derry is John Hume's city, where thirty years earlier he had been a leader of the civil rights movement that first sparked world media interest in the Ulster crisis. The black-and-white images of Hume, drenched by a police water cannon or battered by their batons or thrown against a wall by British troops, still occasionally flash across the screen as filmmakers retell the story of those early civil rights struggles. But just as important for Hume, Derry is also the first city where the Catholic majority, so long excluded from municipal power, finally assumed the reins of government. In doing so they gave him a model of how the Ulster crisis might eventually be resolved, with Catholics and Protestants rotating the position of mayor. By 1995, Derry was the model of civic responsibility and power sharing. Hume wanted to apply its lessons to the whole of Northern Ireland.

As the evening at the White House wore on, as happens in any Irish occasion, the guests took over the entertainment. Hume and Adams got up on the stage and formed a duet. Not surprisingly, the audience wanted to hear another rendition of "The Town I Loved So Well." Clutching microphones, the representatives of the two strands of Irish nationalism, the constitutional and the violent, for seventy years in bitter confrontation with each other, joined together in song. Some were moved to tears at the sight. The other guests linked arms. As the duet wound up, one veteran observer of the Ulster situation remarked with characteristic Ulster sarcasm, "Adams should've been singing 'The Town We Bombed So Well.' " After all, he said, it was the Provisional IRA's bombing campaign in the early 1970s that reduced much of the city center to a wasteland of bombed buildings and boarded-up shops. Sarcasm and irony long ago became part of the mental armory of the Ulster temperament; they serve to ward off any temptation to become too optimistic and enthusiastic about the future.

By the time the two wings of Ulster nationalism had united in song, President Clinton and his wife had retired. So had the Irish prime minister, the representatives of Ulster loyalism, John McMichael and Joe English, along with their companion, Billy Blair. They had stolen out just before the Adams-Hume duet got started. In spite of the evening's claim to be a celebration of the new consensus that was said to be emerging in Ireland, no one had thought to include in the scheduled entertainment a song from the loyalist, Protestant tradition. There had been no rendition of "The Sash," the Protestants' most stirring song. It had been, in the end, in spite of all the euphoria about a new era dawning, a very nationalist occasion, with the Protestants there almost as an afterthought.

In a minor way that was an indication of underlying problems that as yet had not surfaced, though they lurked not far beneath the bubble of euphoria and would soon test its thin skin. From 1993 onward, the entire peace process had been very much a Nationalist-generated affair. Britain stood suspiciously to one side, waiting, watching, mistrustful of the Provisional IRA, which it had grown to grudgingly respect as a wily if vicious opponent, adept at changing tactics to ensure its survival. Meanwhile, though the Ulster Protestants were prepared to make their case in the United States and elsewhere, given the opportunity, they were not entirely happy with what they saw going on around them: Years of violence had deepened the sense of paranoia in a community that believed it was under constant threat from Irish republicans bent on breaking its links to Britain and absorbing it into a new Irish state. That centuries-old paranoia that various campaigns of IRA violence had reinforced was not going to be overcome by a few visits to the White House and a Saint Patrick's Day party.

Nor was there much euphoria outside the White House at the spot where two solitary protesters from Northern Ireland, Thomas Clark and Lisa O'Hagan, were picketing. They were drawing attention to the fact that in spite of the Provisional IRA's "cessation of military operations," it continued to attack alleged criminals. Customarily, the Provisionals carry off the suspects, beat them with cudgels and baseball bats, and/or shoot off their kneecaps. (On occasion they "execute" them by shooting them in the head.) Thomas Clark explained that his son, Malachy, was one such victim. After the Provisionals beat him, he killed himself in despair and fear.

"We're not here to harass Clinton," said Clark, "but just to give Gerry a spin." When asked why Malachy had been singled out, his father replied, "He was found with a bag of glue in his pocket."

Glue-sniffing is a favorite escape for many youths in the poor neighborhoods of Belfast where unemployment is endemic and welfare a way of life as a second generation of the unemployed come of age. The Provisionals act as a kind of surrogate police force, trying to control drug dealing, petty crime, and what they deem "antisocial" behavior, which can include anything from glue-sniffing to child-molesting. They have fulfilled this role since the early 1970s when it became impossible for the Royal Ulster Constabulary, the local Protestant-dominated police force, to operate in a normal fashion in the Catholic ghettos.

Thomas Clark's son, Malachy, is not listed as a victim of the Ulster crisis. Yet in some ways he was as much a victim as any of those deliberately gunned down or blown up. Twenty-five years and more of relentless violence, concentrated mostly in working-class areas, had taken its toll, morally and psychologically, as well as economically and socially. There were the obvious signs that accompany social and economic disintegration. There was a marked rise in crime, for instance, in once closely knit neighborhoods where a few years before it would have been possible to go away for the weekend and leave the front door unlocked without fear of a break-in. In circumstances where it was a common occurrence to see people gunned down for their political or religious affiliations, petty thievery or drug taking must have seemed a small offense to unemployed youths with no hope of a future.

Behavior had changed in other, quite radical ways. Profound sexual repression and conservatism had given way to a confused hedonism. There was a rapid rise in out-of-wedlock births, with schoolgirls having babies at ages as young as fourteen and fifteen. As one sixteen-year-old pupil at a Belfast Catholic girls' school remarked to a filmmaker, "Our school is going to need a maternity ward next to it."

People were left to lament the loss of the old decencies and customs that had once characterized life in the poor quarters of Belfast, both Catholic and Protestant, while still being uncertain and fearful of what would replace them. The Victorian world of hard work and worship that had produced those decencies seemed as far away and out of date as the grainy black-and-white photographs of the *Titanic* sitting in its dock in Harland and Wolff, the Belfast shipyard that built it.

The guests that attended the White House Saint Patrick's Day party that evening paid little attention to the protests of Thomas Clark and Lisa O'Hagan, nor could they address the underlying social and economic ills that they represented. It was not the time to stop and take heed of such details. Their minds were focused on the bigger picture—what they saw as the first real chance of peace since the Troubles began those long, blood-bespattered decades ago. They were convinced that a historic breakthrough in Anglo-Irish relations was in the making such as had not been seen since Ireland was partitioned more than seventy years earlier.

There was surely cause to be optimistic. By March 1995 the Provisional IRA's cease-fire had endured for more than six months; the loyalist groups, too, had succeeded in keeping their men under control, creating the longest cessation of paramilitary violence that Ulster had experienced. But those who looked closely at the Ulster situation noticed several disturbing signs: Not only did the Provisional IRA continue its "policing" role, as it inflicted vicious violence on those such as Malachy Clark who displeased it, but even as celebrations were being held in the White House, plans were being hatched in Belfast to launch a campaign against alleged drug dealers. This campaign would lead to a wave of murders carried out by the IRA under the pseudonym "Direct Action Against Drugs," known by the acronym DAAD, with all its connotations of sinister patriarchal violence.

Meanwhile, in the poor working-class Protestant neighborhoods, the old sectarian hatreds had not gone away. Late in December 1994, a Catholic student called Noel Lyness had drifted into a loyalist area of Belfast, drunk. The next morning his battered body was found dumped in an alleyway. The underlying tensions and fears that had characterized Ulster for generations remained.

As the guests headed back to Ireland, plans were being drafted for a Northern Ireland Investment Conference to be sponsored by Clinton in Washington the following May. There was talk of the first ever U.S. presidential visit to Belfast before the year was out. Hopes were high. But in Ulster, history is a stubborn ghost that is not easily laid to rest. It would haunt the hopes of the peacemakers.

The violence had ended, more or less, but the conflict remained. The politicians and paramilitary chiefs left the East Wing of the White House to go home to the difficult task of dealing with the roots of that conflict. The conflicting claims and aspirations of Catholic and Protestant, nationalist and unionist, republican and loyalist, had somehow to be resolved before the fault lines that lie deep within Ulster society began to grind against each other again, bringing the potential for renewed death and destruction. Hope was not enough to deal with history. It rarely is. In Ulster, history has vanquished hope so often that it seems an act of folly to expect it to exist.

It is the aim of the following pages to elucidate why this should be and how it came about. This will be done based on the premise that the Troubles, usually described in accounts as one seamless period—which some say began in 1969 and others in 1968 and still others in 1966—in fact breaks down into three fairly distinct phases: 1966–1977, 1977–1994, and 1994 to the present.

A few of those who were at the Washington party in March 1995 were formative influences in the first two, 1966–1977 and 1977–1994, and were there to shape the third and perhaps final phase. In each of these phases the nature of the Troubles changed in noticeable ways, though the underlying conflict remained the same.

PART I

THE TROUBLES 1966–1977

· ONE ·

RETURN OF THE GUNMAN

1966–1969

THE CONFLICT known as the Troubles began ingloriously in a Belfast side street with the murder of an old woman. Two drunk men emerged from an alleyway, their raincoats pulled up around their faces. One of them hurled a Molotov cocktail across the street at a Catholic-owned liquor store. He missed and hit the house next door, the home of Matilda Gould, a seventy-seven-year-old Protestant widow who lived there with her son. Unable to climb the stairs, she slept in the front room on the ground floor where the bomb landed.

The first sounds of a conflict that would endure for more than thirty years were the crash of glass from a breaking window, the whoosh of flame as a gasoline bomb burst, and the screech of pain as the burning liquid splashed over Mrs. Gould. Rescuers found her crumpled behind the door, burning.

It was 10:40 P.M. on May 7, 1966. And Northern Ireland was, technically speaking, at peace.

Within weeks of the firebombing there were two more killings. This time both victims were Catholics, picked more or less at random. The first was a drunk named John Scullion; he was shot on his way home while singing an Irish republican ballad. The second, Peter Ward, an eighteen-year-old bartender, was ambushed as he left an after-hours drinking den in the Protestant Shankill area of Belfast in the early morning of June 26.

The Troubles, most assumed, were a thing of the past, a name given to the turmoil of the early 1920s when the Irish Republican Army fought to drive the British out of Ireland. The IRA succeeded in securing twenty-six of the thirty-two counties. Unionists wanted no part of an independent Ireland. They formed their own six-county state, Northern Ireland, carved out of the nine historic counties of the northern province of Ulster, where loyal Protestants possessed an overall majority, imposing their will through violence and intimidation on a recalcitrant Catholic minority. Belfast became its capital, an industrial boomtown, a jewel in the crown of the British Empire, and a bulwark against the nationalism that was threatening to engulf the whole of Ireland.

Between 1922 and 1966, Northern Ireland settled into two more or less homogenous blocks, Nationalist and Unionist, Catholic and Protestant. In many ways they were mirror images of each other. The Nationalists were exiles from the Irish nation; in their exclusion they clung to their religion as a mark of cultural identity; politically, they dealt with the Northern Ireland state by ignoring it. The Unionists were also a community under threat—a minority within the island of Ireland. In 1920, Lord Edward Carson, the founding father of Northern Ireland, calculated that three of the nine Ulster counties with a Catholic majority, Monaghan, Donegal, and Leitrim, would have to be ditched. But counties Derry, Antrim, Tyrone, Armagh, and Down would give Ulster Protestants the homeland they sought. Unfortunately for Ulster Unionists, the prospect of a uniformly "loyal" Northern Ireland proved illusory. There were loyal parts, a majority of them, but in other places in Northern Ireland, Catholics formed a local majority. Northern Ireland was a state based on numbers, and numbers by their very nature have a habit of changing. With this inbuilt insecurity and separated from their parent nation, Britain, Protestants clung to the symbols of their Britishness: the Union Jack flag, the Royal family, and their own particular rituals that celebrated their triumph over popery and nationalism. The most famous of these were the parades organized by the Orange Order, a "brotherhood" of Protestants that had been created in the eighteenth century to fight Irish republicanism. That is, Northern Ireland was comprised of two communities who shared the same area but owed their allegiances to different nations. This difference was the fault line on which the state rested.

By 1966 the IRA numbered its adherents in Belfast on the fingers of two hands. Northern Ireland's Catholic population had failed to respond to its last summons to arms when in 1956 it launched a border campaign to "free" the remaining British-controlled corner of Ireland. The IRA's sporadic attacks against police stations, cross-border bridges, and bus stations sputtered out, barely noticed, in 1962. A liberal Unionist prime minister, Captain Terence O'Neill, was now leading Northern Ireland's parliament at Stormont, promising reform and the integration of the minority Catholic population into the economic and political life of a state that Protestant Unionists had completely dominated since its foundation in 1921. It was the 1960s, after all, the age of the Beatles, Muhammad Ali, John F. Kennedy, manned space flight, free love, and civil rights. Never in human history had change occurred at such a rapid pace. But for some in the backstreets of working-class Protestant areas of Belfast, that was precisely the problem.

Matilda Gould, John Scullion, and Peter Ward were the victims of a small group of working-class Protestant loyalists who called themselves the Ulster Volunteer Force and whose professed aim was to defend Northern Ireland against Catholic subversion.[1] The fiftieth anniversary of the 1916 rebellion stirred their fears; their prime minister's overtures to Catholics and appeals that they should be treated with "due consideration and kindness" were seen as evidence of weakness and betrayal. Their idea of "defense" was to vandalize Catholic-owned premises in Protestant areas and scribble anti-Catholic graffiti on Catholic property—just prior to the firebombing, "Popehead" had appeared on the Catholic premises next door to Mrs. Gould's home—and kill "IRA" men.

A statement issued in the name of the UVF in May declared: "Known IRA men will be executed mercilessly and without hesitation." However, in 1966, IRA men were rare in Belfast, and when the UVF's halfhearted attempts to find them failed, it did what loyalist extremists have always done: killed the most vulnerable Catholic. Anyway, to loyalists such as Andrew Augustus Spence, known as Gusty, the founder of the UVF, a Catholic was by definition an IRA man.

Spence was a lantern-jawed former British soldier who had served as a military policeman in Cyprus. He worked as a steel-fitter in Harland and Wolff shipyards, whose workforce was almost entirely Protestant and the biggest employer in Belfast. When Spence and his gang were arrested in connection with the killing of Peter Ward, of which they were later convicted, one of them, Hugh McClean, blurted out, "I am terribly sorry I ever heard tell of that man Paisley or decided to follow him. I am definitely ashamed of myself to be in such a position."

The Reverend Ian Kyle Paisley was a big, braying anti-Catholic fundamentalist preacher who told men like Spence what they wanted to hear: that the Catholic threat to Ulster was real, part of a vast conspiracy organized from Rome; its agents were the IRA, liberal Unionists such as Terence O'Neill, the ecumenical movement as represented by the World Council of Churches, communists, and socialists; its conspirator-in-chief was the Pope. "Go into any Roman church in this city," begins a typical specimen of Paisley's preaching, circa 1964, "and what do you see? It's like Madame Tussaud's in London. Legions of graven images! Gaudy and vulgar, and an abomination in the sight of God. Equally rank in the nostrils and nauseating are the sanctuary lamps and candelabras placed before the sickly prints of the Virgin and other saints. These are the trappings of the great whore of Babylon and the Scarlet Woman. . . . Are you prepared to be party to this base surrender, to be Lundies and Papists?" (Lundy was a seventeenth-century traitor to the Protestant cause.) His favorite trick was to present an ex-nun to regale his outraged congregation with pornographic tales of convent life, a mixture of sexual fantasy and dubious theology that exercised an irresistible charm over a handful of mostly repressed social misfits.

Paisley drew most of his support from the fringe of the Protestant community, a murky world of crackpot religious extremists, bigots, and gunmen who set up paramilitary organizations that were usually unknown to anyone other than the handful of men that formed them. This was part of a hallowed Ulster Protestant tradition where the need for unofficial militias went back to the eighteenth century. There were at least three different groups using the name UVF. Paisley formed the Ulster Protestant Volunteers in the spring of 1966, the same year that Spence set up his version of the UVF.

Though many of Paisley's associates ended up behind bars for violent crimes, Paisley himself spoke out against acts of violence and avoided arrest on anything more serious than an offense for disorderly behavior. But his followers clearly regarded his public condemnations of violence as a mere fiction and acted accordingly. They used the UPV headquarters in Belfast to hide their arms. When Paisley discovered weapons there, he ordered the UPV member who had hidden them to remove them at once.

The preacher possessed the presence of mind to make sure his follower carried them out the back door, not the front, which he believed was under police surveillance. "If you let those fellows get away with the likes of that, they'd finish us all," he is reported to have remarked, somewhat disingenuously.[2]

A visitor to Belfast at any time since about the mid-1880s would have found gangs of men like those around Spence and Bible-thumping bigots of Paisley's type. It was a hive of fundamentalist faiths and apocalyptic visionaries whose doomsday rhetoric stirred up poor Protestants against the increasing number of Catholics flooding into the city after the Famine of 1847. Catholics were also hungry for jobs and houses. Their large families swarmed in the narrow streets of the Falls Road, just a few hundred yards away from their Protestant neighbors on the Shankill. Moreover, the newcomers traditionally aligned themselves with Irish nationalism. Tension led to clashes and widespread rioting, which in 1886 became so bad as to "assume the character of a civil war."[3] With the rise of the shipbuilding, ropeworks, and linen industries, Ulster became more closely bound economically to Britain and the empire. The severing of those bonds, Protestants feared, would mean the destruction of Ulster's prosperity and status as the only industrially developed part of Ireland.

It remained in 1966 a Victorian city, conservative, pious, and industrious, with work and worship dominating the lives of its citizens, both Catholic and Protestant. The working classes lived in the narrow streets that clustered around the mills and factories in little two-up, two-down redbrick row houses with black slate roofs. It was a city that even then still smelled of coal smoke and candle wax, tobacco and hemp. They were a God-fearing people, reared on religious as well as political dogmas, to whom sin and damnation were as real as the shriek of the factory horn that called them to work in the morning. On Sunday, Belfast shut down. Pubs, restaurants, and cinemas were closed. The children's parks were locked, the swings chained. Like the God of the Old Testament, Ulster had a low opinion of pleasure.

Political change or perceived change made the fault line between the Protestant and Catholic communities shift a little, and the tension released itself in outbursts of rioting and sectarian murder, as much a feature of Belfast life as the gaunt industrial chimney stacks and the church spires that dominated its skyline.

Beyond the low hills that surrounded the city was a world of small, mostly ugly nineteenth-century towns. As in the city, the two communities rubbed against each other, close together yet segregated. The pattern of land distribution dated back to the seventeenth century when James I began the Plantation. English and Scottish settlers supplanted the local, rebellious Celtic warlords. Though the cultural and linguistic links between Scotland and Ulster were far older, the Plantation was a traumatic change, representing the overthrow of the old order of Celtic aristocracy. Protestants farmed the valleys, and Catholics for the most part were left with the smaller, poorer farms among the hills, wresting a meager living from a few stony fields. "Every bullet and every bomb exploded in Northern Ireland," wrote a local historian, "is laid to the blame of a monarch dead these three centuries."[4]

In 1966, the Northern Ireland Unionist Party was celebrating almost fifty years in government. Northern Ireland was, in effect, a one-party state, unique in Western Europe. Voting patterns were as fixed as the Plantation. Of the state's 1.5 million population, around 65 percent were Protestants, the rest Catholic, which kept the Unionists in power year after year, decade after decade. Though a substantial and growing minority, Catholics were politically passive. Nationalist politics was embodied in the Nationalist Party—though "embodied," suggesting life of some sort, is perhaps the wrong word. By the mid-1960s the party was effectively a corpse, killed off by its own verities, one of which was its steadfast refusal to recognize the reality of the Northern Ireland state. Its politicians, when elected to the parliament at Stormont, refused to deal with their Unionist counterparts or act as an opposition in any way. Its goal of achieving a united Ireland through ignoring partition was as far away as ever. During the entire period from 1921 until the 1960s, the Nationalist Party failed to get any reform passed that would benefit the Catholic population or address their grievances.

Catholics were still barred from certain jobs, such as in the Harland and Wolff shipyards. Few found their way into the civil service, and those that did remained on the lower scales. By 1966 only 4 percent of those earning £2,000 (roughly $4,000) were Catholics. In Derry, Northern Ireland's second city, with a large Catholic majority, only 32 of the city's 177 municipal employees were Catholics. Northern Ireland's housing standards were among the worst in the United Kingdom. With outdoor toilets and no bathrooms, some houses dated back to the 1840s. For working-class Catholics the situation was made worse because some local housing authorities, dominated by Unionists, favored their fellow Protestants when it came to allocation of new homes. This was especially noticeable in the west of Northern Ireland, where there was an overall Catholic majority. In County Fermanagh, for example, of 1,589 postwar houses built, 1,021 went to Protestants, 568 to Catholics.[5] The distribution of houses had profound political implications in areas where Catholics were in the majority but Unionists still managed to hold on to the running of local authorities who allocated jobs and houses. It enabled the Unionists to gerrymander the ward system to ensure more Unionists were elected than Nationalists. Thus in Derry, Unionists, though in the minority, were able to hold twelve of the twenty council seats. However, discrimination was an accepted part of Ulster society and practiced on both sides. In some areas where Nationalists held power, such as Newry in south Down, that they should hire "their own" was taken for granted.[6]

Catholics lacked political leadership. A twenty-seven-year-old teacher of French, John Hume, wrote in *The Irish Times:* "Weak opposition leads to corrupt government. Nationalists in opposition have in no way been constructive. . . . Leadership has been the comfortable leadership of flags and slogans. . . . There has been no attempt to be positive, to encourage the Catholic community to develop the resources they have in plenty to make a positive contribution in terms of community service." Hume founded the Derry Credit Union to help working-class Catholics save money in order to buy their own homes. He was a new type of Nationalist that was emerging in the mid-1960s. His mother worked in a shirt factory, and his father was unemployed. Discrimination barred young working-class Catholics like him from skilled manufacturing jobs. A growing number took the route of higher education, effectively moving into the middle class, to become lawyers, teachers, journalists, and academics. They wanted wider horizons than the narrow, sectarian politics of Northern Ireland seemed to offer. And thanks to British education reforms enacted in 1944 and later extended to Northern Ireland, Hume was able to go to a university, where he studied French. One of the first times Hume spoke in public was in a college debate in 1959, when he argued in favor of Ireland joining the Common Market (later the European Community). One of the benefits, he said, was that it would gradually make the border irrelevant.

Traditional Nationalist politicians regarded such arguments as heretical. How could partition not be relevant? It was like telling a Catholic that there was no such thing as original sin. But Hume's contemporaries were as impatient with Nationalist verities as they were with the status quo and the unaddressed grievances on which it rested. They wanted change. The problem was, there existed no vehicle to effect that change. But in August 1966, just as Spence and his gang were going to trial for the murder of Peter Ward, a small group of republicans and political activists quietly met to create one.

An urge to make an old vehicle of change, the IRA, relevant to modern Ireland inspired the meeting. Since the debacle of the 1956–1962 border campaign, a powerful group arose within the IRA who saw the trench-coated gunman—the symbol of the IRA's ethos—as a prop that must be carried off the stage of Irish history and dumped. The romantic nationalism that came out of the barrel of his gun would have to be replaced with something else, something more relevant to a country whose most popular television show was *Top of the Pops*, on which swarms of miniskirted young women and longhaired young men gyrated once a week to the music of the Beatles and the Rolling Stones. At the August meeting, a handful of disgruntled IRA men, left-wing intellectuals, Communist Party members, and trade union activists talked of infiltrating the trade unions to make contact with sympathetic Protestant workers. Like Hume, they were convinced that the old sectarian barriers that divided Catholic from Protestant would crumble. All that was needed was a program around which both Catholics and Protestants could unite. It was an optimistic, progressive vision, based on the left-wing assumption that given the opportunity, Catholic and Protestant workers would realize they shared common economic interests that outweighed the old nationalist ideologies and sectarian beliefs still dividing them.

The unity of Catholic and Protestant workers was the Holy Grail of Irish socialism and, to a lesser extent, republicanism. Progressive left-wing republicans had pursued it since the beginning of the twentieth century. And each time they failed to find it. But in 1966 it seemed right to try again. There were hopeful signs. A Labour government was in power in Britain under the leadership of Harold Wilson. Several Labour Party MPs were known to be keen to reform Northern Ireland and expose its abuses. In February the Catholics of west Belfast had elected Gerry Fitt to

Westminster. Fitt was a member of the small Republican Labour Party. He was a bluff and jovial former dockworker, a lifelong trade unionist, the sort of Belfast man who looks as if he was born wearing a cloth cap and with a pint in one hand and a betting slip in the other. In Westminster, Fitt formed alliances with interested Labour MPs to press for the British government to take a more active role in Northern Ireland affairs. For left-wing republicans this seemed to be part of the general movement toward change that was in the air in the 1960s.

On January 29, 1967, a second meeting was held, this time in Belfast. The original group had expanded considerably to include members of the tiny Ulster Liberal Party and the Northern Ireland Labour Party. A liberal Unionist was co-opted onto a steering committee. Out of this, the Northern Ireland Civil Rights Association was born.

Its constitution proclaimed its goals:

1. To defend the basic freedoms of all citizens
2. To protect the rights of the individual
3. To highlight all possible abuses of power
4. To demand guarantees for freedom of speech, assembly, and association
5. To inform the public of their lawful rights

The group also demanded the abolition of the Special Powers Act, draconian security legislation enacted in the early years of Northern Ireland when the IRA was still a menace. This allowed the Northern Ireland police, the Royal Ulster Constabulary, wide powers of arrest, including detention without trial. There were also calls for the abolition of the B-Specials, a part-time constabulary set up during the Troubles of the 1920s, whom Catholics regarded as sectarian.

NICRA's tactics of marches and sit-downs would be based on the campaign for black civil rights, which at the time was reaching its climax in the United States.[7] In 1968 it took to the streets as a result of a housing protest. Austin Currie, a Nationalist MP for east Tyrone, wanted to draw attention to the case of a nineteen-year-old Protestant woman, a secretary for a local Unionist, who had been allocated a house over the heads of 269 people on the waiting list, many of them Catholics with large families. Attempts to raise the matter in Stormont proved fruitless. Currie recalled the advice of Labour MP Paul Rose who was active on the Northern Ireland issue. "No British government, including this one, will intervene to remedy injustice in Northern Ireland unless you people there force it to," he told Currie. On June 20, 1968, Currie, his wife, and a local farmer broke into the disputed house and squatted.

"The media arrived within the hour. . . . After three and a half hours the bailiffs arrived with a sledgehammer. The door was smashed down and we were ejected none too gently into the lenses of the waiting media. That night the BBC news from London for the first time carried a report of injustice in Northern Ireland. Paul Rose rang to congratulate me. The process of forcing the British government to intervene to remedy injustice in the North had begun."[8]

Two months later, in support of Currie, NICRA organized its first protest march, from Coalisland to Market Square in Dungannon, County Tyrone. A minister in the Unionist government, John Taylor, declared that Dungannon town center was "Unionist territory." The Reverend Ian Paisley and his supporters immediately organized a counterdemonstration, which occupied Market Square to block the civil rights protesters from entering. This was a clash of 1960s culture with fundamentalist, conservative Ulster. But it was occurring on traditional ground. That is, it was the form of the protest as much as its content that spurred Protestant reaction. The issue, as the Protestants saw it, was territorial. To march in Ulster is to stake a claim on a territory. It is to say, "I have a right to march here because this is mine." For this reason traditional parades such as those taking place around July 12 each year are basic expressions of the underlying conflict and over the years have provoked so much violence. Now, the civil rights movement was marching to draw attention not to territorial claims but to fundamental issues concerning injustice and the nature of the state. Their struggle was aimed at a public, legal sphere, where they hoped a consensus could be created on the need for change. But to Paisley and his followers, and to other less militant Protestants also, it was an expansion by the enemy into territory that was not theirs. And they responded as Ulster Protestants always have to perceived threats—with blockades, countermarches, and, ultimately, extreme violence.

NICRA's next march was an attempt to show that its campaign was not about territory but about bridge-building. It was planned for October 5 in Derry city. It would proceed from the Protestant Waterside district and cross a bridge into the west side of the city, which was predominantly Catholic, for a rally in Guildhall Square. However, a few within NICRA and on its fringes had different intentions and effectively took over the organization of the event. A small group of Derry socialists hoped "to provoke the police into overreaction and thus spark off mass reaction against the authorities."[9] The IRA, which had been taking a backseat in these events, also got involved. Their volunteers were ordered to act as "stewards" of the march. When it was announced that a few prominent Labour politicians from Britain would be taking part, the IRA instructed its men to ensure that "if the police lashed out they would connect with newsworthy skulls."[10] When the authorities banned the march, the organizers declared their intention to go ahead, and the scene was set for a nasty confrontation.

Four hundred marchers gathered on a gray Saturday afternoon near the Derry railway station, far fewer than expected. But British and Irish television cameras were there as the Royal Ulster Constabulary blocked the route. Several protesters approached the police cordon to remonstrate with the officers. A baton was thrust into the stomach of one, and he collapsed writhing in pain. The RUC waded into the marchers' ranks, clubbing them to the ground. Westminster MP Gerry Fitt's head was split in front of the television cameras. Meanwhile, a second line of RUC men took the marchers in the rear. A water cannon drenched respectable MPs and militants alike. The demonstrators fled in confused panic into the Catholic west side of the city, the RUC in pursuit. The police were met with stones and gasoline bombs in sporadic attacks that lasted into the early hours of Sunday morning.

For many television viewers in Britain, their first sight of Northern Ireland was that of a policeman batoning a peaceful protester. Their ignorance of the Ulster situation was profound; most assumed that the Irish problem had been settled decades ago. They were shocked not only at the pictures of the violence but at the fact that unlike the English "bobby," the RUC were armed, more like a paramilitary unit than a civilian police force. NICRA effectively exploited the coverage with such slogans as "British Rights for British Citizens." As a result, Northern Ireland was suddenly thrust onto the Wilson government's agenda. For the British, after almost fifty years of keeping the Irish problem at arm's length, it was an unwelcome intrusion.

Wilson ordered the Northern Ireland prime minister, Terence O'Neill, along with two of his more prominent ministers, William Craig and Brian Faulkner, to London where he impressed upon the Unionists the need for reforms. O'Neill announced on his return that the Special Powers Act would be abolished as soon as it was safe to do so; housing allocation would be in future based on a point system; the company vote, allowing businessmen more than one vote, was to be abolished; and there would be reforms in local government, including the abolition of the Unionist-controlled Derry city council. An ombudsman was to be appointed to handle complaints. Craig, a hard-liner who resented British interference, was furious, and once back in Belfast, he stirred up Unionist resistance to the changes with increasingly violent speeches. He depicted the whole civil rights movement as a stalking horse for the IRA. Faulkner, more wily and driven mainly by ambition, bided his time while looking to replace O'Neill as prime minister.

After five years as head of government, O'Neill was in an invidious position. His problems stemmed partly from the fact that he was not a typical Unionist. Educated at Eton College in England, he looked and sounded more like an upper-class Englishman than an Ulsterman. For all the ferocity of their claims to be British, Ulster Unionists deeply suspected Britain, with its changing, multicultural society, its more easygoing morals, and liberal opinions. O'Neill, by accent, education, and class, was tainted and distrusted. His political gestures deepened that distrust among the more hard-line elements in Unionism. In 1965 he had invited Sean Lemass, the Irish taoiseach (prime minister) to Stormont, a harmless gesture in any other but the Ulster political context, with watchtowers and gates as its symbols and betrayal as its rallying cry. He visited a Catholic school and was photographed speaking with nuns. But, in fact, for most of his time as leader, O'Neill had made no serious attempts at addressing Catholic grievances. Instead, he concentrated on economic changes, based on attracting outside investors to Northern Ireland to replace its flagging industries. He hoped that a new prosperity would result that would dissolve traditional sectarian differences, and Catholics would live like Protestants as contented Ulstermen and -women. By 1968, however, it was too late for such long-term solutions. O'Neill was trapped between his enemies within Unionism and the growing anger and impatience of Catholics.

"Patiently endured so long as it seemed beyond redress, a grievance comes to appear intolerable once the possibility of removing it crosses men's minds," observed Alexis de Tocqueville of the days leading up to the French Revolution and the end of the ancien régime. "For the mere fact that certain abuses have been remedied draws attention to others and they appear more galling."[11] O'Neill's promise of change unleashed forces that the ancien régime of Unionism could not contain.

NICRA branches mushroomed all over Northern Ireland, and other groups sprang up. More militant left-wing students created People's Democracy; among them was a young woman called Bernadette Devlin. John Hume, worried that left-wing republican influence was too strong in NICRA, established the Derry Citizens' Action Committee. More demonstrations followed, and O'Neill appealed for calm. "Ulster stands at the crossroads," he said on a television broadcast as 1968 came to a close. "Our conduct over the coming days will decide our future. For more than five years now I have tried to heal some of the deep divisions in our community. I did so because I could not see how an Ulster divided against itself could hope to stand. . . . What kind of Ulster do you want? A happy and respected province in good standing with the rest of the United Kingdom? Or a place continually torn apart by riots and demonstrations and regarded by the rest of Britain as a political outcast?"

NICRA responded favorably to O'Neill's speech and said it was temporarily halting its demonstrations. But the People's Democracy declared it would hold a long march from Belfast to Derry, beginning on January 1, 1969. One of its leaders said that it would be modeled on Martin Luther King's march in 1966 from Selma to Montgomery, Alabama, which "exposed the racist thuggery of America's Deep South and forced the U.S. government into major reforms."[12]

It was a self-fulfilling prophecy. On the fourth day of the one-hundred-mile trek, with an RUC escort, the marchers reached Burntollet Bridge outside Derry. A mob of loyalists, several hundred strong, lay in wait. According to Bernadette Devlin, "A curtain of bricks and boulders brought the march to a halt. From the lanes burst hordes of screaming people wielding planks of wood, bottles, laths, iron bars, crowbars, cudgels studded with nails, and they waded into the march beating the hell out of everybody."[13]

The police did little to protect the marchers. As they staggered into

Derry, bloodied and battered, riots erupted in the Catholic Bogside district where vicious clashes occurred with the RUC. Three hundred people were injured, and Catholics accused the police of running amok.[14]

O'Neill succumbed to British government pressure to set up an inquiry into the disturbances. His enemies within his own party saw their opportunity. Brian Faulkner resigned from the cabinet, accusing O'Neill of abdicating the powers of the Stormont government. Craig attacked him for not standing up to the British and being unable to lead the Unionist Party. Almost fifty years of single-party rule at Stormont, during which Unionists were left to their own devices, made some forget that sovereignty lay not in the Belfast parliament but in Westminster. In a desperate bid to bolster his position, O'Neill called a general election for February 24.

For the first time since 1920 and the divisive debate over whether or not Northern Ireland should comprise six or nine counties, the Ulster Unionist Party began to fragment. Pro-O'Neill Unionists stood against anti-O'Neill Unionists, and former colleagues bitterly denounced each other. Paisley stood under the label of Protestant Unionist and challenged O'Neill in his own constituency. A similar fragmentation occurred on the Nationalist side. Civil rights campaigners such as John Hume and Austin Currie ran in constituencies formerly the domain of the old Nationalist Party. In Belfast, Gerry Fitt's Republican Labour Party sought to broaden its base among Nationalists and trade union activists.

The election result was a failure for O'Neill and the moderate Unionists. Though his majority—twenty-seven pro-O'Neill Unionists as against twelve anti-O'Neill MPs or undecideds—seemed solid, it was not the overwhelming endorsement of his policy he felt he needed. Most embarrassingly of all, Paisley, his nemesis, came within fifteen hundred votes of taking his seat. Catholics also failed to support pro-O'Neill Unionists. His attempt to build a bridge between moderate Unionists and moderate Nationalists collapsed under Paisley's jeers that "bridges like traitors go over to the other side." The election dubbed the "crossroads" election (after O'Neill's speech of the previous December) showed that a significant block of Ulster's Protestants were taking the road of extremism. It also showed that Nationalists were following a different road from that of the old Nationalist Party. The party's overall vote dropped catastrophically to 6 percent. Civil rights activists, including Hume, took three seats from Nationalist Party MPs. In Belfast, where the party had never been strong, it ceased to exist. Republican Labour with two seats was now the voice of Belfast Nationalists.

The realignment that took place in February 1969 would set Northern Ireland's political mold for the coming decades. Two months later it saw the election to Westminster of Bernadette Devlin, a twenty-one-year-old student, civil rights campaigner, and the youngest MP for fifty years. The left-wing IRA leadership supported her campaign as a way of bringing civil rights issues right into the heart of the British political establishment. Her maiden speech was a fiery attack on British government policy, and she warned that if British troops were sent to Ulster, "I should not like to be either the mother or sister of any unfortunate soldier stationed there."

Wilson, perhaps misreading the February election result as a clear-cut victory for moderate Unionists, continued to press O'Neill to make reforms, especially to introduce one-man, one-vote for local elections. He moved to introduce the reform. Militant loyalists were more frustrated than ever. O'Neill was still in power, bending to British pressure and as ready as ever, as they saw it, to sell out. On the gable walls in Protestant areas of Belfast was scrawled: "Gusty Spence Was Right."

After Spence was imprisoned for life, his organization, the UVF, merged with two smaller groups on the Shankill Road using the same name. One of these was no more than a gang of street thugs who liked to beat up any Catholics who wandered into their area. Among its members, however, were Davy Payne and Jim Craig, men who would later rise to prominence in loyalism's violent underworld. In the spring of 1969, UVF elements linked up with members of Paisley's Ulster Protestant Volunteers. On March 21 they bombed a Catholic church in County Antrim. On March 30 an electricity substation in Protestant east Belfast was struck. Three weeks later, a few days before O'Neill was to announce the abolition of the property vote in local elections, a wave of explosions rocked Ulster. The targets, as before, were water and electricity utilities, including Belfast's reservoir.

Paisley alleged it was the work of the IRA. But RUC intelligence pointed in a different direction, and O'Neill was told that the attacks were the responsibility of Protestant extremists linked to the UVF. O'Neill had banned the UVF in 1966 after the first wave of murders. It now exacted its revenge. On April 28, demoralized and disheartened, his hope of a moderate center embracing Catholic and Protestant broken, O'Neill resigned.

At the trial in April 1970 of one of those accused of taking part in the bombing campaign, it was revealed that the bombing conspiracy also involved members of Paisley's UPV. It was stated that the defendant, Sam Stevenson, a UPV man and a member of Paisley's Free Presbyterian Church, "was not the man who conceived the idea, nor had he a mind subtle enough to consider the long-term implications of his conduct."[15] It was suggested that the mysterious mastermind of the plot to remove O'Neill was Paisley himself. Over the years, though he has been associated with violent organizations, there has never been hard evidence to connect Paisley to violent acts. He himself condemns violence. But there is evidence (as already noted) that he knew members of his UPV were acting illegally at times. The organization's constitution, which forbade Catholics to join, advocated using whatever "legal" means were necessary to uphold the constitution. However, it contained a clause that stated, "When the authorities act contrary to the Constitution, the body will take whatever steps it thinks fit to expose such unconstitutional acts."[16] This was easily interpreted by extreme loyalists as meaning that through violence they could rid themselves of someone like O'Neill whom they considered a traitor.

Brian Faulkner lost the Unionist leadership contest to James Chichester-Clark. Right-wing Unionists who hoped for stronger leadership were soon disappointed. Chichester-Clark would face the same dilemma as his predecessor, caught between insecure and angry loyalists, British government pressure for reform, and increasingly belligerent Nationalists, some of whom began thinking that if Protestants can use violence to achieve their aims, then perhaps the age of the trench-coated gunman was not yet past.

· 2 ·

FOR MOST CATHOLICS the IRA was a derisory organization, real only to a handful of old men, superannuated republicans, and a few paranoid loyalists. By the 1960s it was being kept alive in Belfast thanks to a handful of republican families such as that of Gerry Adams, whose father was an IRA veteran imprisoned in the 1940s. But it was politics as well as family tradition that pushed Adams to join while still a lanky teenager. The attempt to make the IRA relevant again attracted Adams and a few other working-class Belfast Catholics. The new left-wing politics the IRA leadership in Dublin espoused made sense, as did the republican movement's involvement with the burgeoning civil rights campaign as a way of broadening the IRA's appeal beyond the romantic images of gun battles on picturesque hillsides and stoical martyrs facing firing squads for "the cause." "The civil rights movement had done more in a few weeks to damage Unionist structure than decades of IRA activity," observed one republican activist.[17]

However, for many older veterans the new course was a dangerous diversion from the main aim of the IRA, which was to fight for the thirty-two-county republic they believe was betrayed in 1921 with the partition of the country. Belfast IRA men like Billy McKee and Joe Cahill, whose republican creed was forged in the 1940s and 1950s, believed the politicization process would mean the end of the IRA. According to McKee, "The IRA would've been phased out but for the Troubles. By 1969 it was bankrupt."[18] Money was being used not to buy weapons but to keep the movement's newspaper, *The United Irishman,* from closing. The veterans' discontent intensified as the civil rights movement came under attack from extreme loyalists. They had some support among the leaders in the south. Sean MacStiofain, who was head of the IRA's intelligence-gathering department, sympathized with their predicament. He complained bitterly that "the Irish Republican Army had been bogged down in politics to the point where young girl students from northern universities had left it far behind in revolutionary initiative."[19] MacStiofain, an Englishman by birth and a former corporal in the RAF, was a fanatical republican and Irish language devotee who had served a prison term in England in the 1950s for stealing arms. He demanded the IRA take retaliatory action against police officers who had been seen hitting demonstrators during riots. He said they should be shot. Fortunately, cooler heads within the IRA's ruling body, the Army Council, quickly squashed that proposal, realizing it would play right into the hands of right-wing Unionists. But in April 1969, under growing pressure from their more militant members, the Army Council placed all volunteers on full alert and sent a number of fully equipped units north to take up "defensive" positions. This sounded more impressive than it actually was; the number of men involved was no more than a few dozen at the most. In Belfast, however, the IRA ignored the leadership's caution and early on moved from "defensive" into "offensive" mode.

Between April 20 and 21 their younger activists carried out a series of firebomb attacks on post offices.

Adams's bartending job was taking second place to his IRA activities. The Unionist response to the civil rights movement had moved the situation beyond NICRA's demands for reform and brought "the existence of the six-county state into question."[20] MacStiofain agreed. Without informing other members of the Army Council, he collected ammunition from arms dumps in the south, as well as a few hand grenades and guns, and quietly transported them to Belfast where they were handed over to the IRA's intelligence officer in the city.[21] The authority of the Dublin leadership was being further undermined as individual republicans, convinced that a major confrontation was looming, set up secret training camps.

Summer, when thousands of Orange parades take place, is always the most dangerous time in Ulster. As the evenings lengthened, riots erupted and spread beyond Belfast and Derry to rural towns such as Armagh, Lurgan, and Dungannon. Those parades that passed Catholic areas came under attack from youths throwing bottles and stones. Orange halls were torched. Not since the 1880s had rioting occurred on such a scale. Northern Irish Catholics, sensing change was in the air, were aroused from their stupor; they were no longer content to sit back and be spectators at a display of Protestant hegemony designed to humiliate them. In Belfast fierce sectarian street battles broke out along the fault line where the two communities met: Unity Flats, a Catholic apartment project at the foot of the loyalist Shankill; Ardoyne, one of an archipelago of Catholic ghettos in loyalist north Belfast; and near the streets that joined the Protestant Shankill to the Catholic Falls. Adams spent his lunch hours touring the threatened areas and helping locals, he says, prepare for their defense. He did so without the support of the IRA Army Council, which "in no way was prepared for any sort of military defense, never mind an offensive. It was, instead, engaged in political semantics."[22] MacStiofain implored Cathal Goulding, the IRA chief of staff and one of the architects of the new republican strategy, to "take heed of the warnings we were relaying from our threatened comrades in the north. On the very brink, the 'politicals' still refused to do anything."[23]

Goulding, a left-wing Dubliner, deeply distrusted the militant Belfast republicans. It was a feeling shared by many southern radicals that went back to the 1920s when the IRA in the northern capital emerged as "defenders" of Catholics first and republicans second and retaliated against Protestants for attacks on Catholic streets. In the 1930s, Peadar O'Donnell, like Goulding a socialist republican who wanted to turn the IRA into a radical left-wing movement, commented, "We haven't a battalion of IRA men in Belfast, we just have a battalion of armed Catholics."[24] He might have been expressing Goulding's fears that an injection of arms into the city would be like throwing gasoline on a fire. The IRA leadership wanted to avoid a sectarian conflict, not provoke one—especially since they knew they could not protect isolated Catholic areas should they come under sustained attack.

Belfast republicans, however, saw armed action as a deterrent to attack, a way of letting their enemies know they were able to defend themselves. In July, in the maze of narrow streets near the Falls Road, RUC patrols were attacked with handguns and hand grenades. Though there were no serious injuries, it made the police nervous and convinced angry loyalists that the old enemy was back, getting ready to strike at them. In mid-July, at the height of the Orange marching season, a Catholic mob tried to burn down an Orange hall in Dungiven in south County Derry. The police intervened and killed Francis McCloskey, a sixty-seven-year-old Catholic, during the riot. On July 17 another Catholic, Samuel Devenney, whom the RUC had injured in a confrontation in Derry three months earlier, died. Their deaths provoked further demands within the IRA for stronger action as the police were increasingly viewed as anti-Catholic and not to be trusted with the protection of Nationalist areas.

Young IRA activists in Belfast, including Adams, led Catholic mobs in attacks on RUC stations on the Falls Road in early August, in one case battering down the station door with a telegraph pole. Loyalists revenged themselves on vulnerable Catholics. Unity Flats, at the foot of the Shankill, became a favorite target. In rioting around the flats on August 2, involving loyalists, Catholics, and the RUC, the police fatally injured a sixty-one-year-old Catholic, Patrick Corry.

The resources of the three-thousand-strong police were being stretched. Paisley and other Protestant extremists demanded that the part-time constabulary, the B-Specials, be deployed to aid the RUC. However, Chichester-Clark hesitated, knowing that it could produce a backlash from enraged Catholics who hated the Specials as a thoroughly sectarian unit.

The Apprentice Boys were a Protestant group, a "Loyal Order," rather like the Orange Order but older. The group was formed to commemorate events dating back to the seventeenth-century war of succession between the Protestant King William of Orange and the Catholic King James II, during which Catholic forces besieged Williamite Derry and, legend has it, were kept successfully at bay thanks to the action of thirteen loyalist apprentice boys. The Apprentice Boys held its main march on August 12. Traditionally, the marchers' route took them along the city's seventeenth-century battlements that looked out over the impoverished Catholic neighborhood of the Bogside. Some marchers contemptuously hurled pennies at the Catholics in the streets below. As the march came to an end, it was met with a torrent of stones, bottles, and nails. The RUC moved against the Catholic rioters, who had erected barricades around their district. The Bogsiders were prepared, with thousands of gasoline bombs ready. The worst riot so far of the Troubles resulted, lasting two days. For the first time the RUC, exhausted and stretched to near breaking point, lobbed tear gas canisters into the rebellious streets. But the rioters quickly found an antidote in water and vinegar. The Northern Ireland prime minister, facing the worst crisis in the state's history, sent units of the B-Specials to Derry to relieve the weary and demoralized police force. It only led to a further deterioration of the situation. On August 14 the Northern Ireland authorities requested the intervention of British troops.

In the Northern Ireland capital, meanwhile, an even more disastrous breakdown occurred. As news spread about the riots in Derry, NICRA called for demonstrations throughout the province. Local IRA men helped organize mob attacks on police stations along the Falls Road. Rioters set fire to a few vulnerable Protestant businesses, including a car showroom and a flour mill. Their aim was to take the pressure off the besieged and barricaded Catholics in the Bogside, which was now being proclaimed Free Derry. But sectarian animosity in Belfast was always more deadly.

Mobs of loyalists from the Shankill descended on the Falls, torching Catholic homes along the streets linking the two thoroughfares, only a few hundred yards apart. Gunshots reverberated along the narrow streets. A few armed IRA men were spotted flitting from alleyway to alleyway. Billy McKee began evacuating Catholic families along Divis Street, at the foot of the Falls. Along with three other IRA veterans, Seamus Twomey, Liam Burke, and Liam Price, he took up position in a primary school that commanded a view of the streets leading into their area from the loyalist district. They were joined by seven or eight local teenagers. Between them they possessed six handguns and an old submachine gun. As the loyalist mob approached, the IRA men opened fire, wounding eight Protestants.[25]

The RUC, jittery and expecting an IRA ambush, riddled the Divis Flats, a Catholic apartment block, with a general-purpose machine gun mounted on an armored car, shooting a nine-year-old boy, Patrick Rooney. As the boy was whisked away in an ambulance, his father was left to scrape his son's brains off the bedroom wall with a spoon.[26] Rooney was one of eight killed in Belfast during the night of August 14 and the early hours of the following day. They included a Protestant, Herbert Roy, shot dead not far from the school where McKee and his men were stationed, and an off-duty British soldier, Hugh McCabe, who like Rooney died in the Divis Flats complex as a result of police gunfire.[27] A fifteen-year-old republican, Gerard McAuley, was among the dead, killed by a loyalist sniper during an attack on Bombay Street, which was Catholic and close to the border with the Shankill area. Thirty-eight houses of the sixty-three in the street were destroyed. As the day dawned over the smoldering ruins in street after street, the scene resembled the aftermath of the blitz.[28]

When British troops took up positions in Derry on August 14 and then in Belfast on the next day, things calmed down. Catholics welcomed them with open arms and cups of tea. A few people returned to the homes from which they had fled the night before. Nineteen-year-old Geraldine O'Regan, a Catholic, was due to be married in two weeks. She found her home a burned-out ruin. "I walked down this street, and I seen all the destruction around me and . . . you couldn't really understand it, you couldn't take it in. . . . Our house was burnt to the ground, and all the houses around it were burnt. And the Protestants . . . were shouting down at us and laughing at us. . . . My whole political thinking changed at that point."[29]

The hope hatched in the early 1960s, which envisioned a different world where Catholic and Protestant would live side by side, was reduced to ashes. It was the figures rooted in the violent past, once derided as historical anomalies, who now shaped events.

· TWO ·

OUT OF THE ASHES

1969–1972

THE CHARRED SHELLS of homes and factories smoldered between the Falls and Shankill roads, the smell of smoke and burning gasoline everywhere. Gaunt streets of gutted houses stood abandoned.

Troops patrolled the uneasy city, uncoiling rolls of barbed wire to separate the Protestant and Catholic working-class communities, where the mood of uncertainty was mixed with anger. Where was the legendary IRA and the UVF when they were needed most? As usual, Catholics and Protestants looked at the same events and came to opposite conclusions. The burnings proved to Catholics that the IRA was woefully inadequate as a defense force. The killings of two Protestants, meanwhile, convinced loyalists that they had been right all along: The IRA was back on the offensive.

Resentment was turned on their leaders. "Paisley blotted his copybook in August 1969. I remember when it was still pretty hairy, when there was still fighting going on in Percy Street [between the Shankill and the Falls], and he was saying, 'Let me down there to my people, I'm going down to my people.' Women were holding on to his arm and saying, 'No, you can't go down there.' He wasn't making much attempt to get away from them. Men were just standing there with their arms folded looking at him and saying, 'Look at that eejit.' After that, people said: 'Where were you when we wanted you? You started this thing, and then where were you when we needed you?' "[1]

Around the Catholic streets the slogan "IRA = I Ran Away" appeared on walls. The Dublin leadership was blamed and accused of being out of touch with the realities of Ulster. IRA Chief of Staff Cathal Goulding, committed to transforming the IRA from a cabal of militarists into a left-wing organization relevant to modern Ireland, came under attack from two different generations. IRA veterans such as Billy McKee regarded as folly the efforts of the reformers to "phase out" the IRA when it was most needed. "Money was being used to keep *The United Irishman* [newspaper] going instead of buying arms. The first rule of the IRA was defense of the people."[2] McKee's reputation, gained from the twelve years or so he had spent in jail for IRA activities, was enhanced as one of the "defenders of the Falls" in Saint Comgall's School. Younger republican activists like Gerry Adams, less than half McKee's age, were at one with him in feeling that the Army Council in the south could no longer be trusted to take the necessary steps to protect northern Catholics.

According to Adams, "The republican movement of the 1960s had proved incapable of responding adequately to events as they evolved in the Six Counties."[3] They believed that the movement would have to reverse its course if it was to survive. Agreement developed between the young street fighters of Belfast and the aging traditionalists, who after years of isolation and derision suddenly saw the prospect of an IRA reborn. But in the meantime it was galling for them to look on powerlessly as Catholics welcomed British troops with cups of tea as their saviors from loyalist mob rule.

The British government, too, saw its approach to "the Irish question" go up in smoke in the fires of August 1969. Since the 1920s, Britain's aim had been to insulate itself from the Irish question, which from the 1880s on had proved so disruptive to British political life. Partition was a means of keeping the problem at a safe distance. The Unionist parliament in Belfast was left to run things much as it liked, while the Irish Free State suppressed the remnants of militant Irish republicanism south of the border. Over the decades, Ulster was kept firmly on the margins of British political life. In 1923 the Westminster parliament ruled that "matters of administration for a minister in Northern Ireland could not be discussed" in the British parliament.[4] Even among educated English people not much was known about Northern Ireland or even if it was still a part of the United Kingdom.[5] The main link between the two parliaments was financial, with Britain shoring up a failing Ulster economy through yearly disbursements from the British treasury. But even that relationship was left mostly undiscussed. According to Richard Crossman, who was a minister in the cabinet of the Wilson government, "Neither Jack Diamond [chief secretary to the treasury, 1964–70] nor the Chancellor knew the formula by which Northern Ireland gets its money. In all these years it has never been revealed to the politicians, and I am longing to see whether now we shall get to the bottom of this very large and expensive secret."[6]

With Harold Wilson in power after 1964, Labour Party activists, among others, felt that the party should press for a United Ireland. The prime minister was known to be in favor of a united Ireland, at least in principle. His government was, after all, one of reform, which some in the party thought should encompass changes in Northern Ireland. But Wilson was effectively overruled. Any kind of intervention—other than nudging Terence O'Neill to do the right thing—was regarded as too risky. As the crisis deepened, Unionists were warned that if they requested troops, Stormont would have to be suspended and direct rule imposed. However, it was a threat meant only to discourage Stormont from seeking such aid. Direct rule would have breached the British principle of minimal intervention. When the crisis broke in August 1969 and intervention became inevitable, it was delayed, and when it came, it was minimal. Committing the Prince of Wales's own regiment to the Bogside in Derry on August 14 and the Second Battalion of the Queen's Regiment to the streets of Belfast the following day was viewed as a holding operation, no more. The troops were there to give Chichester-Clark time to push through the necessary reforms. Once confidence in the police was restored, they would leave. If Britain could be said to have a strategy, that was it. When the troops did go in, they were under the control of the Unionist government, although their legal status was somewhat confused.

On August 19, Wilson's government tried to reassure jittery Unionists that the status of Northern Ireland within the United Kingdom was not threatened and that "the border is not an issue."[7] This, the first Downing Street declaration, at the same time welcomed reforms in local government elections, public housing allocation, and other steps to ensure that equality of treatment for all the people of Northern Ireland would be guaranteed. It was a reminder to the Unionists that while Northern Ireland was still part of the United Kingdom, it would have to change.

The Northern Ireland prime minister, Chichester-Clark, undertook a sweeping security review. Lord Hunt chaired a commission on the police. It recommended that the RUC be disarmed and civilianized, and the B-Specials be abolished and replaced by a reserve force. A locally recruited military unit, the Ulster Defense Regiment, would be raised under the control of the British army.[8]

Loyalists were already in a state of agitated insecurity, convinced that the IRA was active again. At the beginning of September, Jackie Todd, a Protestant vigilante, was shot dead near a barricade in north Belfast—the third Protestant to be murdered within as many weeks. Soon arms, including .45 Smith and Wesson long-barreled revolvers and .32 and .38 pistols, were being sold on the Shankill. During the riot on October 9 with which loyalists greeted the Hunt Commission's recommendations, the British army fired on the crowd, killing two Protestants. Loyalists replied using the recently acquired weapons and shot and killed Constable Victor Arbuckle. Thanks to the Hunt reforms, Constable Arbuckle was unarmed at the time.

Arbuckle's death was a reminder of the crucial role loyalists have played in creating the Ulster crisis, a role that tends to be forgotten. Between 1966 and 1969, they launched a murder campaign, bombed a prime minister out of office, burned down hundreds of homes, and murdered a policeman.

The only organization on the Shankill that contributed to the violence was the Shankill Road Defense Association, a gang of vigilantes under John McKeague, a blond-haired Paisleyite with a taste for teenage boys.[9] Other Shankill Road Protestants, also vigilantes but less prominent and certainly less flamboyant, began quietly to meet in local clubs to plot a course of action.

The meetings were divided into two parts, the first devoted to recruiting those who were prepared merely to man the barricades, and the second to identifying those prepared to take the war into the Catholic areas, those who believed that attack was the best form of defense. Charles Harding-Smith, a truck driver and hod carrier, dominated these gatherings, which were attended by a handful of local toughs and street fighters. While not a hard man himself, he knew how to attract them.

Throughout 1970 the Protestant vigilantes remained a ramshackle amalgam of different defense groups. There was no centralized command

and not even an agreed name. Harding-Smith wanted the loose alliance to be called the Ulster Volunteer Force, but since there were already organizations using that hallowed name, it would have caused confusion. Eventually McKeague's idea of calling the collection of vigilantes the Ulster Defense Association was accepted. The loyalist vigilantes established a training camp in the little fishing port of Kilkeel in south Down in June 1970. The training consisted mainly of arms drill under the guidance of Jim Finlay, a former British soldier. It was not much use for men who were about to become assassins, but it built up a camaraderie among them. As Harding Smith's power grew, he clashed with the volatile McKeague, accusing him of stealing funds. McKeague was expelled but still continued to cause trouble. He set up his own group with a comic-book name, the Red Hand Commandos. As a warning, Harding-Smith's men firebombed the shop above which McKeague lived with his aging mother. Mrs. McKeague was burned to death, and the UDA claimed its first victim—a Protestant old-age pensioner.

The violence of August 1969 also provoked a crisis within the IRA and Sinn Fein, which brought to the surface the underlying tensions and distrust between the Dublin leadership and the majority of republican activists in Belfast. The uncertainty and distrust that the Dublin IRA felt went back to the 1920s. Even when the IRA was at the height of its power under Michael Collins, it balked at the prospect of a full-scale assault in Ulster. IRA men from the north advised Collins against it, pointing out that the kind of guerrilla war the IRA fought successfully in parts of southern Ireland—especially in west Cork and Kerry—could not be sustained in Ulster where the majority of the population was hostile to republicanism. The ever present prospect of loyalist counterterror directed against innocent Catholics (particularly in Belfast) was also an important factor in restraining the IRA's activities in the north. During the civil disturbances following the formation of the Northern Ireland state, the IRA's actions in Belfast provoked a ferocious Protestant backlash. Republicans retaliated with attacks on Protestants. Left-wing activists such as Peadar O'Donnell long regarded the IRA in the north as a Catholic defense force with reactionary potential.[10] He fiercely criticized the Belfast IRA for its failure to build relations with the Protestant working class and accused it of possessing "a bigotry that is dangerous to the cause they have at heart."[11] O'Donnell's expectations were absurdly high; like all left-wing republicans he completely misunderstood the nature of the Ulster Protestants' connection to Britain, seeing it as an "artificial" link that could be broken if the right socialist policies were presented to them. In the 1960s the IRA leadership again took up this line, arguing that militant loyalism would die out because British imperialism no longer had any use for it. It was only a matter of time before the Protestant working class would be won over to revolutionary socialism—provided the republican movement could make them see its relevance. In the intervening thirty years, the IRA in Belfast went into a disastrous decline, precipitated partly by the defeats of the 1920s. It played no part in the 1956 border campaign. And it was peripheral to the republican analysis that followed the collapse of that campaign in 1962.

For Goulding, faced with a new crisis and many republicans clamoring for a northern campaign, the lessons of the 1920s still applied. He and his supporters on the Army Council pressed ahead with their politicization program, demanding that the movement change its constitution to allow elected Sinn Fein members to take their seats in the parliaments in Belfast, Dublin, and London.

Infuriated, the anti-Goulding faction of the IRA in Belfast staged a coup against his supporters and replaced Liam McMillen, the officer commanding the IRA in the city, with Billy McKee. The Belfast IRA then announced that it was breaking off relations with the Army Council in Dublin.

An extraordinary convention of IRA delegates was held in mid-December 1969 to debate the leadership's proposals to recognize the three parliaments—in effect, to accept the reality of the 1921 settlement. The traditionalists asked that a two-thirds majority should be required if such drastic changes were to be enacted, but they were overruled. The IRA's intelligence chief, Sean MacStiofain, warned that if the change came about, "those who accepted it would forfeit the right to describe themselves as the Irish Republican Army."[12] But the main proposals passed with a simple majority.

Opposition to Goulding crystallized around MacStiofain, the forty-one-year-old Londoner. Hurried meetings followed with opponents of the new course, including McKee and Seamus Twomey, who had taken part in the Saint Comgall's School action in August, and two prominent veterans of the 1956–62 campaign, Daithi O'Conaill and Ruairi O'Bradaigh. A new IRA emerged from these gatherings, intent on remaining faithful to traditional republican goals and methods. O'Conaill was elected its first chief of staff, but he declined. MacStiofain was then chosen—the first time in the history of the republican movement that an Englishman filled that role.[13] Because a full-scale army convention had yet to formalize the new structures and personnel, the organization called itself the Provisional IRA.

Murals soon appeared in working-class Catholic areas of Belfast showing a crudely drawn phoenix rising up from the flames. Under it was written, "From the ashes of '69 arose the Provisionals." The name stuck.

The Provisional IRA was a dangerous mix of dogma and determination. Purist republicans from the south such as O'Bradaigh and O'Conaill joined forces with embittered and angry Belfast men like McKee. They shared a contempt for conventional parliamentary politics. The Holy Grail of a United Ireland would never be obtained through surrendering to the temptations of compromise, however alluring. To their zeal was added the impatience of the young left-wing activists of Adams's generation who wanted action, as did the third element in the mixture: the recruits from the local Catholic defense groups that manned the barricades in embattled areas such as Ardoyne in north Belfast and were ready to retaliate against Protestants. The ethos of the early Provisionals was decidedly Catholic—McKee, the first commanding officer of the Belfast organization, was a daily communicant. The dogmatism of the pulpit and the narrowness of the Belfast ghetto made for a ruthless combination.

However, for Belfast activists like Adams the most important thing was that there was now a leadership in Dublin in sympathy with their need for guns. Shortly before the split, he and a few like-minded republicans took measures into their own hands and attended an unauthorized arms training camp across the border in County Leitrim. On the way back to Belfast, their car crashed, and one of his companions, IRA man Liam McParland, was killed. Adams was suspended from the IRA. But by then the Goulding faction in Belfast was already under siege, and his suspension was soon lifted. Although Adams joined the Provisional faction, he maintained friendly contacts with many who stayed with Goulding and was suspected of leaning in that direction by McKee, who said that Adams once told him "the split was right but for the wrong reason."[14]

In January, at the Sinn Fein ard fheis (party conference), the two sides fought it out again at a political level. Once again the majority voted in favor of the Goulding proposals. Sinn Fein split, and O'Bradaigh led 257 delegates out of the convention to form the Provisional Sinn Fein, of which he became president.

The Goulding IRA became known as the Officials and then the Stickies, thanks to an adhesive Easter lily emblem that its members wore and distributed during the commemoration of the 1916 Easter Rising.[15]

Among the first tasks the Provisionals set themselves was the acquisition of an arsenal. Like earlier generations of Irish republicans, they turned to the United States. In New York, George Harrison, a fifty-four-year-old Brink's security guard who traced his roots back to County Mayo in the west of Ireland, was watching the developments in Ulster with interest and concern. An uncompromising republican, Harrison became involved in supplying weapons to the IRA in the 1950s. His main link was through another American-based republican activist, Eoin McNamee. In August 1969, McNamee wrote to Harrison from the Bogside, at the height of the riots, with the smell of burning gasoline in his nose, asking for assistance. Harrison raised and dispatched several thousand dollars—perhaps the first money from the United States to reach Nationalists in this phase of the conflict. Later, McNamee, who supported the Provisional faction, arrived in New York, and Harrison handed over what few weapons were left from the early 1960s. McNamee shipped them back on a regular Aer Lingus flight from Kennedy Airport. "The inspection at the airport was easy at the time," said Harrison.[16] McNamee helped set up a meeting between Harrison and Daithi O'Conaill, who came to New York in January 1970. Harrison and Liam Cotter, another exiled republican who was part of the 1950s arms smuggling network, met with O'Conaill in a restaurant near Central Park. O'Conaill asked if they would be prepared to help with the "armed struggle." "There's no problem with that," they told him.[17] O'Conaill met with other Irish Americans such as IRA veteran Michael Flannery, who agreed to start a fund-raising organization, Irish Northern Aid. Harrison and Cotter kept their activities far apart from those of the fund-raisers and succeeded in establishing a regular supply of guns and ammunition that gave the Provisionals the firepower to take on the British army.[18]

· 2 ·

THE COZY relationship between Catholics and the British army deteriorated rapidly during the early months of 1970. Restless and aggressive youths challenged the army, which having replaced the RUC was forced into a policing role it was not equipped to handle. The first serious confrontation took place in Derry in March when a crowd attacked an RUC station and injured twelve soldiers. But it was the windswept and desolate housing developments on the outskirts of Belfast, places such as Ballymurphy where Adams lived, that saw the worst violence. These sprawling estates erected in the early 1950s were areas of high unemployment, and the Provisionals took hold quickly over their large populations of bored and listless young men.

In Ballymurphy, relations between the people and the troops became strained after Adams and other local Provisionals organized a picket of the nearby army base to protest soldiers inviting local girls to their weekly disco.[19] Pent-up frustration and daily friction between youths and troops boiled over at the beginning of April. Mobs of Catholics and Protestants who lived nearby confronted each other, with the army in between. Local residents armed with hurling sticks, clubs, and rocks fought hand to hand with the soldiers. Other army units lobbed CS gas canisters into the streets. Army units known as snatch squads would suddenly dash from the ranks to seize an identified mob leader and drag him back. Youths turned this tactic against the army. They deliberately lured snatch squads into cul-de-sacs, which they sealed with barbed wire, trapping the troops and pelting them with stones and bricks. Many Protestants who lived in or near Ballymurphy were driven from their homes.

In June 1970, to the dismay of Nationalists, the authorities failed to ban an Orange parade that skirted Catholic streets in north Belfast. Serious riots flared up on June 27. Provisional IRA snipers opened fire on the Protestants rioters and killed three. The same night, in the east of the city, loyalists attacked the isolated Catholic Short Strand area. Billy McKee arrived on the scene to support the local IRA, and a gun battle broke out around Saint Matthew's Catholic Church. Another two Protestants were shot dead, along with one Provisional IRA man. McKee was wounded and smuggled across the border to a hospital. The next day loyalists ejected five hundred Catholic workers from their workplace at the Harland and Wolff shipyards.

The intervention of the Provisionals confirmed their primary role as a Catholic defense force; it was strongest in areas like the Short Strand and north Belfast where Catholics felt most vulnerable.

The situation continued to deteriorate throughout the spring and summer of 1970. In April the "general officer commanding" (GOC) in Ulster, General Sir Ian Freeland, warned bomb throwers that they would be shot. In June he warned that anyone seen carrying a weapon would be shot on sight.

Increasingly, Catholics saw the British army as just another instrument of Unionist rule, no better and even worse than the RUC.

On July 2 the army made an arms find in the lower Falls district, an area loyal to the Official IRA. A mob trapped the search team, and snipers fired on troops surrounding the neighborhood. General Freeland decided a show of force was needed and launched a rescue mission. Troops went in firing CS gas, sending residents choking through the narrow streets. Soldiers smashed their way from house to house, kicking down doors and tearing up floorboards. They hauled off a small horde of weapons, twenty-eight pounds of gelignite, over twenty thousand rounds of ammunition; they made 337 arrests.[20] The Official IRA "took on" the army to show they could defend their area as well as PIRA, wounding eighteen soldiers. The army killed four civilians during the operation, including a visiting photographer from England.[21]

Freeland imposed a curfew that was not lifted (except for two hours to allow women to shop) until 9 A.M. on July 5. He later justified the Falls raid as a major success because of the arms found. However, in Northern Ireland it is the political consequences of every military or violent act, not its tactical success, that determines whether it is judged a "success" or otherwise. By this measure, the Falls Road Curfew, as it came to be known, was a political disaster for British policy in Ulster:

> *It can be argued that the failure to ban the 1970 Orange parades, and the massive arms searches and curfew in the Lower Falls area which followed, was the last chance to avoid the catastrophe that has since engulfed Ulster. . . . Until the spring of 1970, most Catholics regarded the troops as their protectors. The Lower Falls operation*

> *changed everything, though the Army was merely doing its job and reacting to events. . . . Following the events of early July, PIRA grew from fewer than 100 activists in May–June to roughly 800 in December 1970.*[22]

Embarrassingly for the government, it was discovered the curfew had been illegally imposed.

The momentum was now behind the Provisional IRA. Though the Provisionals concentrated on "defensive" operations, they occasionally carried out more aggressive actions, like the January 1970 bombing of a RUC station on the fringe of west Belfast. Two weeks after the Falls Road raids, a bomb exploded with no previous warning at a bank in the heart of the city, injuring thirty people, two of them seriously. A UDR vehicle was blown up near Derry and two soldiers injured. When the British GOC warned rioters they would be shot, the Provisionals countered that they would retaliate. At the end of July, troops shot dead nineteen-year-old Daniel O'Hagan during a riot in north Belfast. On August 11 a booby-trapped car left near Crossmaglen in south Armagh exploded and killed two RUC men, Constables Samuel Donaldson and Robert Millar.[23] They were the first members of the security forces to die at the hands of the IRA in the current Troubles. They were the exception. Of the nine victims of the Provisional IRA in 1970, seven were civilians, five of them Protestants. The disproportionately high number of civilian deaths would remain a characteristic of the ensuing conflict.

A second Provisional army convention was held in September 1970, ratifying the decisions made the previous December and reelecting MacStiofain as chief of staff. In the meantime, in Belfast, the Provisionals prepared to go on the offensive. Many of those joining the organization were former British soldiers, who brought with them valued experience in weapons training.

The Provisionals began to enforce their own version of law and order in Catholic areas of Belfast. Ordinary crime was comparatively rare in Belfast, but where it appeared, the Provisionals knew there was a likelihood also of informing, since criminals often bargain with the police, offering information in return for leniency. Arthur McKenna and Alexander McVicar, two petty criminals operating in Adams's area, were shot to death on November 16. The killings served as a warning that there was a new law enforcement organization in the district and that it would deal brutally with transgressors. The new year, 1971, began with the murder of the first alleged informer, John Kavanagh, a neighborhood drunk who was accused of speaking to the police. The Provisionals dragged Kavanagh to the banks of a polluted river in west Belfast, shoved a gun in his mouth, and "executed" him.

· 3 ·

THROUGHOUT 1970, violence pushed civil rights issues into the background. Northern Ireland was seen more and more as a security problem, a view that gained strength when the British general election of June 18, 1970, brought the Conservative Party to power, with Edward Heath as the new prime minister. Unionist and Conservatives were traditional political allies. Unionists could expect a more sympathetic hearing from London to their argument that the fuss over civil rights was merely a front for the IRA. But the Conservative government shared with its Labour predecessor the same aversion to becoming more involved in Ulster than was absolutely unavoidable. The new Home Secretary, Reginald Maudling, arrived in Northern Ireland on July 1 to be greeted by a swarm of conflicting views and opinions. He left a few hours later exasperated and confused. Insofar as he was able to formulate a consistent policy, it was one of letting the Unionists get on with whatever it was they were doing. On the return flight to London he exploded: "For God's sake, bring me a large scotch. What a bloody awful country!"[24]

"With the advent of a new British government," wrote one of the founders of the civil rights movement, "there appeared to be changed attitudes. The Unionists' 'harder line' directives went into the Catholic areas to re-establish 'law and order.' Force was met by force. . . . The army was now, according to them, and with appropriate support from Westminster, acting in a proper way and doing what every loyalist and Unionist required. . . . Beating the minority back into submission."[25]

Against the background of militarization, within the Nationalist community a major political realignment took place. Civil rights leader John Hume had long called for "a new political movement based on social democratic principles . . . that must provide what has been severely lacking at Stormont—a strong energetic opposition to conservatism—

proposing radical social and economic policies."[26] Hume made the constitutional status of Northern Ireland central to the new political movement he envisioned. But any change in that status would only come about with the consent of the majority. This was heresy to traditional nationalism, which saw partition as Britain's way of retaining control over part of Ireland. Hume's view implied that partition was a product of the Protestants' wish to stay out of a United Ireland, not of a British desire to dominate.

Gerry Fitt, the Republican Labour MP, shared Hume's view, as did Paddy Devlin, a former IRA man and member of the Northern Ireland Labour Party. In August 1970 they got together with a few members of the old Nationalist Party (by then almost defunct) and civil rights activists to form the Social Democratic and Labour Party.

The SDLP was woven from three different political strands within nationalism represented by left-wing trade unionists, the civil rights activists, and the former members of the Nationalist Party. Unlike the Nationalist Party, the SDLP would actively engage with Unionists, and, if elected, its members would take their seats in both the Belfast and London parliaments. Among the party's aims, as embodied in its constitution, were "to organize and maintain in Northern Ireland a socialist party . . . to promote the cause of Irish unity based on the consent of a majority of the people of Northern Ireland." It aligned itself with other social democratic parties "at an international level" and would "cooperate with the Irish Congress of Trades Unions."[27]

Fitt and Devlin gave the new party a base among the Catholic working class in Belfast. Both were blunt-speaking, working-class politicians with strong links to the unions. Austin Currie, whose house-squat had helped start the civil rights movement in 1968, brought into the party some of the rural bastions of the Nationalist Party for which he was an MP. Hume's popularity in Derry gave the SDLP an almost impregnable base in that city among Catholics of all classes. Other prominent members of the new alignment were Paddy Wilson of Republican Labour and Ivan Cooper, a Protestant and a leading civil rights activist. But the SDLP never succeeded in attracting more than the occasional Protestant. The Alliance Party founded in the same year siphoned off many politically moderate Protestants, some of them former supporters of Terence O'Neill.

Because of his position as a Westminster MP, Fitt was appointed SDLP leader, with Hume as his deputy.

In 1971, Hume wrote: "To create a truly united country we need a truly united people, not a united piece of earth. In that task we need not to overcome the Northern Protestant but to seek his cooperation, help and assistance."[28] The creation of the SDLP was an attempt to translate that vision into practical politics. It was a struggle to introduce rational politics into what was fundamentally an irrational situation where the clash of conflicting absolutes drowned out reasoned argument. It was not that the Provisionals did not have politics as such—they did, as well as a political program for a new Ireland, *Eire Nua;* it was that their aim had become secondary to the methods they were using to achieve it.

The Provisional IRA despised SDLP pragmatism as weakness and cowardice. The moral basis for its vision was a semimystical incantation of sacrifice and martyrdom where absolutes reigned: the absolute right of a vague entity, the "Irish people," to an independent united Ireland, and the IRA's absolute right to use violence to achieve it. Provisional leaders scorned the SDLP as the "Stoop Down Low Party."

• 4 •

IN THE eighteen months between August 1969 and January 1971, the IRA was brought back from the verge of extinction. The Provisionals alone could now muster about one thousand activists, concentrated mainly in Belfast, the Officials somewhat fewer. Opposed to them were seven thousand regular British troops, four thousand Ulster Defense Regiment members, and just over three thousand RUC officers, aided by about six hundred reserve constables. The struggle over civil rights was transformed into an incipient guerrilla war, with Belfast as its cockpit. The city's three battalions were the first to organize and the first to demonstrate a willingness to "defend" their areas with violence. They were also the first to go on an all-out offensive. The strategy was two-pronged, consisting of attacks against soldiers and policemen in tandem with a bombing campaign aimed at "economic" targets. The aim was to make Britain's link to Northern Ireland so expensive that it would be forced to withdraw.

MacStiofain believed that if the British army lost forty men, the government would come under irresistible pressure to pull out. This assumption was naive but typical of the failure of the Provisionals' mainly Dublin-based leadership to realize the crucial role that Protestants played in the equation. The strength of their resistance to British withdrawal was not taken into account. Instead, the Provisional leaders believed that once soldiers started coming home in boxes, the clamor would be so great in Britain that the link would be cut. But even those republicans with a more skeptical view of this program were swept along by the desire for sheer revenge that gripped the nationalist ghettoes in the wake of army raids, searches, and general harassment.

However, the most important factor that would determine the course of the Provisionals' campaign was one that had little to do with strategies worked out in Dublin or the political analysis of ideologues. The Provisionals were a ghetto force first and foremost, and responded to events in their neighborhood, often taking actions that disregarded the leadership's instructions. After all, it was far away in Dublin. According to McKee, MacStiofain, though chief of staff, "knew nothing about what was going on in the North."[29]

Although MacStiofain liked to give the impression that the decision to kill British soldiers was not made until February 1971, in fact the Provisionals had been targeting them since at least the summer before.[30] That they did not succeed in killing any was as much a matter of luck as policy. That changed on February 6. After a series of vicious riots, a patrol of the Royal Artillery came under Sterling submachine gun fire on the New Lodge Road in north Belfast. The hail of bullets killed twenty-year-old Gunner Robert Curtis, the first British soldier to die in Ireland in over fifty years.

"At long last the step had been taken."[31]

His killer, Billy Reid, had never used a Sterling before.[32] He was a member of the Provisionals' Third Battalion in north Belfast, the most active of the three that made up the Belfast Brigade and the most dangerous IRA unit in the whole of Northern Ireland. Of the fifty-nine security forces' fatalities that year, twenty-one died at the hands of the Third Battalion, including seven RUC officers. Snipers killed most, using the back alleyways to escape. But the Third Battalion showed it was flexible when it came to tactics.

A Scottish regiment stationed in north Belfast soon gained a reputation for harassing the locals and even provoked complaints from some Protestants. On the night of March 10, three members of the regiment, two of them brothers, were drinking in a city center pub where they met three IRA men from the tough Ardoyne neighborhood in north Belfast. They were lured to an isolated roadway with the promise of women. The three soldiers were urinating at the side of the road when their drinking companions shot them dead.

The IRA issued a statement denying responsibility. MacStiofain claimed that his men only targeted on-duty military personnel. As usual, however, the Dublin leadership was being left to try to explain events over which it exercised little control. It was later admitted that the Belfast Provisionals had lied in the hope that the killings would be blamed on Protestant extremists and would cause friction between them and the British.[33] The incident led to a widespread investigation during which Billy McKee was arrested. He was charged and convicted of possession of explosives.

The killings provoked a crisis for the Unionist government. Four thousand workmen put down their tools at the Belfast shipyards and marched on the city center to demand the introduction of internment without trial against the IRA. Many Unionists agreed with them. The British resisted, partly because the army advised against it and partly due to a fear of being sucked more deeply into the Ulster morass. Unionist Prime Minister Chichester-Clark then asked London for three thousand more troops. When the Heath government sent him thirteen hundred, he resigned.

Frustrated and still determined to get internment, the Unionist Party turned to Brian Faulkner. A dapper little businessman and a cunning politician, Faulkner had made his name in two areas: commerce and security. During the IRA's border offensive, Faulkner had used internment without trial to break the back of the campaign. In the 1960s, as O'Neill's commerce minister, he had helped bring new industry to Northern Ireland. But it was his reputation as a "law and order" man that won him Unionist support in 1971.

The Provisionals' other tactic, the bombing campaign, was also bringing the Northern Ireland government pressure from those who wanted a quick solution to the worsening security situation. There were sixteen bombings in January, thirty-eight in February, thirty-one in March, and thirty-eight in April. May saw forty-three, and June forty-four. In July the number of bombing attacks jumped to ninety-four.[34] The attacks were often reckless. On May 25 a Provisional bomber threw a suitcase packed with explosives into the hallway of the Springfield Road RUC station, in the Falls area. A group of women and children standing nearby were ushered to safety just before it exploded, killing Sergeant Michael Willets, who was between them and the blast. A baby on the opposite side of the street was flung from its pram and buried under the rubble. Miraculously, the baby had a fractured skull but survived. When the fatally wounded soldier was being carried out of the station on a door, used as a makeshift stretcher, a crowd of youths began to jeer and scream obscenities. "My reaction was one of total disbelief that anyone could be so inhumane," commented Lieutenant Colonel Peter Chiswell, who was in command of the unit at the time.[35]

The rapid growth of the Provisional IRA caught the RUC unawares. It was overwhelmed. Its small crimes special unit, which replaced the Special Branch, lacked informers. A new generation of gunmen and activists was emerging, about which the police possessed only a few clues. This lack of reliable information made the British hesitate to use internment.

However, Faulkner was besieged. The IRA menace was growing, and without some drastic action, how could the government prevent the prospect of a militant Unionist backlash? British Secretary of State for Defense Lord Peter Carrington thought there might be a way of actually utilizing internment to gain the much needed information. He reached an arrangement with Faulkner and the police. Army intelligence officers would instruct the RUC in secret methods for extracting information from a group of prisoners who would be specially selected from the internees.[36] They were sensory deprivation techniques. They had been used in every colonial war that Britain had fought since the late 1940s, but this fact was not widely known.[37]

The Provisionals were expecting internment. From the beginning of the summer its members were ordered to take the necessary precautions, the most obvious being not to stay at home. IRA operatives watched the airport and seaports, noting the steady influx of troops. However, the British still hesitated. It was only after an army swoop on July 28 failed to disrupt IRA operations that the final decision to go ahead was made. The operation was code-named Demetrius.

At around four A.M. on August 9, people in the Catholic areas of Belfast and Derry awoke to a deafening noise. Women were banging garbage-can lids on pavements, the traditional signal that the security forces were approaching. Thousands of troops stormed into the ghettos, with a list of 452 suspects; 342 people were taken, including a few members of NICRA and the student group People's Democracy. According to MacStiofain, only 56 Provisionals were caught in the net.[38] Gerry Adams was one of those most sought, but he watched quietly from a distance as soldiers wrecked his home, dragging off his father and a younger brother.[39] The Catholic districts were raked with gunfire as battles broke out between loyalists, the IRA, and the army. Within a few hours fifteen people lay dead, all but one of them civilians. They included a Catholic priest, Father Hugh Mullan, and a fourteen-year-old boy, Desmond Healey. Twenty-five hundred Catholics were driven from their homes near Protestant areas, and in north Belfast, Catholics drove out Protestant neighbors. Whole streets were ablaze. In the Ardoyne, Protestants burned down two hundred houses after evacuating them rather than hand them over to Catholics.

"By now the entire area was in a state of insurrection," wrote Adams of Ballymurphy.[40]

One-third of those arrested were released within two days. Twelve of the remaining 237 were hooded and flown by helicopter to an old Royal Air Force base in Ballykelly, County Derry. For six days they were subjected to the nightmare of sensory deprivation: spread-eagled against a wall for up to sixteen hours at a stretch, always hooded and denied sleep while a noise like the roar of a jet engine drowned out the sound of everything else. They were beaten if they fell, then dragged before Special Branch officers for questioning before being sent back to the wall again. During the six days they were kept on a diet of bread and water. The effect was to induce a kind of psychosis. "I thought I was going mad," said one victim, nineteen-year-old Joe Clark from west Belfast.[41]

When details about the treatment began to emerge, there were demands for an inquiry, which led to the setting up of a committee under Lord Parker. A member of his committee, Lord Gardiner, declared that the techniques were illegal. For this reason, he argued, the army could not have used them in any authorized fashion. "If any document or Minister had purported to authorize them, it would have been invalid because the procedures were and are illegal by domestic law and may also have been illegal by international law."[42]

Yet no charges were ever brought against those involved in what was one of the most egregious acts of illegality in the Troubles. It was part of a pattern that would lead to further, bloodier violations of human rights.[43]

The political cost of internment far outweighed whatever intelligence-gathering benefits might have been gained. It was aimed solely at the

Catholic community; not one loyalist was interned.[44] The authorities defended themselves by arguing that loyalists did not pose a significant threat at the time. Catholics, at the receiving end of UVF sniping attacks, were not convinced. Internment succeeded in alienating the entire nationalist community from the state and its security forces. From August 1971 the IRA's grip on the working-class nationalist neighborhoods tightened, turning them into no-go areas for the army and police.

The SDLP had walked out of Stormont on July 8 to protest a British army shooting in Derry. Although uncomfortable with the abstentionist tactic, internment made it impossible for the party to reenter parliament without losing all credibility with nationalists. It organized a rent-and-rates strike to protest internment, but the initiative still lay with the Provisionals.

Internment was a political disaster for Faulkner, partly because it was so obviously a military failure also. Within days of its introduction, practically the entire Provisional Army Council held a press conference in a school in Ballymurphy to flaunt their freedom. And British army casualties were rising drastically. Between February 6 and August 9, eleven soldiers were killed; in the weeks following internment, thirty-two died. The IRA was emerging in other areas where it had lain dormant for years, such as south Armagh. On August 29 the Provisional IRA shot dead a British soldier, Ian Armstrong, in Crossmaglen. Other units became active in Tyrone, Fermanagh, and Down. The number of explosions soared. In September, 179 took place, the highest until then. Among the targets was a Protestant pub on the Shankill Road, which was bombed on the 29th of that month, killing two customers and injuring thirty.[45] The Provisional IRA leadership again denied responsibility, but it was suspected that the north Belfast units were involved. The sectarian element that was present in the Provisionals from the start now asserted itself. Another Protestant pub was bombed a few days later, but fortunately with no fatalities.

Because internment was so obviously a failure, it did nothing to placate Unionist and loyalist militants. If anything, it convinced loyalists that they would have to take the "offensive" themselves to thwart the IRA menace. The pub bombings in the heartlands of loyalist Belfast were added provocations.

The loyalists who gathered around Charles Harding-Smith were getting ready to strike back. "We were trying to sort out the wheat from the chaff—establishing who had what weapons, who was prepared to do what. It was a weeding-out process," said one of the UDA men who attended the meetings that were taking place in loyalist areas.[46] The organization was building crude bombs. A premature explosion in September killed two of its men, John Thompson and Jim Finlay, the ex-soldier who had been a UDA training officer. Immediately after their funeral, a UDA meeting was held in a school hall to discuss the organization's future. Harding-Smith and a gang of his backers walked up the hall and unbuttoned their jackets, revealing an array of pistols. It was the first time that the UDA militants publicly displayed their weapons. The two hundred people in the hall began to applaud. The time for action had come. Harding-Smith was elected chairman and began amalgamating the loosely coordinated defense groups into a sectarian murder machine.[47]

Loyalists revenged themselves for the pub attacks. At the beginning of October 1971, UDA men threw a bomb into a pub known for traditional Irish music, but the only fatality was Winifred Maxwell, a forty-five-year-old Protestant. On December 4, after an IRA sniper shot dead a Protestant teenage girl, loyalists targeted a pub known as an IRA haunt. En route they panicked and left the bomb at McGurk's Bar, the nearest Catholic pub. At 8:45 P.M. one of the thirty customers in the bar shouted, "Somebody has put a stink bomb in here." Seconds later a blinding flash and loud bang brought the building down. An underground gas pipe erupted, asphyxiating and burning those trapped in the rubble, from which fifteen corpses were eventually dug, including that of the owner's wife, Philomena, and fourteen-year-old daughter, Marie.

A week later the Provisionals bombed a furniture store on the Shankill, killing four people. As rescuers dug out the dead, they found the remains of one-year-old Colin Nicholl and two-year-old Tracey Munn, along with that of an old-age pensioner, Hugh Bruce, and twenty-nine-year-old Harold King.

The dark winter months closed in rapidly as 1971 ended, with no sign that the security forces were making any progress against the republican uprising. The city center emptied before evening fell, and people fled home along roads rendered pitch black because the street lamps were out; they were often forced to make the journey on foot after the city's public transport collapsed because of hijackings, burnings, and riots. A makeshift service of taxis was struggling to replace the buses. Among Catholics, thousands of families disrupted by internment and evictions faced Christmas without a father or a home. By the beginning of 1972, over nine hundred Catholic men were being held without trial, leaving women to struggle as best they could.

And worst of all, the killings continued relentlessly. Catholic children, Protestant children, old-age pensioners, teenage girls—their broken bodies littered Ulster's landscape as the New Year dawned.

· THREE ·

THE BLOOD-DIMMED TIDE

1972–1977

IN DERRY, Northern Ireland's second largest city and the scene of the first civil rights clashes, the IRA took longer to organize. The city, with a solid nationalist majority, did not have the sectarian problems that haunted Belfast, and therefore the Provisionals were not called upon as a "defense" force to guard against loyalist attack. Their rivals in the Official IRA thrived in the city's lively left-wing political environment, where Trotskyists, communists, and Marxist militants of various varieties debated traditional republicans. It was not until August 10, 1971, that the Derry IRA managed to kill a soldier.

The authorities were notified that on January 30 a NICRA march against internment would be held in the city's Catholic Bogside, followed by speeches from Bernadette Devlin, other MPs, and civil rights activists. The government had banned all marches in Northern Ireland from August 9, 1971, but Chief Superintendent Frank Lagan, the head of the Derry RUC, advised Major General Robert Ford, the new general officer commanding British forces, that the march should be allowed to proceed and the organizers prosecuted later. In his estimation the police would be able to control the situation, and the army would not be needed because intelligence suggested that the IRA would not be involved in the demonstration. Technically speaking, the British army was in Ulster as an aid to the civil power, which gave Chief Superintendent Lagan, as head of the police, the authority to order the army's intervention or not. However, Lagan was informed that the military had orders to "contain" the march within the Bogside. On January 24, Ford told Lieutenant Colonel Derek Wilford, the commander of the First Battalion of the Parachute Regiment, to prepare to conduct an "arrest operation" on January 30, meaning going after the "hooligan element" if it should attempt to penetrate the streets on the fringes of the Bogside that led to Derry's city center. But First Parachute Battalion was given a standing order not to engage in running battles in the streets that led into the Bogside itself, for fear of falling victim to IRA snipers. Lagan had been superseded, his advice ignored. Major General Ford would be in Derry himself to observe.

The decision to overrule Lagan was made at a high political level, though the actual responsibility for this has never been determined. Nobody would ever be held accountable for the disastrous events that followed.

Frank Lagan's prediction of a relatively uneventful demonstration seemed to be proving true. On that Sunday afternoon the several hundred youths who had earlier indulged in the ritual stone throwing at the security forces on the border of the Bogside began to disperse while the main crowd gathered to listen to the speakers at "Free Derry Corner" in the heart of the nationalist area. Then, shortly before 4 P.M., the first army units arrived.

Since internment, barricades had effectively sealed off the Bogside. The first of these lay a few hundred yards away from where the crowds were milling around and moving toward Free Derry Corner. As the troops crossed the first barricade, they opened fire, wounding two civilians, one of whom, John Johnson, a passerby, died months later of his wounds. The troops continued toward the Bogside, with others arriving in a convoy of ten vehicles. Leaving their armored carriers, the paratroopers fanned out in a rapid and disciplined deployment, some toward nearby blocks of flats. It was 4:10, and already the wintry twilight was setting in. It was then that the "arrest operation" began in earnest. According to Agnes Hume, the sister of the SDLP leader, "One Saracen knocked a man on the ground and a soldier jumped out. He kept the man on the ground by battering him with the butt of his rifle and another soldier shot at this man from very close range. Then the soldiers seemed to go berserk and were shooting everywhere. Women and children were running for cover, screaming."[1]

At the same time, unknown to the crowd below, members of the Royal

Anglican Regiment were in positions on the walls overlooking the Bogside. At least two of them were equipped with sniper's rifles.

Seventeen-year-old Jackie Duddy was the first to be shot dead that afternoon, hit in the back as he ran up the street toward Free Derry Corner. Within minutes and in the same area, others would follow. Patrick Joseph Doherty, age thirty-one, was crawling along to avoid the paratroopers' guns when he was shot in the buttock and died. Hugh Gilmore, a teenager, died next, after being shot, possibly by two different soldiers. Forty-one-year-old Bernard McGuigan had taken cover not far from where Gilmore was hit. An eyewitness, Geraldine Richmond, said they heard a wounded man cry out, "I don't want to die [by] myself, I don't want to die [by] myself." McGuigan responded, "I can't stand this any longer. If I take a white handkerchief out they will not shoot me." He did so. But as he crossed to aid the wounded man, he was shot in the head. The force of the bullet that killed him was such that it blew off the back of his skull.[2]

John Young, William Nash, and Michael McDaid were killed immediately after McGuigan as they stood at a barricade near Free Derry Corner, picked off from the walls overlooking the Bogside where the Royal Anglicans were stationed.[3]

As the paratroopers moved swiftly toward Free Derry Corner, they killed Michael Kelly and Kevin McElhinney, and cornered James Wray, Gerald Donaghy, Gerald McKinney, and William McKinney (no relation) with a group of terrified demonstrators in a courtyard. Eyewitnesses saw William McKinney being shot while going to the aid of a wounded man; they claim Donaghy and Gerald McKinney were gunned down at point-blank range even though they had their hands on their heads in a gesture of surrender. Gerald McKinney's last words were "Don't shoot, don't shoot."[4]

The shooting finally stopped at about 4:30, but the lying about what happened had just begun. It was to last some twenty-five years.

At first the British army claimed that eight of the thirteen dead were wanted, known terrorists and found with weapons. Within hours this claim was modified to four wanted IRA men. They said one of the dead, Gerald Donaghy, had been found with four nail bombs in his pocket. Within two days even these claims were almost totally abandoned as it was admitted that none of the dead was on any wanted list, nor had any been found with weapons; the claim against Donaghy was repeated at a subsequent inquiry but later retracted. This did not discourage the British from asserting, however, that the troops had been fired on first, if not by those shot dead then by IRA snipers operating either from behind the barricades or from the surrounding buildings. The GOC, Major General Ford, was categorical: "There is absolutely no doubt that the Parachute Battalion opened up only after they were fired on."[5]

There is evidence that republican gunmen were present that afternoon. A man firing a pistol was seen by some civilian witnesses. In December 1991, Channel Four in London claimed that the Official IRA had fired at soldiers. A week after Bloody Sunday, the author spoke with a wounded man who said he was in the Official IRA. He said soldiers had shot him in the buttock after he had opened fire on them. But he claimed that he fired only after the British troops had begun shooting. There is no way of determining the accuracy of this last claim. But the fact that not one soldier was injured during the course of the operation suggests strongly that there was no concerted IRA effort (either Provisional or Official) to either lure the troops into a gun battle or engage with them in response to their raid into the Bogside.

Civilian eyewitnesses rejected allegations of an IRA presence or any attempt to use the demonstration for cover in order to launch an attack on the army. Their version was simple: Soldiers murdered people without provocation, in cold blood. The clash between these two versions of the events of January 30 would last for decades. A British government inquiry into the shootings, headed by the lord chief justice of England, Lord Widgery, did not resolve it. In a report published in April 1972, his sharpest criticism of the behavior of British troops on what nationalists were calling Bloody Sunday was in his conclusion. He wrote:

> *Each soldier was his own judge of whether he had identified a gunman. Their training made them aggressive and quick in decision and some showed more restraint in opening fire than others. At one end of the scale some soldiers showed a high degree of responsibility; at the other, notably in Glenfada Park [where James Wray, Gerald Donaghy, William McKinney, and Gerald McKinney were shot] firing bordered on the reckless. These distinctions reflect differences in the character of the soldiers concerned. . . . None of the deceased or wounded is proved to have been shot whilst handling a firearm or bomb. Some are wholly acquitted of complicity in such action; but there is a strong suspicion that some others had been firing weapons*

> *or handling bombs in the course of the afternoon and that yet others had been closely supporting them.*[6]

Widgery arrived at his conclusions through studiously ignoring the statements the Northern Ireland Civil Rights Association collected from some five hundred civilian eyewitnesses, choosing instead to rely on the testimonies of the soldiers and their officers. Most important, he avoided the question of who held the overall responsibility for ordering the troops into action. The testimony of Chief Superintendent Lagan, who had said that the use of the army would not be required on January 30, was kept until the very last days of the inquiry. Though Lord Widgery acknowledged that the decision to override the civil authority had been made at a level higher than that of the chief constable and the GOC, he did not pursue the question of who it was who had defined the task of the paratroop battalion. Widgery offered no explanation as to how it was that the troops exceeded their orders not to penetrate into the Bogside. As with the question of the authorization of the illegal methods of interrogation (known commonly as "the five techniques"), the question of who bears the ultimate responsibility for the massacre that afternoon in Derry has never been fully answered.

However, in a statement in the House of Commons two days after the event, British Prime Minister Edward Heath admitted that the plan to "contain" the January 30 demonstration had been drawn up in consultation with the Joint Security Council, chaired by Northern Ireland Prime Minister Brian Faulkner, and was known to ministers in the British government. Of these, Reginald Maudling, the Home Affairs minister, and Lord Carrington, the secretary of state for defense, would have been the most crucial in formulating Ulster security policy. Carrington had already given the go-ahead to one illegal procedure, the use of the sensory-deprivation techniques, nine months earlier. It was he who would have had to have sanctioned the use of the First Para in Derry on January 30 for the aggressive "arrest operation."

For nationalists, the most damning aspect of the Widgery enquiry and report was the failure of the lord chief justice to decide on whether the soldiers had acted illegally. When it came to the Ulster question, Britain's preeminent legal authorities seemed to have dozed off between 1970 and 1972, substituting disingenuous and tautological arguments for objective evaluations of what happened.

It took over twenty years for evidence to emerge that would wake them up. In *Eyewitness Bloody Sunday,* journalist Don Mullan compiled a series of eyewitness statements collected in 1972 but never admitted as evidence before the Widgery tribunal. New evidence also emerged. At the beginning of 1997 a paratrooper later known as "Para AA," who had served with the First Para, approached an Irish journalist claiming that he had been on duty on January 30 in Derry and witnessed several of the killings. He said that the previous day an officer had told them to get some "kills." His statement, which was passed on to the Irish government, confirmed civilian eyewitnesses' accounts of unarmed demonstrators being shot while wounded or trying to surrender. He also stated that Widgery tribunal members doctored soldiers' original statements to make them conform to an acceptable version of what happened. Para AA continued: "I was then interviewed in an office by two Crown lawyers on Lord Widgery's team. I rattled off everything I had seen and had done. The only thing I omitted were the names and the manner in which people had been shot; apart from that I told the truth which I wanted to convey. Then to my utter surprise one of these doddering gentlemen said, 'Dear me, Private 027, you make it sound as though shots were being fired at the crowd, and we can't have that, can we?' And then proceeded to tear up my statement. He returned ten minutes later with another statement which bore no relation to fact." Para AA was informed that this would be the statement he would use when going before the inquiry.[7]

Channel Four News in London compiled an investigative report that was broadcast on January 17, 1997, including tapes made of army and police radio messages in Derry on January 30, 1972, and a medical expert's analysis of some of the forensic evidence relating to the killings of Young, Nash, and McDaid. The radio intercepts gave no indication whatsoever of any nail bombs being thrown or of shots fired at First Para. Instead they indicated that soldiers were firing from Derry's walls. The medical examination supported the allegations that the shots that killed Young, Nash, and McDaid were fired from a position or positions on the walls overlooking the Bogside.

Twelve days later, on January 29, 1997, Channel Four News reported that a member of the Royal Anglican Regiment had confirmed that at least one army sniper was operating on the walls. Like Para AA he has not been named. But their versions of events of Bloody Sunday, which are supported not only by other eyewitness accounts but also by independent forensic and ballistic evidence, constituted an overwhelming case for reopening the Bloody Sunday inquiry. At the beginning of 1998 the new Labour prime minister, Tony Blair, announced that the case would be reexamined. By the summer of that year, preliminary hearings had begun.

The impact of Bloody Sunday reverberated throughout Ireland. On February 2, 1972, a mob attacked the British embassy in Dublin and burned it to the ground. Thousands of workers went on strike in protest. In Australia, dockers refused to unload British cargo ships. In the United States, Irish Northern Aid's money-raising efforts met with increasing success. Figures filed with the Justice Department show that between January and July 1972, NORAID collected $313,000, compared to $128,000 for the previous six months. (This figure is but an indication of how much was actually raised, since considerable sums were brought into Ireland by hand and never declared.) Meanwhile, the Harrison arms network in New York was getting into its stride and by the end of 1972 was sending between two hundred and three hundred rifles and several hundred thousand rounds of ammunition a year to the Provisionals.

Bloody Sunday's most important impact was at home. On March 22, 1972, the British government informed Brian Faulkner that it was taking over full security powers for the province. When Faulkner responded that Unionists could never accept this watering down of the Stormont regime's authority—already his own right wing was coalescing around a new militant movement called Vanguard—the British prime minister announced, on March 24, the imposition of direct rule from London and the suspension of the Northern Ireland parliament. Six days later the 1920 experiment came to an end, and Britain took full responsibility for the bloody mess it had helped create. Internment marked the failure of the ordinary system of law and order to cope with the security crisis. The end of Stormont meant the collapse of the political structure that had sustained that system.

Over the next quarter of a century Britain would try other versions of devolved government for Ulster, but the old majority-rule regime that had been in place for over fifty years was gone forever.

· 2 ·

BEFORE THE suspension of Stormont, murder had already become part of Ulster's daily routine. Between August 1971 and March 30, 1972, there were more than 1,130 bomb explosions and more than 2,000 shootings. These claimed the lives of 158 civilians, 58 soldiers, and 17 RUC men, while 2,505 civilians, 306 soldiers, and 107 policemen were injured. However, in the six months following the suspension of Stormont, violence increased drastically. There were 9,536 shooting incidents: 264 civilians died, as well as 108 soldiers and 9 RUC members, with 2,634 civilians, 535 soldiers, and 195 policemen injured. Only the number of explosions showed a slight decline.[8]

There were two main reasons why violence rose sharply. Both were linked to Stormont's suspension. The first was that the Provisional IRA took credit for bringing down the Unionist government and assumed that suspending Stormont was a sign that Britain was weakening in its commitment to Northern Ireland. As a result, the Provisionals' leaders were encouraged to launch an all-out offensive while at the same time opening up contacts with the government in the hope of negotiating a British withdrawal. Meanwhile, loyalist paramilitaries viewed the end of Stormont as an appalling betrayal, the inevitable consequence of the perfidious policies of successive British governments that had abolished the B-Specials, disarmed the RUC, cosseted the civil rights movement, and failed to deal successfully with the IRA menace. They were confronting the end of Ulster as they knew it. Loyalists would respond to the crisis with the most vicious sectarian campaign that Northern Ireland had yet experienced. It would last for almost twenty-five years.

From a small band of neglected old men, the IRA in Belfast had become, by early 1972, stronger than at any time in its entire history, with hundreds of recruits and many thousands of supporters. Most of these new republicans came from nonrepublican backgrounds, and almost all were working class. Middle-class Belfast remained largely unaffected by the trauma that was going on around it. The quiet, prosperous avenues in the south of the city and along its eastern fringes on the County Down coast rarely had their tranquillity disturbed.

One of those most eagerly overseeing the republican movement's rapid growth was Gerry Adams, who throughout 1971 and early 1972 was commanding officer of the Provisionals' Second Battalion, based in the mid-Falls area. He established his republican credentials during a feud with the local Official IRA in which one of their Ballymurphy members was shot and seriously wounded. The man was paralyzed for the rest of his life. In mid-1971, on the run from the security forces who had already snatched his father and at various times would put his brother, two of his cousins, and his uncle Liam Hannaway behind bars, Adams took time off from guerrilla warfare to get married to Colette McArdle in a church in west Belfast. Outside, troops scoured the streets, with Adams near the head of their wanted list, as the ceremony proceeded.

What few rules the Provisional IRA established to give its war a moral context began to dissolve, and with increasing rapidity following internment and Bloody Sunday. At the beginning of the campaign there was a rule about attacking members of the security forces only while they were on duty. Any pretense about obeying it was abandoned after internment was introduced. The Provisionals targeted the local militia, the Ulster Defense Regiment, whose members were easy to locate. One of the first to be murdered at home was Sean Russell, who lived in the Ballymurphy area, Adams's stronghold. Gunmen from the Second Battalion shot him dead on December 8, 1971. In the very first week of 1972, gunmen from the Second Battalion struck again. Raymond Denham, an off-duty RUC reservist, was shot while at the factory where he worked near the Falls Road. Over the following days the Provisionals in north Belfast killed another off-duty UDR man and an off-duty policeman.

Seventeen days after Bloody Sunday, Provisional gunmen in Derry kidnapped a Catholic bus driver, Thomas Callaghan, who was also a part-time member of the UDR, and "executed" him. At first there were cries of horror that men should be gunned down out of uniform, often in front of their families, but within months it had become just another routine Ulster killing.

A novel contrivance—so simple that it now seems incredible that anyone actually had to invent it—helped propel the Provisional IRA to new heights of violence: the car bomb. It would change terrorist tactics throughout the world. It first devastated Derry's city center in March 1972. The same month, a one-hundred-pound car bomb killed seven people—two of them old-age pensioners—and wounded one hundred in Donegall Street in the center of Belfast. For the first time television viewers came home to scenes of policemen scooping burned and unrecognizable parts of human beings into plastic bags. The Provisional leadership justified the tactic by saying that it tied down hundreds of troops and policemen, drained the British coffers of money in compensation payments, and that, anyway, they always gave warnings. But the telephoned warnings were frequently inaccurate or confusing. In the Donegall Street bombing, the warnings actually led the police to shepherd people into the street where the car bomb was waiting to explode. The storm of condemnation that followed the blast contributed to the leadership's decision to call a temporary truce, lasting seventy-two hours. It was also a signal to the British, now directly embroiled in the Ulster crisis, that they were dealing with a disciplined movement that under the right conditions could bring about a permanent halt to the violence. The Provisionals, having gotten rid of Stormont, now wanted face-to-face negotiations with the "real" enemy.

The violence resumed with even greater fury in April 1972. On the 14th, there were twenty-three explosions across Northern Ireland. Provisional IRA snipers in the narrow streets of west and north Belfast continued to pick off troops on foot patrol on almost a daily basis. In rural areas, especially Armagh, the Provisionals favored land mines, which soon made the roads around the south of the county unusable for the security forces.

While the Provisionals were going for a final push, their former comrades in the Official IRA stumbled from one disastrous mistake to another. After Bloody Sunday, their operations officer, Seamus Costello, dispatched a bombing team to Britain to wreak revenge on the Parachute Regiment. A former British paratrooper drove a van bomb to the gates of the regiment's headquarters in Aldershot. When it went off, it killed six cleaning ladies and a Catholic chaplain. Shortly afterward, Joe McCann, an Official IRA leader from Belfast, along with two other gunmen, attempted to assassinate the Stormont minister for home affairs, John Taylor. Though hit over twenty times, Taylor survived, thanks to the inaccuracy and low velocity of the antiquated Thompson submachine guns that the gunmen used.

McCann was as militant as any Provisional but had stuck with the leadership of Cathal Goulding for political reasons. However, he remained close to Adams; the two had joined the junior wing of the IRA at around the same time. In May 1971, McCann ambushed an army patrol in Belfast, killing Corporal Robert Bankier, the first fatality the Official IRA claimed. During internment, McCann made a name for himself as one of the most dangerous operators in Belfast in a series of gun battles with British troops. By 1972 he was on the army's most wanted list. Under the circumstances, his decision to return to his native Markets area near the Belfast city center seemed foolhardy, especially since he refused to disguise himself. On April 15 police spotted McCann as he got off a bus. A patrol of paratroopers gave chase. McCann, unarmed, dashed down a side street, desperately trying to push through one front door after the next. On that day all the doors happened to be locked. He died in a hail of bullets.

When news of McCann's death spread, working-class areas of Catholic Belfast and Derry erupted in a series of gun battles. Within twenty-four hours the Officials killed three soldiers. It would be their last show of strength against British forces. The Official IRA Army Council had made up its mind that political violence in Northern Ireland was counter-productive. Already there were worrying signs of growing loyalist militancy, with a series of "unexplained" murders of innocent Catholics in Belfast. Goulding and his supporters on the Army Council feared the violence would provoke a Protestant backlash.

The Official IRA in Derry gave Goulding the excuse he needed. William Best, a young Derry Catholic who was in the British army, came home on leave to the Bogside, where a group of Official IRA men kidnapped him. Pleas for his release were ignored. His body was found dumped on a vacant lot. It outraged local Catholics, and they marched to the Official IRA's Derry headquarters to demand that they get out of the area. Eight days later, on May 29, the Official IRA announced an open-ended cease-fire. It said it was doing so in compliance with the wishes of the people it represented in Northern Ireland but warned that it reserved the right to retaliate against the British troops or "sectarian" forces. The decision left many members of the Officials unhappy and suspicious of Goulding's long-term intentions. This was especially so in Belfast, where the leadership's overtures to loyalists in its attempts to link up with the Protestant working class were regarded as naive.

Two weeks after the Official IRA cease-fire, the Provisionals met with John Hume and Paddy Devlin in Derry. For Hume and for the SDLP, the period since internment had been one of continuing frustration since ordinary politics became impossible. But there had been feelers put out between the recently appointed secretary of state for Northern Ireland, William Whitelaw, who effectively ruled the province, replacing the Stormont government, and the Provisional Army Council. Hume acted as a go-between and passed on to the British the Provisionals' terms for talks. The most important was that IRA prisoners should not be treated as common criminals but granted "political status." Billy McKee was leading a group of republicans on a prison hunger strike to win special privileges, such as the right to wear their own clothes and to refuse to do prison work. Political status, a traditional IRA demand, was an acknowledgment that its acts were politically motivated. In the eyes of republicans, it was recognition that they were prisoners of war. The Provisionals also wanted an independent observer at the meeting and demanded that it not take place at Stormont. The Heath government acceded to all their demands. The Provisionals responded with a declaration that they would call a cease-fire on June 26. Ulster held its breath.

Earlier, on March 14, just ten days before Stormont's suspension, Adams's life on the run had come to an end when troops raided the house in which he was hiding. He was taken to the Springfield Road RUC station where a Special Branch officer eventually identified him. For thirty-six hours he was punched, slapped, and kicked around; a Special Branch officer threw a fit, went for his gun, and wrestling free from his colleagues' efforts to restrain him, attempted to shoot the prisoner. The gun was unloaded, which suggests the police were indulging in histrionics. Adams was interned. But the Provisional IRA cease-fire entailed a happy consequence for him. In June he was whisked from prison to freedom as one of the delegates the Provisionals named to meet with the British government.[9] The others were Army Council members MacStiofain, O'Conaill, Seamus Twomey (a veteran from the August 15 shoot-out in Divis Street), Belfast IRA leader Ivor Bell, Adams's Derry contemporary Martin McGuinness, who had graduated from the Officials to command the city's Provisionals, and a Sinn Fein representative, Myles Shevlin.

On July 7, en route to the Belfast airport, where an RAF helicopter awaited the delegation, one of the two cars carrying them broke down.[10] It was an omen. The delegates were flown to Oxfordshire and then taken to Chelsea, the heart of fashionable London, where at the gracious home of a junior minister in the Northern Ireland office they came face-to-face with the British government's supremo in Northern Ireland, William Whitelaw. His rather moonlike face was that of a northern English gentleman farmer who listened with some bemusement to MacStiofain's main demand for a British declaration of intent to withdraw by 1975. The other demands, such as the reduction of the military presence in Catholic areas and the ending of internment, were possible under the right circumstances; in fact, the British had already begun to release those held without charge. But Whitelaw told MacStiofain that the Protestants might react violently if Britain were to announce an intention to pull out. MacStiofain dismissed this fear. The Provisionals' fundamentalist republicanism had no place in it for Protestants other than that of dupes of British imperialism who would come to their senses when the British told them to. They saw the threat of a Protestant backlash as a bluff Britain used for its own insidious purposes. The gulf between these two positions was unbridgeable. The Provisionals would maintain this view of Ulster's Protestants, refusing to acknowledge that there is legitimate, indigenous opposition to republicanism within Ulster—opposition that exists independent of Britain's interests. It is, of course, a self-serving incomprehension, allowing republicans to prolong the fiction that they are fighting on behalf of the whole Irish nation.

After the meeting Whitelaw commented with undisguised disdain: "The meeting was a non-event. The IRA leaders simply made impossible demands which I told them the British government would never concede. They were in fact still in a mood of defiance and determination to carry on until their absurd ultimatums were met."[11]

Adams kept his counsel at the talks, saying nothing. He had not wanted the meeting in the first place and cautioned the southern IRA men that the British were more interested in gathering information about them than in seriously negotiating. Both he and Ivor Bell, who was a close friend and a committed socialist, dressed down for the occasion to show their scorn for it. In contrast, MacStiofain and O'Conaill saw themselves as being in a similar position to that of Michael Collins when he went to meet the British in December 1921 to negotiate the treaty—except, of course, they were now going to end the partition that came about as a result of those talks.

The reality was that, unlike Collins, the Provisionals had no political machine to translate whatever military strength they possessed into an expression of popular support—Provisional Sinn Fein hardly existed as a political organization. The Provisionals had sprung from a "purist" republican tradition that regarded politics and the fighting of elections rather like Paisley regarded the Catholic Church—as a source of temptation and vice. The blandishments of constitutional politics had to be spurned at all costs since they would lead to compromise. The Belfast Provisional leader Billy McKee expressed it best when he called Sinn Fein "a bloody anchor around our neck."[12] But neither, in the end, did MacStiofain and O'Conaill have a military machine anything like that which stood behind Collins. Events would soon expose their crippling military and political weaknesses.

The British were supposed to report back with their response to MacStiofain's demands inside a week. But within two days of the London meeting the cease-fire collapsed. Given the Provisionals' dismissal of Protestant opposition as irrelevant, it was ironic that what ended the slim hope of peace was the UDA. It blocked a Catholic family from occupying a house that a Protestant family had vacated. The British army refused to intervene to break up the UDA blockade of the street. On the July 13 the Provisionals fully resumed their campaign, killing three soldiers in west and north Belfast. Loyalists were threatening to impose their own "no-go" areas unless the British dismantled the IRA's strongholds. The British did not sit back for long. Four thousand extra troops were sent to Ulster to take part in a huge invasion of the Catholic working-class "no-go" areas. Militant Protestant action had forced the British to act yet again.[13] The republican barricades were dismantled on July 31 without the IRA firing a shot. Its forces melted away to resume their campaign of hit-and-run.

By July 1972 the feared Protestant backlash had begun, although many—including the British, the RUC, and the IRA, each for their own reasons—refused to recognize it. For the next two years it would dominate the future of Ulster, acting as a check on nationalists' ambitions and frustrating Britain's most ambitious attempt to reach a settlement and extricate itself from the Irish quagmire.

• 3 •

JOHN WHITE was nineteen years old when rioting and burning consumed west Belfast in 1969. One day, shortly after the August upheavals, White was stopped at a Catholic barricade near the Falls Road and given a bad beating. He became a Protestant vigilante. In 1971, White was still a vigilante, manning barricades in the Shankill area and attending meetings of the various defense groups that were coming together slowly to form the UDA. Then two events hardened him. The first was the bombing of the Four Step Inn pub on the Shankill Road in September 1971, which killed a friend, Ernie Bates. White had lived next door to Bates's family.

"The Four Step Inn was a paramilitary hangout," White admits, "but Ernie was just an Orangeman." No one claimed responsibility for the attack, but it was almost certainly the north Belfast Provisionals' work. Then the following December, White encountered the funeral of one of the two "Balmoral babies" killed in a Provisional IRA bombing of the Balmoral furniture store. "I saw the father carrying the little coffin," White remembers. He joined the UDA shortly afterward. "I wanted revenge, I wanted to protect my community, and I wanted to stop the IRA," said White.[14]

Within a month he was involved with UDA strongman Charles Harding-Smith in a gunrunning effort. A local gun dealer had put the UDA in touch with an English dealer who told the loyalists that he had access to a large haul of AK-47s, the powerful Russian-made automatic rifle that would later become the Provisionals' trademark. With the guns going at £250 ($450) each, the UDA raised £500,000 for the deal, mostly, says White, from members' subscriptions. After a few meetings in London, everything seemed ready to go. The UDA made the arrangements to have the arms shipped to Belfast.

In January 1972, White, Harding-Smith, and the English gun dealer met at the Hilton Hotel in London to clinch the deal, along with another man who turned out to be a member of the RUC Special Branch. Harding-Smith and White were arrested. White is convinced that the English contact was, in fact, a member of MI5, the British internal intelligence-gathering service. White and Harding-Smith were held for eleven months in Brixton Prison, only to be acquitted in court on the grounds that they had been "entrapped." When they got back to Belfast in December 1972, White was amazed at the change in the ramshackle league of vigilantes that he and Harding-Smith had left behind.

Throughout 1972 the Protestant backlash manifested itself in two ways. In public, disaffected Ulster Unionist Party politicians such as William Craig set up rival political organizations. Paisley had established his own party, the Democratic Unionist Party, in September of the previous year. Craig, who since 1968 had been the chief voice of right-wing obstructionism within the UUP, launched the Vanguard movement on February 9, 1972, threatening, "If and when the politicians fail us, it will be our duty to liquidate the enemy."[15] On March 18 he held a mass rally in Belfast with leather-jacketed men in serried ranks and with motorcycle outriders escorting his car, like an ominous revival of 1930s fascism. But in spite of the impressive numbers—sixty thousand showed at the first rally—and violent talk, Protestant resistance did not coalesce around Vanguard, which tried to bridge the gap between paramilitary menace and political respectability, ground that the Reverend Ian Paisley already occupied.

The real backlash began in a much more low-key but far more deadly manner on the day before the founding of Vanguard. On February 8 a forty-nine-year-old Catholic, Bernard Rice, was walking along the Crumlin Road, north Belfast's main thoroughfare, when gunmen shot him dead from a passing car. There was no claim of responsibility. The RUC issued a statement calling it a "motiveless murder." Mrs. Rice thought differently. Two days after her husband's murder she said that he had been killed "because he was a Catholic."[16] Mrs. Rice was right. The killers were members of the Red Hand Commandos, John McKeague's virulently sectarian organization. For a time they operated out of the UDA's office on the Shankill Road. The bigger organization occasionally lent them guns.

By then the UDA itself was ready to go into action. Behind the vigilantes lurked four killer squads, comprising thirty-eight men. The biggest team was in White's area of the Shankill Road, with twenty members; its leader was an ex–British soldier and former UDR man. His second-in-command was Davey Payne, on whom his colleagues would soon jokingly confer the nickname "Psychopath." The north Belfast UDA had a smaller team of six gunmen. A third group was based in the oldest loyalist area of Belfast, Sandy Row, near the city center. It also had six members, as had the fourth hit team. It operated across the Lagan River in east Belfast, where Tommy Herron, the former hotel doorman who had become UDA vice chairman, held sway.

These men would kill approximately 80 of the 121 victims of sectarian assassination (the vast majority of them in Belfast) who helped make 1972 the worst year of the conflict. The Provisionals murdered most of the rest.

The aim of the UDA's death squads, according to White, was "to terrorize the terrorist. It was one community attacking another."[17] At first, victims were gunned down on the street or at home. But in May, when the UDA set up a series of no-go areas in response to those in the Catholic districts, the nature of the killings changed. A more frightening pattern emerged with the discovery of the body of Gerard McCusker, a twenty-four-year-old Catholic, in a vacant lot in the Shankill area. His hair had been pulled out, his face was badly bruised, and his wrists were broken. According to the UDA, McCusker's killers believed that he knew the names of IRA men, and he was brutalized in order to force him to talk. As the summer weeks passed, this kind of brutalization grew even more ferocious. Herron's UDA squad in east Belfast kidnapped twenty-three-year-old Henry Russell, one of the few Catholics to have joined the UDR. On July 13 his badly beaten and almost naked body was found with burn marks and with a cross branded on his back. Terror began to take hold of the Catholic community, who feared that a loyalist Jack the Ripper was prowling the streets. The torture and beatings were a feature of all four death squads. Nine days after Russell was murdered, the rumors had more sensational material on which to feed. In the early hours of July 22, the UDA stopped local Irish folksinger Rose McCartney and her boyfriend, Patrick O'Neill, at a roadblock on the Crumlin Road. Both were taken to the UDA's Shankill Road headquarters, above a pub called the Bricklayer's Arms, where their heads were covered while the Psychopath set about interrogating them, badly injuring O'Neill's hand in the process. Present in the room was east Belfast supremo Tommy Herron. Unfortunately, the cover slipped from one of the victims, who caught a glimpse of Herron. This sealed their fate. After making McCartney sing a song, their killers bundled the two into the back of a car, drove to an empty field, and machine-gunned them to death.[18]

Rose McCartney was the first Catholic woman to fall victim to the Shankill Road UDA, and rumors spread throughout west Belfast that the "Ripper" had struck again, inflicting terrible mutilations on her.[19] White's theory about "terrorizing the terrorist" at least worked insofar as it terrified the population that supported the Provisional IRA. But since working-class Catholics did not trust the security forces to protect them—between July 31 and December 31 only three Protestants were charged with murder—sectarian killings may have enhanced the position of the IRA. Nor did the UDA's killings do anything to curb the Provisionals' campaign, which proceeded throughout 1972 with increasing recklessness. Nine people were killed in a series of twenty-two bomb explosions in Belfast on July 21, a day of panic and death known as Bloody Friday. Ten days later another nine died when three car bombs exploded in the peaceful village of Claudy in County Derry. Included among the dead were two children. A sectarian element was noticeable in this atrocity, as all three bombs were left near Protestant-run businesses.[20]

In the closing months of 1972, the Provisionals' armed campaign showed the first signs that it was running out of steam. In each month for the first eight months of the year, the Provisionals detonated well over 100 bombs, reaching a peak of 196 during the bloody days of July. But in the last three months, the average fell to under 100. In December there were only 64 IRA bombings.[21] The army's saturation of Catholic areas made it increasingly difficult for the IRA to mount bombing runs. Perhaps more important, they were losing the moral ground they had held since internment. The slaughter of civilians in Provisional bombing attacks, whether "accidental" or not, undermined whatever claim they might have had to being the "defenders" of Catholics. It allowed the Dublin government—which, thanks to internment and Bloody Sunday, was reluctant to clamp down on the movement—to adopt a more stringent approach.

On November 19 Sean MacStiofain, the Provisionals' chief of staff, was arrested and sentenced to six months in jail for IRA membership. He went on a hunger and thirst strike, which he abandoned after a week. Although he refused food until January, it was a futile exercise, invoking less and less sympathy even among Provisionals. Meanwhile, the introduction into the Provisionals' arsenal of a new weapon, the RPG-7 rocket launcher, while potentially deadly, did not halt the group's military decline. But it did signal the beginning of a relationship that in the coming years would prove very fruitful for the IRA. A consignment of these Russian-made weapons was flown from Libya to a small airstrip in Kerry, where they were unloaded and sent north. Army Council member Joe Cahill had made the contact with Colonel Muammar Qaddafi. A Canadian had piloted the consignment. He and his plane were later lost over the Atlantic. The rocket was first used on November 28 in an attack on a RUC base in Fermanagh, which killed a police officer. Fortunately for the security forces, in the Provisionals' hands the device proved erratic and unreliable.

As a sign of the Irish government's increasing confidence, it introduced the Offenses Against the State Act, a draconian new bill that allowed the authorities to jail anyone as a member of an illegal organization simply on the word of a policeman. The debate on the measure went on against the background of the UDA's campaign, which spread beyond Belfast to Derry—where UDA gunmen murdered five people in a machine-gun attack on a pub—and into the Irish republic. After bombing a pub and a soft drinks factory in Donegal, the UDA issued a rare statement in which it claimed responsibility for the incidents. It concluded: "We warn the Eire Government to clamp down on the IRA. Every time the IRA strike in the North we will strike twice as hard in the south."[22] During the debate on the new antiterrorism bill in the Dail (the Irish parliament) on December 1, two car bombs exploded in Dublin, killing two men and injuring eighty. The Belfast UVF was responsible, though it never publicly acknowledged the attacks.

In the panic following the bombings, parliamentary opposition to the Offenses Against the State Act collapsed, and it was made law.

When White returned to Belfast from London shortly after this, he shared the satisfaction of the UDA leaders, who looked upon the last twelve months as a period of great advancement for the organization. It had been instrumental in forcing the British to dismantle the nationalist no-go areas, blocking the government from making concessions to the IRA, and frightening the Irish political establishment into taking a harder line with militant republicans under its jurisdiction. The Protestant backlash was achieving results; the problem was that few seemed to recognize it, at least publicly. The RUC persisted in describing the sectarian killings as "motiveless murders," and the IRA insisted that they were the work of undercover British agents. Neither the British government nor the Irish government rushed to proclaim Protestant involvement in widespread terrorism. Each had its own reason for ignoring the facts—the security forces because they did not want to be distracted from their war against the IRA, and the British because they did not want to be forced to start introducing internment against Protestants for fear of provoking a bigger backlash. And, anyway, in late 1972 they were phasing out internment. The Irish government was afraid to recognize Protestant violence in case it should legitimize the Provisionals' claims to be the Catholics' defenders.

As for the Provisionals and the Officials, they both refused to accept the extent and depth of Protestant opposition to their goal of "uniting" all Irishmen; they preferred to ascribe the sectarian killings to the sinister machinations of their "real" enemy, the British. So it was that in early 1973, John White began thinking of ways to make the point that loyalists were behind the murder campaign and were prepared to continue until the IRA stopped.

White had rejoined the Shankill Road section of the UDA, which was now organized, like the Provisionals, into a pseudomilitary structure consisting of "companies." The Shankill Road unit became "C" company. By early 1973, White was third in command and soon afterward became "C" company's representative in the Inner Council, the UDA's ruling body. According to White, "C" company was responsible for "90 percent" of all the sectarian killings in the west Belfast area from 1972 until about 1976.[23]

The UDA campaign escalated in February 1973 with a hand-grenade attack on a bus carrying workers to an east Belfast factory. By then the UDA had murdered almost one hundred people. It had also engaged in several gun battles with the British army after riots in Protestant areas left two civilians dead, provoking Tommy Herron, the UDA's vice-chairman, to declare, "The British army and government are now our enemies."

Yet of the 364 people who were being held without trial as of February 3, 1973, not one was a loyalist. The police argued that this was because loyalist violence was neither sufficiently "organized" nor systematic enough to warrant such a response. The authorities maintained that "maverick" gangs were carrying out the killings. Herron, fearing internment, did his best to reinforce this notion. As a ruse he issued a statement "warning" the killers that unless they stopped, the UDA would act against them. In fact, Herron had been one of the murder campaign's main organizers. As White's testimony reveals, this was a politically convenient fiction that the police chose to accept. After the hand-grenade attack, however, the outcry from nationalists forced the authorities to act for political reasons, regardless of whether or not their security arguments about the nature of the sectarian campaign were legitimate. On February 5 the first two loyalists were interned. Within a few days five more were arrested. Among them was John McKeague, the erratic leader of the Red Hand Commandos, and several UVF members, although their contribution to the sectarian violence was slight. There was a burst of protest from the Protestant community, with marches, demonstrations, and a series of strikes that quickly degenerated into widespread rioting, looting, and general disorder, antagonizing ordinary, respectable Protestants who regarded their own paramilitaries with suspicion if not outright hostility. There was no foundation of sympathy on which the UDA could build a coherent protest movement against internment.

The introduction of internment against loyalists highlighted the UDA's dilemma about acknowledging its responsibility for the sectarian murder campaign. If it claimed the killings, then the authorities would have no other option but to crack down harder on the organization, interning its leadership and declaring it illegal as they had done with the UVF and IRA. But by not claiming responsibility, the political point of the murders was lost. In May 1973 the UDA held a conference in an east Belfast hotel, attended by some fifty leading members. There was a battle for the chairmanship between east and west Belfast, with Herron and Harding-Smith the respective contenders. It was resolved with the election of a "compromise" candidate, Andy Tyrie, a founding member of the organization in west Belfast. Tyrie, portly and bespectacled, mustached like a Mexican bandit, was a quiet background figure. To Herron and Harding-Smith he seemed malleable enough to serve as a puppet. It was after his election that the contentious issue of claiming responsibility came up again. John White and another UDA man suggested a simple solution: Invent a different name for the UDA's hit squads. The name they came up with was the Ulster Freedom Fighters.

Tyrie agreed. In fact, it fitted in with his own plans. He appointed an overall "military" commander to take charge of the UFF. He would choose those men from the four murder gangs regarded as the most reliable and ruthless to head UFF cells in each area. Things would be systematized. Members of the west Belfast unit were given instructions on, among other things, the use of the knife. One of their commanders, who favored this method of killing, demonstrated how the victim was gripped from behind and the jugular cut across from left to right. "The assassin must always make sure to stand behind the victim to avoid being drenched in blood," he said.[24] He acknowledged that only a few men were capable of killing with the knife.

A death list of SDLP politicians was drawn up, with Gerry Fitt at its head. A UFF cell from C company, with White in charge, waited to abduct Fitt from a bar in central Belfast. When he didn't show up, they grabbed his election agent and SDLP city councilor, Paddy Wilson, along with his companion, a Protestant woman, Irene Andrews, with whom Wilson was having an affair. They were taken to a remote quarry outside Belfast and stabbed and shot to death. Andrews was stabbed over twenty times in her head and body; Wilson had over thirty stab wounds, and his throat had been cut from ear to ear. One of the killers remarked that stabbing a woman to death was like "sticking a knife in a pillowcase."

At 1:30 A.M. on June 26 a call to a Belfast newspaper in the name of

"Captain Black, Ulster Freedom Fighters," gave the location of the bodies. They were found three hours later. According to White, this was the first time that the name UFF was used to claim responsibility for a murder. "There will be more deaths in reprisal," said the caller.[25]

Shortly after the double murders, White was arrested and detained without trial. One of the UDA's most prolific killers would remain behind bars for two years. After August the sectarian murder rate began to drop drastically as more of the UDA's hit men were deposited in Long Kesh, reaching a peak of around thirty. This put considerable strains on the UDA's economic resources, since the organization was expected to contribute money to the families of its interned and imprisoned members. It was shortly after a fund-raising drive for prisoners' families that Herron disappeared, only to be found murdered in a ditch along a country road southeast of Belfast on September 16. The murder fueled conspiracy theories for decades and to date remains unsolved.[26]

By the end of the year there were around seventy-five loyalists interned, as well as over five hundred republicans. In December 1973 there was only one sectarian murder in Northern Ireland. Internment was hurting both the UDA and the Provisionals. The decline of the paramilitaries allowed the British government to launch a daring political initiative to solve the Ulster crisis, one that would give Catholics governmental power and an institutional link to the Irish republic.

• 4 •

IT WAS ALWAYS the intention of the British government to keep Northern Ireland on the margins of British politics. Its first instinct, having removed Stormont, was to put something in its place that would have the support of the nationalist population. Following the announcement of Stormont's suspension, Prime Minister Heath appealed to Northern Ireland's Catholics: "Now is your chance," he said in a television broadcast. "A chance for fairness, a chance for peace, a chance at last to bring the bombings and killings to an end."[27] Britain could only reinstate a devolved government that would keep Ulster at arm's length with the help of the moderate Nationalists, whom the SDLP represented. But the party ignored a British appeal to all the parties to meet to discuss political options in Darlington, England, in September 1972. Only the UUP, the Northern Ireland

Labor Party, and the Alliance Party showed up. As long as internment existed, the SDLP's room for political maneuver was limited: It could not ignore the alienation of the Catholic population. However, Britain's professed intention of ending internment as soon as it was feasible, along with its publication of a plan that advocated an assembly with a power-sharing executive and an Irish dimension for a future Northern Ireland government, allowed Fitt and Hume to lead their party into elections in June 1973 for the proposed new assembly. The Provisionals opposed the plans, calling on Nationalists to boycott the elections. They accused the SDLP of a sellout; after all, the party had pledged itself not to take part in any Ulster political institution until internment ended. But Hume and Fitt had calculated wisely. Sinn Fein had not one single elected official in Northern Ireland. Southern traditionalists like O'Conaill and O'Bradaigh dominated the Provisionals' thinking at this time, and a moribund Sinn Fein reflected their scorn for the ordinary political process. Their boycott proved ineffective, and the SDLP won nineteen of the seventy-eight proposed seats, which represented 22.1 percent of the vote. As Michael Farrell has pointed out, this made the SDLP "the biggest anti-Unionist parliamentary party in the history of the state."[28] The SDLP could claim four positions on the power-sharing executive.

Things were more confused and more difficult on the Unionist side. Faulkner, the UUP leader and Northern Ireland's last prime minister, was ambivalent about the British proposals; eventually he committed himself to supporting them but with the intention of changing them so that they would be more palatable to Protestants. Ex–Unionist Party member William Craig and the Reverend Ian Paisley opposed the plans vociferously. A poll in March, which the British included as part of the overall plan and which showed an overwhelming majority in support of partition, did not appease loyalist fears about long-term British intentions. And loyalists were especially incensed at the idea of a Council of Ireland, linking Northern Ireland to the republic. Craig and Paisley ran against the plan, as did a group of Unionists led by John Taylor, who had survived the Official IRA's assassination attempt the year before. The Unionist result boded ill for the future of the proposed executive. The anti-power-sharing Unionists won twenty-seven seats, while Faulkner's supporters took twenty-two. As Britain would find time and time again, the struggle to create a moderate consensus among Unionists proved much more difficult than among

Nationalists, who were more willing to compromise. Still, Heath pushed ahead, trying to make Faulkner into a Terence O'Neill for the 1970s.

A four-day conference was held at Sunningdale, England, beginning December 6, 1973. In attendance was the SDLP, the Faulkner Unionists, the Alliance Party, British government ministers, and ministers from the Irish government, led by William Cosgrave, whose Fine Gael–Labor Party coalition had just ousted Jack Lynch. An agreement was hammered out making the Council of Ireland a fourteen-member body responsible mainly for economic and social matters. In return, the Irish government agreed to recognize the right of the majority in Northern Ireland to remain part of the United Kingdom for as long as they wished. Britain undertook to review internment and release more prisoners by Christmas, and to make the RUC more acceptable to Catholics. The Irish agreed to intensify the offensive against the Provisionals, an undertaking very congenial to Cosgrave whose Fine Gael Party was traditionally antirepublican. Its partner, the Irish Labour Party, was hardly less enthusiastic.

In the words of Farrell, "Sunningdale was the high point of British strategy in Ireland. It was a masterpiece of balance and ambiguity."[29] But for over twenty years the Sunningdale Agreement would stand more as a gloomy reminder of the dangers of ambitious reform than as a beacon showing the way forward.

Unionist opposition quickly hardened around the United Ulster Unionist Council. Its members disrupted the assembly with noisy protests, which intensified when the executive took power in January 1974. Brian Faulkner was appointed chief executive, and Gerry Fitt was his deputy. John Hume held the post of minister for commerce, with his colleagues Paddy Devlin and Austin Currie holding the ministries of health and social services, and housing, respectively. It was poetic justice that Currie, who started the civil rights protests in 1968 by squatting in a house, should have ended up in charge of all housing allocation in Northern Ireland. Unfortunately, no one had the time or the inclination to savor it. Faulkner resigned as Unionist Party leader in January 1974 after a vote of the party's leadership body rejected the power-sharing settlement. The SDLP did not help matters by trumpeting the new arrangements as a triumph for nationalism. In a speech in Trinity College, Dublin, on January 17, SDLP assembly member Hugh Logue proclaimed the Council of Ireland as "the vehicle that would trundle the Unionists into a United Ireland," to the discomfit of Faulkner, who was desperately trying to convince his demoralized supporters that it was a defense against a United Ireland.

A British general election the following month gave the anti-Faulkner Unionists a chance to show their strength. They did so, triumphantly. United Ulster Unionist Council alliance candidates dominated by Paisley and Craig took eleven of the twelve Westminster seats, leaving Faulkner's supporters without any; Gerry Fitt was returned as the sole pro-power-sharing representative. The SDLP split the Nationalist vote in two marginal constituencies, Fermanagh–South Tyrone and Mid-Ulster, with the result that anti-power-sharing Unionists took the seats from independent nationalists Frank Maguire and Bernadette McAliskey (née Devlin). McAliskey's defeat marked the end of the era of the "new" Nationalist politics based on civil rights demands.

The election also returned a Labour government, under Harold Wilson, who had been out of office since 1970. He appointed Merlyn Rees as the Northern Ireland secretary of state. This was not the confident Labour Party that had tackled the Ulster crisis in 1969, pushing reforms through in spite of loyalist ire, but one that seemed mainly peeved that the situation had not yet gone away but, in fact, had become much, much worse. Tension in loyalist parts of Belfast spilled over into riots and gun battles with the British army. The Ulster Volunteer Force, dormant for two years, resumed its campaign of sectarian violence, murdering sixteen people in the first months of 1974, mainly in Belfast, and threatening further havoc if the British tried to enforce the power-sharing agreement. But Wilson, on a visit to Northern Ireland in mid-April, responded to Unionist threats with a flat statement saying there was no alternative to the Sunningdale Agreement.

On March 23, 1974, a hitherto unheard-of loyalist group, the Ulster Workers Council, issued a statement demanding fresh assembly elections and warning that there would be widespread disruption if its demands were not met. The UWC was, in fact, a small group of loyalist workers that had recruited trade union shop stewards from the power stations. It had the support of the UDA as well as several smaller loyalist paramilitary groups. At first it was ignored. Unionist politicians like William Craig were wary of being linked to loyalist working-class militants; their last attempt to organize work stoppages in February 1973 in protest against the internment of Protestants had collapsed in disorder. When the UWC announced the beginning of a "constitutional stoppage," or general strike, on May 14 to oppose the power-sharing executive, it was greeted with a certain amount of skepticism. However, what was happening became startlingly clear soon thereafter when hooded UDA men appeared on the streets of the Protestant port of Larne and forced shops to close in "support" of the UWC's call. UDA roadblocks soon appeared all over Protestant areas of Belfast, bullying workers to return home. Factories and shops began to shut down. Meanwhile, UWC supporters in the main power plant near Larne began running down the province's electricity supply. On May 16, Craig declared that Sunningdale must be scrapped and if it was not, its supporters had to realize that "there will be further actions taken against the Irish republic and those who attempt to implement the agreement."[30]

The following morning, May 17, 1974, the UVF in Belfast hijacked two cars on the Shankill Road and stole a third from the city's dockside. They drove the vehicles to south Armagh, where mid-Ulster UVF men loaded them with bombs. The cars continued south toward Dublin. That afternoon a fourth car was stolen from a parking lot in Portadown. It, too, was taken to south Armagh and loaded with explosives.

In a parking lot just outside Dublin, at around 5 P.M., the bombs in the three cars from Belfast were armed and then, with their timers ticking away, driven into the city. Two were left on the north side, on Parnell Street and Talbot Street. The driver of the third car bomb seems to have been trying to get close to the Irish parliament in Kildare Street on the city's south side. A bus strike may have complicated matters for the UVF team, and the car was parked instead on nearby South Leinster Street near a wall of Trinity College, on the other side of which was the university's playing fields.

People were leaving work for home, getting ready to face the tribulations and confusion of the bus strike, when at 5:27 P.M. the two bombs in Parnell Street and Talbot Street exploded almost simultaneously and without warning. Six minutes later the South Leinster Street bomb went off.

The explosions were heard all over Dublin, as black clouds of dust and debris spiraled into the sky. The blasts shredded passersby with tangled metal and slivers of glass as shop windows were shattered. Their force was such that the bodies of two victims, a man and woman, hurled through a shop window in Talbot Street, were found fused together.[31] A young family, the O'Briens, was wiped out—the husband, John, age twenty-three; his wife, Anne, twenty-two; and their two children, Jacqueline, seventeen months, and Anne Maire, five months. Among the dead was a thirty-year-old Frenchwoman, Simone Chetrit, who was working as an au pair in Dublin and was planning to return to Paris on May 19.[32] In South Leinster Street, twenty-one-year-old Anne Massey was hurrying to meet her husband-to-be, who was to give her a ride home. She passed the car bomb just as it exploded.[33] Her body lay covered with a policeman's coat, only her platform boots protruding. Not far from her lay the body of a man who had been reduced to smoldering cinders. An old man lay nearby, screaming, one foot missing and his legs smashed, as the ambulances raced through the traffic-jammed streets to the disaster zones, which reeked of sulphur, burning gasoline, and cordite.

At 6:42 P.M., as the stunned Irish capital was coming to terms with the horror, the fourth car bomb exploded in Monaghan town, outside a pub. It killed seven people, including two old-age pensioners. The death toll from the four explosions climbed as the hours ticked by and the corpses were identified. The final victim did not die until June 24, bringing the toll to thirty-three dead, making May 17, 1974, the bloodiest day in the history of the Ulster conflict. The bombings remain the greatest crime in the history of the Irish republic, a crime for which no one has been convicted.[34]

Meanwhile, the UWC, aided by the UDA, tightened its grip on the province's lifeline, choking off fuel, food, and electricity supplies. People had to cook out in their gardens, making the best of the unusually sunny May weather. Rumors swept the Catholic districts of Belfast that the next stage of the loyalist plan to overthrow the government was to launch all-out attacks on vulnerable nationalist areas. Two Catholic brothers were shot dead in their bar near Balleymena on May 24 for refusing to close it. Faulkner, Fitt, and two other executive ministers flew to London to plead with Wilson to send the troops in to dismantle the UDA barricades and take over the fuel depots and power plants. Wilson hesitated to use the army against the massed ranks of the UDA and UWC, especially since their support seemed to be growing. Instead, he launched a vituperative attack on the loyalists—on behalf of British taxpayers who, he said, "have seen the taxes they have poured out without regard to cost—over 300 million pounds a year with the cost of the army on top of that—going into Northern Ireland. They see property destroyed by evil violence and are asked to pick up the bill for rebuilding it. Yet people who benefit from this now viciously defy Westminster, purporting to act as though they were an elected government, spending their lives sponging on Westminster and British democracy and then systematically assault democratic methods. Who do these people think they are?"[35]

Wilson's response to the UWC-UDA challenge was typical of his government—petulant and weak. Two days after his speech the army took over twenty-one gasoline stations, provoking the UWC, which warned that it would completely close down the power stations, water, and sewage works. Ulster was on the verge of collapse when Faulkner begged Rees to open talks with the strike leaders. Rees refused, and on May 28, Faulkner resigned as the head of government—for the second time in just over two years. "It is . . . apparent to us," said Faulkner, "from the extent of support for the present stoppage that the degree of consent needed to sustain the executive does not at present exist. Nor, as Ulstermen, are we prepared to see our country undergo, for any political reason, the catastrophe which now confronts it."[36]

When the news of the executive's collapse reached loyalist ears, bonfires were lit across the province, and Protestants took to the streets to celebrate. Faulkner, like O'Neill before him, was dispatched into the political wilderness for daring to compromise. He would not return.

Ironically, in Faulkner's footsteps went the UDA. Its role in the events of May 1974, though pivotal, brought it no political rewards; instead, Unionist politicians took credit for having "saved" Ulster and made sure that the paramilitaries were kept out of mainstream Unionist politics. Andy Tyrie's successful management of the UDA during the strike made him the most powerful figure within the organization. Tyrie, embittered at the Unionists' treatment of the UDA, launched his organization on a quixotic political quest, which would bring it to Libya and New York, and meetings with the SDLP and the Provisionals.

As for the SDLP, the fate of the power-sharing experiment was an especially bitter blow. Hume concluded that it was no use searching for a political solution within the confines of Northern Ireland. He began a long pilgrimage that would take him beyond London and Dublin to Brussels, Boston, and Washington, looking for a way out of the bloody deadlock. His quest would last for twenty years.

Britain's most ambitious attempt to restructure the 1921 settlement had failed disastrously. Immediately after the collapse of the executive, the British announced a "constitutional convention" in which all the political parties could take part, but it would be no more than a talking shop. In the future, successive British governments would adopt a more cautious approach to searching for solutions to the Ulster problem. Indeed, there would be no more ambitious political schemes for the province for over a decade. Britain would concentrate on finding ways to contain the violence. For the British, Ulster had become primarily a security problem.

• 5 •

IN THE AFTERMATH of the power-sharing executive's fall, the Provisional IRA was left to contemplate the new political landscape and completely misread it. Its leading ideologues, Daithi O'Conaill and Ruairi O'Bradaigh, came to the conclusion that Britain's failure to take on the UWC meant it was making ready to withdraw from Northern Ireland. They declared 1974 the "Year of Victory."

It was a startlingly inappropriate declaration, given the state of the Provisionals' military machine in Ulster. Internment had cut a wide swath through its ranks, and most of the younger, northern-based activists who had come to the fore in 1971 were behind bars. Adams, the commanding officer of Belfast, was grabbed (for a second time) in July 1973, along with Brendan "The Dark" Hughes, the man who had taken over the Second Battalion, and Tom Cahill, Joe Cahill's brother and a prominent member of the Belfast brigade. After a heavy beating, Adams was sent to Long Kesh. Shortly afterward, Adams's successor as commanding officer, his close friend Ivor Bell, was arrested and joined Adams in the internment camp. By then there were 578 prisoners being held in Long Kesh without trial, all but 29 of them republicans.[37] The Belfast units were especially badly hit. As a result, by 1974, IRA activity in the city had dropped drastically. During the first six months of the year, only three British soldiers were killed in Belfast compared to sixteen in the same period the year before. In September, Billy McKee, who had been commanding officer of Belfast until his arrest in March 1971, was released. He says he was shocked at what he found. "There was no IRA [in Belfast] when I got out, thanks to internment," he said.[38] For a period in the fall there was no one to take over as commanding officer. So how was the Army Council in

Dublin going to deliver its "Year of Victory"? The Provisionals were active, it is true, in rural areas such as Tyrone and south Armagh, where land mine attacks were proving effective against British forces. Soon the south Armagh IRA acquired the kind of reputation that the north Belfast IRA had enjoyed in 1971 and 1972. But the Provisionals knew that no matter how successful, the rural battalions were too easily isolated. The war would not be won unless they could strike at commercial and military targets in urban areas. With the Belfast Brigade temporarily crippled, they looked to England.

When MacStiofain was chief of staff, there had been no attacks in England. Under the brief reign of Joe Cahill, his successor, the Belfast Provisionals carried out a quick bombing raid in London to coincide with the border plebiscite in March 1973.[39] But it was under Seamus Twomey, who took over as chief of staff from Cahill, that England was first subjected to a concerted bombing campaign. An army bus was bombed in February 1974 as it drove along the M62 motorway, killing twelve people, nine of them soldiers. Among the dead were two children, ages five and two. In July a bomb exploded at the Tower of London, killing a woman tourist. In October the Provisionals bombed a pub frequented by British troops in Guildford, Surrey, and five people died, four of them off-duty members of the British army and two of them teenage girls.[40] More attacks followed. Most occurred without warning. The worst incident took place in Birmingham toward the end of November.

Birmingham, with its large Irish population, was central to the IRA's 1970s English campaign. Explosives carried in cars from Belfast would arrive there on a regular basis. The Birmingham IRA had been responsible for thirty-eight attacks in 1973, causing only one fatality, an army bomb-disposal officer. An effort had been made to concentrate on damaging property and avoiding civilian deaths. With the proclamation of 1974 as the "Year of Victory," that changed. On the evening of November 21 the Provisional IRA targeted two popular downtown Birmingham pubs, The Mulberry Bush in the landmark Rotunda building and The Talk of the Town, located underneath the tax office in nearby New Street. The bombing team of two men planted the first bomb in a duffel bag in The Mulberry Bush and a few minutes later left the other in a small brown suitcase in The Talk of the Town, three hundred yards away. Both pubs were packed that evening. At 8:11 P.M. a telephone operator at the *Birmingham*

Post and Mail received a warning: "There is a bomb planted in the Rotunda and a bomb in New Street . . . at the tax office." It came six minutes before the first blast at The Mulberry Bush. That blast killed ten people. It was heard at The Talk of the Town, just minutes before the bomb exploded there, killing eleven.[41]

Shortly afterward, in a wave of anti-Irish sentiment, six Irish immigrants—Hugh Callaghan, Patrick Hill, Gerry Hunter, Richard McIllkenny, Billy Power, and Johnny Walker, all longtime residents of Birmingham—were arrested. Five of them were picked up on the night of the pub blasts as they were on their way back to Belfast for the funeral of an IRA man who had earlier killed himself in a bungled bombing in nearby Coventry. They suffered severe beatings before being charged and later convicted of the worst mass murder in British history. Their convictions were overturned sixteen years later, following a long campaign to prove their innocence.[42]

The Provisionals denied responsibility for the bombings, though shortly before they occurred, Daithi O'Conaill had given an interview warning that the English campaign would be stepped up. Along with Twomey, he was convinced that this would finally persuade Britain to leave Ireland. The Provisional IRA commander in Birmingham, who ordered the bombings, was said to have remarked, "Three or more of those and the Brits will pull out."[43]

Britain's first response was to introduce the Prevention of Terrorism Act, which allowed police to hold suspects for up to seven days without charging them and to expel people from Great Britain. In announcing the new bill, Home Secretary Roy Jenkins said, "These powers . . . are Draconian. In combination they are unprecedented in peace time. I believe they are fully justified to meet the clear and present danger."[44] There was considerable irony in the fact that the Northern Ireland problem, which had developed as a protest against the lack of certain civil rights in one part of the United Kingdom, was now forcing the government to suspend many of the same basic rights throughout the whole of Great Britain.

Although the no-warning bombing campaign in England did not in the end force Britain from Northern Ireland, it undoubtedly had something to do with the reopening of contacts between the government and the Provisional leadership, if only with the aim of getting the IRA to stop. With Protestant clergymen acting as go-betweens, contact was renewed. The

Provisional Army Council called a cease-fire on December 20, 1974, its first since June 26, 1972. After a false start, followed by more bombings in London, the cease-fire was renewed indefinitely on February 10, 1975. In return for a cessation of IRA attacks in Britain and on military targets in Ulster, the British agreed to release one hundred prisoners within two weeks, with the aim of ending internment completely, withdraw between three thousand and four thousand troops, de-escalate the British presence in Catholic areas, permit wanted IRA men to carry weapons and return to Northern Ireland without fear of arrest, and allow Sinn Fein to open seven "Truce Monitoring Centers" throughout the province. The government also said it would hold further talks with the IRA and draw up a formal truce agreement. A further condition for the cease-fire, which was not made public, was the transfer of Gerry Kelly, convicted of the London bombings of March 1973, from an English jail to Long Kesh, an indication of Kelly's status within the movement even at this early stage.

The British government's public acknowledgment of its arrangement with the Provisional Army Council alarmed the Irish government and the SDLP. Both were disturbed about the prospect that the Wilson government had made a secret deal behind their backs, one that could provoke a vicious Protestant backlash and reprisals in the Republic by fueling rumors of a British withdrawal plan. This is exactly the interpretation that Provisional leaders O'Bradaigh and O'Conaill were advocating as they sought to deliver on their 1974 "Year of Victory" slogan.

For six months a high-ranking British official, James Allen, liaised with the Belfast commanding officer, Billy McKee, as Long Kesh was emptied of its inmates. Whatever the aim of the meetings, one thing was plain: They did not end the violence. On the contrary, it grew worse. Loyalists, anxious about the government-IRA contacts, launched another round of sectarian killings, and the Provisionals responded in kind. Both the UDA and the UVF were now active, the UDA using its nom de guerre UFF, which the government had banned in November 1973. (This had prompted one UDA man to ask, "How can you be convicted of belonging to an organization which doesn't exist?"[45])

From late 1974 the Provisionals' campaign in Belfast ceased to be aimed at the security forces (between September and December 1974 not one police officer or soldier was killed); its guns instead were turned on Protestants. Nine were murdered in November, compared to eight Catholics.

The sectarian killings would get worse throughout 1975 and 1976, long after the cease-fire, such as it was, had collapsed. Of the 247 people murdered in 1975, only 30 were members of the security forces. The following year there were 297 murders—making it the second worst year in the history of the Troubles; of those, only 52 were police officers or soldiers.

This disproportion between the numbers of civilian and military victims would remain a constant feature of the Ulster conflict. In the single worst incident, on January 5, the Provisional IRA in south Armagh stopped a busload of Protestant workers, lined them up, and shot ten of them to death. The killings were in revenge for a UVF attack in Whitecross, south Armagh, during which three Catholic brothers were murdered.

The various paramilitary groups also fought among themselves. By late 1974 a faction within the Official IRA had formed around Seamus Costello. He feared that the organization's leadership was intent on completely abandoning the armed struggle and endeavored to prevent it. His efforts failed, and he was court-martialed. On December 8, 1974, the split became formal with the birth of a new republican organization. In its political, public guise it was called the Irish Republican Socialist Party. Behind the scenes it was secretly organized as the Irish National Liberation Army. Costello's new alignment attracted much of the Official IRA's support in Belfast and Derry. When the Belfast Officials attempted to stamp out the new group, a feud erupted. On April 28, 1975, a sixteen-year-old gunman named Gerard Steenson shot dead the Official IRA's Belfast leader, Billy McMillen, a veteran republican. In the years to come Steenson would earn a reputation as one of the most feared gunmen in Northern Ireland. Five republicans were killed in the feud.

Six months later, another feud broke out, this time between the remains of the Official IRA in Belfast and the Provisionals. It claimed eleven lives, including that of seven-year-old Eileen Kelly, whom Provisional IRA gunmen murdered while trying to shoot her father. It was hardly surprising that in August 1976 the war-weary population of Belfast, disgusted by what was seen as increasingly aimless violence, should marshal themselves behind two local Catholic women, Mairead Corrigan and Betty Williams, in a short-lived peace movement. It sprang up spontaneously when soldiers shot dead a friend of Adams's, IRA gunman Danny Lennon. His car crashed into Corrigan's sister, Annie Maguire, and her family as they walked along the street, killing three of her children, ages six weeks to nine years. The women organized a march to demand an end to the killings.

The marches, involving both Catholics and Protestants, grew in size throughout the late summer and early autumn, helped by an intense media interest.

Some thought that the movement had the power to isolate the Provisionals, against whom its campaign was chiefly directed. It was wishful thinking. Many in the Catholic ghettos felt the government was manipulating what was a genuine yearning for peace but had become a well-managed media event fronted by naive women. Though the peace movement remained a news story for some months longer, by early 1977 it had spent itself. It brought Corrigan and Williams the Nobel Peace Prize, but it did not bring peace to Ireland.

From inside Long Kesh, Adams watched these developments with growing anxiety. At the core of his criticism was his attitude toward the 1975 cease-fire. Adams suspected that the 1972 cease-fire had been a British ploy to lure the IRA away from the armed campaign with false hopes. He saw the 1975 cease-fire in the same light, except this time it was succeeding.[46] Adams would later claim that at this point the IRA was near defeat. Its drift into sectarian killing and internecine violence was playing right into the hands of British government policy. Although the peace movement was not a threat to hard-core republican support, Adams and others such as Ivor Bell saw it as a worrying symptom. That hard core would always be enough to keep a campaign of some sort going, but it was not wide enough to provide a basis for the Provisionals to expand, leaving them in danger of isolation from the broader Catholic community.

Adams and his associates also came to another conclusion that would drastically affect the future of the Provisional IRA: that contrary to what O'Conaill and O'Bradaigh believed, the British, far from preparing to leave, had merely changed their tactics and were ready to embark on a new offensive that combined both legal and military means to isolate and finally defeat the republican movement. The changes were encapsulated in the terms "normalization," "Ulsterization," and "criminalization." A new legal system was being introduced, supported by a restructuring of the RUC to enable it to take the leading role in tackling the paramilitaries. The Provisionals would have to adjust their strategy accordingly.

The year 1977 was the turning point in the history of the conflict, for loyalists as well as for the IRA. Proof of this came in May when the UDA attempted to duplicate its success against the power-sharing executive.

This time, with the support of Paisley, the militants took aim at Britain's failure to return a majority-ruled government to Northern Ireland and its failure to defeat the IRA. The police and the army moved resolutely against the barricades, arresting obstructers, including Paisley himself. Protestant shipyard workers voted to stay at work. More important, so did the workers in the main power station. After ten days, on May 13, the "strike" collapsed ignominiously.

Ulster was entering a new phase. The most important sign was the drastic reduction in the yearly death rate; after 1977 it would rarely rise above one hundred.[47] Internment had ended with the last detainee being released on December 5, 1975. Security forces' tactics were changing equally drastically. One indication was that the number of houses searched annually fell from a high of 74,914 in 1974 to 20,724 in 1977. It would continue to fall. Widespread street disturbances and open confrontations between the Provisionals and the army became rarer. The no-go areas (with the possible exception of south Armagh) were no more, and civil rights protests had become a historical memory. The "Troubles," in one sense, were over. But, in another sense, they were just about to begin. Ulster was soon to be engulfed in a twilight war of covert action from which it would not emerge for almost twenty years.

PART II

THE TWILIGHT WAR

· FOUR ·

THE POLITICS OF DESPAIR

1977–1981

BY 1977 a pall of despair had settled on Ulster. The optimism of the civil rights days was spent; the destructive energy of the paramilitaries, which seemed for a time as if it might settle the question one way or another, was exhausted; a peace movement had come and gone without changing anything. As for the politicians, the faces of the new men who sprang up in the late 1960s promising change had become as dully familiar as the phrases they used to condemn the murders. The centers of the two main cities, Belfast and Derry, were dead after dark since those fortunate enough not to be touched by the growing unemployment hurried home from their jobs to the safety of their ghetto—Catholic or Protestant, working-class or middle-class.[1] The Peace Line had become a wall fifteen feet high, dissecting west Belfast, a crude expression of the segregation that sectarian violence had imposed on the city. The days of city center dance halls, movie theaters, and restaurants were a memory around which those born in the 1930s and 1940s could weave nostalgic stories about the time when Belfast was a "real" city. Many of the Victorian working-class neighborhoods that had sustained city life were being leveled as planners gouged out tracts of land for access roads to the motorways. Most of the lower Falls was gone, passing into history along with the linen mills where its people had worked for generations. Even the city center pubs fell silent in the evening, their doors barred. In the working-class districts along the main roads out of town or in the surrounding housing estates, there were pubs, but they looked like miniature prisons. Metal cages protected the entrance. From inside, guards scrutinized monitors linked to security cameras trained on the street. Boulders or barrels filled with concrete and connected by iron rods ringed the pavement to prevent car bombers from parking too close to the premises. Drinking in a "legitimate target" was not a very relaxing experience.

Shopping was hardly any better. Long lines formed in downtown city stores as security guards searched shoppers on their way in. They went through bags, pocketbooks, and parcels, and passed detectors up and around customers, monitoring them from head to foot. Belfast and Derry were probably the only cities in the world where customers were scrutinized more as they went into the shop than when they were leaving it. Because of car bombs, parking had long ago been banned from the city center. As a result, commerce drained away to the suburbs. People followed, and the population of the cities fell throughout the 1970s. Soon Belfast began to resemble a midwestern town in the United States, a place from which life fled after business hours. The ghostly atmosphere was augmented by the boarded-up buildings and half-demolished streets, the houses sliced in half and the tattered wallpaper exposed to the sky. Only the Europa, opened in 1969 and Belfast's last remaining downtown hotel, stood as a reminder of what other cities took for granted—that some of the minor pleasures of life were still possible, such as dining out in the evening after a few cocktails in a cheery, anonymous environment. But dining in the Europa was not without its tribulations: By 1977 it had been bombed twenty-eight times.

By then, too, a feature of the cityscape of Belfast and Derry that startled visitors were the heavily armed foot patrols of British soldiers, edging their way slowly around the streets of the working-class housing estates, the constant whir of helicopters circling above them. At night the choppers would swoop low, searchlights blazing, waking every baby for miles around. What could almost have been a normal vision of urban desolation was thereby transformed into something else: a scene from a war movie, perhaps, though what kind of war it was hard to gauge.

For Gerry Adams, released from prison in March 1977, that was a question of supreme importance. He had had four years to think about it. The situation he confronted as he enjoyed his first days of freedom was very different from the one that had existed in 1973. The British government had put in place a whole new battery of legislation, following the recommendations in a report by Lord Gardiner, the same man who in 1972 had advised the government that the use of in-depth interrogation—the "five techniques"—was illegal. His report came to several important conclusions. One was that the use of detention without trial "cannot remain as a long-term policy. . . . The prolonged effects of the use of detention are ultimately inimical to community life."[2] Another was that Special Category status, conferred on paramilitary prisoners in July 1972, "was a serious mistake. . . . We recommend that the earliest practicable opportunity should be taken to end the special category."[3]

A new court system had already replaced internment. A single judge, sitting without a jury, decided on the guilt or innocence of the accused. This followed on the recommendations of Lord Diplock and became known as the Diplock courts. The Emergency Provisionals Act (1973, 1978) replaced the old Special Powers Act and allowed a more flexible interpretation of when confessions might be used in court as sole evidence to convict a suspect. Meanwhile, as Lord Gardiner had recommended, the old prison system of Nissen huts arranged in compounds, which had housed the sudden huge influx of prisoners since August 1971, was replaced by a new cellular prison near Long Kesh, renamed the Maze. The individual blocks were shaped like the letter "H" and soon became known as "H-blocks." It was said to be one of the most secure prisons in the world. As of March 1, 1976, no one convicted of a terrorist offense would be granted Special Category status but would be incarcerated like any other "ordinary" criminal in an H-block cell.

The aim of these reforms was to "normalize" the situation in Ulster by processing suspects through the courts. Putting prisoners in ordinary prison cells and depriving them of the privileges that came with Special Category status "criminalized" the paramilitaries, denying them the opportunity to present themselves to the world as "freedom fighters," whose crimes were "political." The third leg of this plan, "Ulsterization," meant withdrawing the British army into the background and placing the chief responsibility for fighting the paramilitary organizations back in the hands of the RUC. In the long run this would be the only part of the initiative that would succeed.

The new Northern Ireland secretary of state, Roy Mason, who had replaced Rees in September 1976, was also a source of much concern to republicans. Mason was the opposite of Rees. If Rees looked somewhat like an indecisive, bumbling Labour Party intellectual, Mason had the appearance of a stocky, bluff coal miner. He went down the mines at age fourteen and liked nothing better than an opportunity to talk about it. Right from the start he wanted to "take on the terrorists." Even before he was appointed to the Northern Ireland post, as secretary of defense in the Wilson government in early 1976, he had ordered the army's elite undercover unit, the Special Air Service (known in security circles as the Troop) into south Armagh after a series of bloody sectarian murders. Rees had been a student of Irish history. Mason was mainly concerned with winning the present war and not cogitating too much over the outcome of "battles long ago." Indeed, the battle had hardly begun when he declared that it was won, that the IRA was "reeling" or was being "squeezed like toothpaste from a tube."

Neither did he endear himself to loyalists; in fact, he had a more pronounced success against them than against republicans. He sent the RUC in to smash their "strike" in May 1977, dismantling barricades and arresting the ringleaders. Several of the most vicious UVF gangs were arrested and jailed, including the Shankill Road Butchers, who terrorized Catholics between November 1975 and March 1977. The gang's violence was so indiscriminate that of their nineteen victims, nine were Protestant.[4]

If certain kinds of murder can be said to be as revealing as poetry is about the nature of the society in which they occur, then loyalism's deep-seated bigotry had found its most brutally eloquent exponent in gang leader Lenny Murphy. Murphy was a Shankill Road Protestant whose Catholic surname would have been enough to doom him at the hands of the kind of thugs he recruited. His reputation as Belfast's Jack the Ripper rests on the series of frenzied cutthroat killings for which he and his gang became notorious.

In November 1975, Murphy and two others dragged Francis Crossan, a thirty-four-year-old Catholic, into a black taxi driven by Billy Moore. Crossan was beaten with a tire iron, kicked, and had a broken beer glass shoved into his face. The gang drove him to an alleyway off the Shankill Road, where his semiconscious body was laid out. Murphy then set about hacking his way through Crossan's throat with a butcher knife until the spine was reached.

A detective who was among the first on the murder scene recalled it years later: "It was a horrific sight and especially when the body was lifted off the ground because the victim's head was held to the trunk by tissue. I knew I was witnessing something different . . . a more personal type of killing."[5] Thomas Quinn and Francis Rice were beaten and hacked to death in February 1976. Murphy was taken off the streets in March that year, charged and convicted of possession of a gun, which kept him locked up until 1982. But on his instructions his gang continued killing, hatcheting Cornelius Neeson to death in August 1976 and cutting the throats of another three victims: Stephen McCann the following October, Daniel Morrisey in February 1977, and Francis Cassidy in March the same year. After one of their intended victims escaped, the gang was finally identified and arrested. Following a sensational trial, in January 1979 eleven of them were convicted and given forty-two life sentences. Murphy, nicknamed the Master Butcher, emerged from prison three years later as eager as ever to resume his reign of terror. (More about this in chapter 5.)

After the collapse of the UDA strike in May 1977 and the breakup of the UVF gangs, sectarian killings came to a halt and did not resume until February 1978. Along with the Butcher's gang, among those removed from the loyalist paramilitary scene was John White, founder of the UFF. After his release from internment in 1975, he had rejoined the UDA, only to be seized in July 1977. The detectives questioned him about the murders of SDLP man Paddy Wilson and Irene Andrews. White believes that one of the Shankill Butchers gang, who had been arrested at the same time, gave the police information. The interrogation lasted morning, afternoon, and evening for three days, at the end of which White confessed. He was convicted and received a life sentence.[6]

When sectarian killings did resume, they were on a much smaller scale and would remain so for a decade. Like the Provisionals, the loyalist groups had been forced to retrench and consider their future.

The main target of the security forces remained the Provisional IRA. While Mason's declaration of victory was to prove premature, there was no doubt that he was having unprecedented successes against them. A new chief constable, Kenneth Newman, had helped restructure the RUC, setting up four Regional Crime Squads "to target the most active members of terrorist organizations."[7] The squads combined the resources of the Criminal Investigation Division with the Special Branch. They were also responsible for interrogating suspects at the Castlereagh holding center in east Belfast. In this they were helped in obtaining confessions by the court's interpretation of Section 6 of the Emergency Provisions Act, which stipulated that unless it could be proved such confessions were obtained by torture or inhuman or degrading treatment, they were to be regarded as admissible in a court of law. It afforded the police interrogators room to apply a considerable amount of "rough" treatment that did not fit the definition of torture or degrading treatment, though for those on the receiving end the distinction was academic. Confessions began to flow, and the conviction rate soared. During 1976, out of twelve hundred people charged with terrorist offenses, nine hundred were convicted, and 80 percent of them were on the strength of confessions. In August the government felt secure enough in Northern Ireland that Her Majesty the Queen made her first visit to the Province in eleven years, defying Provisional IRA threats.

Certainly, a government that was going to such pains to reform its legal and prison system was hardly planning to pull out of Northern Ireland anytime soon, regardless of what the Provisional IRA leadership might think. By the spring of 1977, that much was obvious to Adams and to the younger Belfast and Derry activists who like him had been drawn into the movement in the 1960s. They realized from the evidence all around them that what they were now involved in was a long war of attrition, with little prospect of an immediate British withdrawal. As Adams saw it, while the Provisionals had been sitting around in their Truce Monitoring Centers waiting for a British withdrawal to begin, the British had pushed ahead with their efforts to normalize, criminalize, and Ulsterize the conflict, bringing the IRA to the verge of defeat.

Adams on his release had taken up a leadership position on the general headquarters staff and was summoned south to work with Seamus Twomey, who had been chief of staff since 1973. Efforts began to restructure the Provisional IRA and Sinn Fein. The public face of this initiative was revealed on June 12 at the Wolfe Tone Memorial in County Kildare. This is one of the two most sacred occasions on the Irish republican calendar (the other being Easter), when devotees look to Tone, the leader of the 1798 rebellion and the man they regard as republicanism's founder. The event has been frequently used as an opportunity for the leadership to announce fresh policies or a new departure. Goulding did so in 1967, proclaiming the republican movement's rededication to left-wing political action. Ten years later, the message was not much different. In a way it harked back to Adams's days as political activist in Belfast, prior to the

1969 upheaval, when he and his colleagues were involved in housing action and other forms of social protest. In order to avoid accusations (which came anyway) that this was a return to the Official IRA "Marxist" line, the man chosen to deliver the speech was Jimmy Drumm, a contemporary of Cahill and McKee, a founding member of the Belfast Provisionals, and a veteran of the 1950s campaign.[8]

Drumm cautioned that the war could not be won if it was fought solely on the issue of the withdrawal of the British army. It had to be broadened into a political struggle, with links forged throughout Ireland to other revolutionary and socialist groups. Clearly this meant Sinn Fein would play an important role, but there would be no cessation of the armed campaign, which was to remain the "cutting edge" of the struggle.

Meanwhile, behind the scenes, the secret reorganization of the Provisional IRA had begun. It was not without its casualties. McKee, who had been commanding officer of the Belfast Provisionals since June 1975, was brought to Dublin and placed in charge of sorting out "internal problems."[9] Others were given a rather more violent send-off. Jack "Fingers" McCartan, who for years ran a social club in west Belfast—a republican front operation—and was involved in corrupt housing schemes, was shot dead one night as he left his club. The killing was blamed on the British army, but it was the Belfast IRA who removed him as part of their "cleanup" campaign.

Just how thorough the reforms were was revealed in December that year, thanks to the arrest of Seamus Twomey. After four years as chief of staff and one spectacular escape—he and two other IRA leaders were lifted by helicopter from the Mountjoy Prison yard in Dublin—Twomey's run came to an end on the southern outskirts of the Irish capital when Irish police stopped his car and arrested him. In a follow-up search of his apartment, they discovered the plans for the restructuring of the republican movement under the title "Staff Report."

It began by sounding an alarm: "The three-day and seven-day detention orders are breaking volunteers, and it is the Irish Republican Army's own fault for not indoctrinating volunteers with the psychological strength to resist interrogation. Coupled with this factor, *which is contributing to our defeat* [author's emphasis], we are burdened with an inefficient infrastructure of commands, brigades, battalions and companies. The old system, with which the Brits and Branch are familiar, has to be changed. We recommend reorganization and remotivation, the building of a new Irish Republican Army."[10] After advocating the creation of the post of education officer as part of the general headquarters staff for training recruits in how to resist interrogation techniques, the report continued:

> *We must gear ourselves towards long-term armed struggle based on putting unknown men and new recruits into a new structure. The new structure shall be a cell system.*

It would consist

> *ideally of four people. Rural areas we decided should be treated as separate cases to that of city and town areas where the majority of our operations are carried out and where the biggest proportion of our support lies anyway.*

The cell system is then described. Each cell is to be under the control of

> *the brigade's/command's intelligence officer. . . . Cells must be specialized into IC cells, sniping cells, execution, bombing, robberies, etc. The cell will have no control of weapons or explosives, but should be capable of dumping weapons overnight (in the case of a postponed operation). The weapons and explosives should be under the complete control of the brigade's/command's Q[uarter] M[aster] and E[xplosives] O[fficer] respectively. Cells should operate as often as possible outside of their own areas; both to confuse Brit intelligence (which would thus increase our security) and to expand our operational areas.*

The report went on to deal with Sinn Fein, the almost nonexistent political wing of the movement that Provisional activists held in contempt. That would have to change. According to the staff report:

> *Sinn Fein should come under army organizers at all levels. Sinn Fein should employ full-time organizers in big republican areas. Sinn Fein should be radicalized (under army direction) and should agitate about social and economic issues which attack the welfare of the*

> *people. Sinn Fein should be directed to infiltrate other organizations to win support for, and sympathy to, the movement. Sinn Fein should be reeducated and have a big role to play in publicity and propaganda depts, complaints and problems (making no room for RUC opportunism). It gains the respect of the people which in turn leads to increased support for the cell.*[11]

When these ambitious plans about Provisional Sinn Fein's role were drafted, there seemed little or no chance of their being realized. Sinn Fein as a unified organization had not fought an election in Ulster since the mid-1950s. After the republican movement split, Official Sinn Fein, whose own strategy was similar to that outlined in the staff report, had entered elections for the first time in 1973. The result was not auspicious. The Officials won only ten seats in the local elections of May and a derisory 1.8 percent of the vote in the June assembly elections, winning no seats.

There also remained within the Provisionals a powerful current running against involvement in politics, particularly electoral politics. After all, one of the reasons for the 1969 split was disagreement with the Goulding-Garland leadership's ambitions for Sinn Fein to become a "real" political party that would take its place in the Dail in Dublin if elected. Men such as O'Conaill and O'Bradaigh who had fought this ideological battle in the 1960s were still powerful figures within the Provisional movement. In 1977, however, it is unlikely that anyone in the Provisionals thought these issues would ever have to be faced again. Sinn Fein's prospects of fighting elections, never mind winning them, seemed remote to say the least. But more important for the movement's immediate prospects, its ability to continue its armed campaign was being seriously challenged. It was a challenge that had to be met by a new chief of staff.

Twomey's successor as chief of staff was Adams's Derry contemporary Martin McGuinness. McGuinness was the first of the 1960s generation of northern activists to head the Provisional IRA. Under him the Derry active service units had devastated the city, reducing its downtown area to streets of bombed and boarded-up buildings. They had also been among the first to carry out a ruthless murder campaign against off-duty UDR men. McGuinness was a devout Catholic who guarded the Provisionals' Derry domain jealously. As a result, the Derry IRA did not tolerate rivals easily.

When the IRSP/INLA started to organize there, the Provisionals tied one of its leaders to a lamppost and covered him with tar.

McGuinness faced severe problems thanks to the new security initiatives. In the first eight months of 1977, compared with the previous year, bombings were down 52 percent, shootings 33 percent, and the death toll fell by 62 percent. The statistics show that September 1977 was the first month since October 1970 in which no civilians were killed in Northern Ireland as the result of political violence. Attacks on the British army and the RUC declined drastically. The Provisionals' campaign became restricted to attacking off-duty UDR men at home or at work. Between September and December only one member of the security forces was killed while on duty: Paul Harman, an undercover soldier shot dead in Andersonstown, west Belfast, on December 14. The IRA's plans to regroup suffered a serious setback when a large arms shipment acquired from PLO sources and destined for the Provisionals was tracked from Cyprus and intercepted in Antwerp, Belgium, at the end of November. As the year ended, *The Irish Times* quoted Mason as declaring that "the tide has turned against the terrorists and the message for 1978 is one of real hope."

The pattern of striking at soft targets persisted into 1978. It was a particularly prominent feature of the Provisionals' violence in rural areas in Fermanagh, Tyrone, Armagh, and Derry where off-duty UDR and RUC men were more vulnerable, often living on isolated farms. On February 8 part-time UDR officer William Gordon got into his car with his ten-year-old daughter, Lesley, sitting next to him. When he started the engine, it detonated an under-car booby-trap bomb (UCBT), which killed them both. Such killings especially angered local Protestants, who viewed them as part of a deliberate IRA campaign to drive Protestant farmers off their land in areas where Catholics were in the ascendant.[12]

Car bombs for the time being became a thing of the past. Instead, the Provisionals used incendiary devices to burn down movie theaters, hotels, offices, shops, and department stores. Women were the key to this tactic. The cigarette-sized bombs were often smuggled into stores inside the soles of the platform boots so fashionable at the time. Throughout the first months of 1978 the Provisionals mounted a concentrated campaign of firebombings, determined to prove that Mason was overly optimistic. By February there were more than one hundred explosions. On the evening of February 17, 1978, the Northern Ireland Collie Club and the Junior

Motor Cycle Club were holding their annual prize-giving functions in the La Mon House hotel in the Castlereagh Hills, a low range of drumlins patchworked with fields overlooking east Belfast. Just before 9 P.M. a warning came that a bomb had been planted. As the staff rushed to clear the dining room, two bombs attached to cans of gasoline and hooked onto security grills outside the main function room exploded. A huge fireball engulfed everything in front of it as dozens of guests were sprayed with burning fuel that stuck to their clothes and flesh. Twelve people were burned to death. Pictures of their blackened, charred remains—hardly recognizable as human beings—were distributed around the country in an effort to make those who still supported the Provisionals realize the cost of their campaign and to remind those who opposed them of the need to continue doing so.

When reporters asked the chief constable if he still thought that the Provisionals were beaten, he replied tersely, "I never made that claim."[13] The message was clear to Mason: Neither should he have made it. Declaring victory was a dangerous business in an unconventional war in which winning or losing was more a matter of perception than established fact.

Something significant emerged in the days following the La Mon House atrocity. In spite of the horror of the bombing and the fact that all of the twelve dead were Protestants, there was no loyalist retaliation. This was the first time since 1971 that the UDA and the UVF refrained from answering a republican outrage with one of their own. The UDA's supreme chairman, Andy Tyrie, maintained that this was because the organization no longer targeted ordinary Catholics but was more selective.[14] The La Mon bombing did lead to a crackdown, however. Among twenty-one republicans arrested in the aftermath was Gerry Adams. He was charged with belonging to an illegal organization. After eight months in custody, the court accepted his lawyer's argument that there was insufficient evidence to convict him of the charge, and he was released. (The evidence consisted of speeches Adams made and pictures of him taking part in an IRA parade in prison.) Sinn Fein turned the situation to their advantage and for the first time went on the propaganda offensive, claiming that the British government was using the La Mon House bombing as an excuse to impede their legitimate political activity through harassing and arresting Sinn Fein members and workers. The party's new feistiness was a sign of things to come.

Another offensive against the Provisionals was under way, and in the end it would prove to be the most effective one. RUC recruitment had increased. The Special Branch, or E Department, was restructured in line with the government's "Ulsterization" plans, the key to which was reestablishing the primacy of the police in security matters. Traditionally, E Department's function had been more or less restricted to gathering information from informers. In the 1970s the department was subdivided into different sections, each with its own specialization. The handling of the human sources of intelligence became the responsibility of E3. Later, a surveillance unit, E4, was developed, specializing in technical sources of intelligence. It oversaw the use of various types of bugging devices and wiretaps to monitor arms dumps and premises used by suspects.[15] These operations were carried out in collaboration with MI5, Britain's internal security service. MI5 agents were tasked to plant listening devices in targeted buildings under RUC supervision.

In 1976 a division, E4A, was set up, modeled on the British army's surveillance unit known as "Det." RUC officers were trained in Close Target Recognizance (CTR)—surveillance techniques such as the use of disguises, selecting and establishing suitable observation posts (OPs), and the following of suspects. Police operators were sent into nationalist areas to maintain surveillance of IRA suspects, often for weeks at a time. It was relatively easy to carry out these operations in rural areas, but in urban centers it was difficult and dangerous. Fortunately for the RUC, in the late 1970s the redevelopment of Belfast provided plenty of abandoned buildings in which E4A could set up OPs. The Special Branch also began working in close collaboration with the army's Special Air Service, which had been in Ulster as a unit since 1976, though before that individual members of the troop stationed there had been attached to other regiments.[16]

The Tasking Coordination Group (TCG) was created in the late 1970s to pool intelligence from police, army, and MI5 sources, and to coordinate a response to planned terrorist operations, "locking together intelligence from informers with surveillance and ambushing activities of undercover units."[17] The first TCG was established in Belfast. Later TCG South, headquartered in Gough Barracks, Armagh, and TCG North, based in Derry city, were created.

The RUC began making dramatic progress in the twilight war during this period, recruiting among others two key figures from the Belfast Brigade who became informers. One, whose police nickname was "DJ," was from west Belfast and was recruited after being arrested for a driving offense. DJ's information would frustrate many IRA bombing operations and lead to the apprehension of some of their top activists. The other "tout" was Maurice Gilvary, the operations officer of the Third Battalion in north Belfast, who according to republican sources provided the information that allowed the SAS to ambush a bombing team as it was about to blow up a post office depot on June 20, 1978. Denis Brown, Jackie Mealy, and James Mulvenna were shot dead in the single biggest strike the troop had so far delivered against the Provisionals, who admitted the men were on "active service" but alleged they were shot without warning and were unarmed. A fourth man, Billy Hanna, a Protestant, who happened to be passing at the time, was also killed. His death was an indication of the risks the authorities took in deploying the firepower and aggression of the troop in built-up areas. In the end, the SAS would be used mainly in the countryside. This operation and others like them highlighted the growing reliance of the security forces on accurate intelligence that allowed them to anticipate paramilitary operations with deadly effect.[18] It also allowed the RUC Special Branch to build up a picture of the Provisional IRA command structure in Ulster from the late 1970s onward.

At this point the Provisional Army Council, under the growing influence of the northern activists, had established two separate commands: Northern and Southern. The main responsibility of the Southern Command was acquiring and storing weapons, raising finance (at first through robberies, later through running front operations such as pubs and clubs), organizing the training of volunteers, and transporting weapons to the "war zone," where Northern Command ran the actual day-to-day operations. Gerry Adams's name was at the top of a list of twenty-seven that the Special Branch made of Belfast PIRA activists. He was listed as being on "Northern Command." Along with the names, the police had details of the license numbers of the suspects' cars, their hair and eye color, addresses, height, and so forth. (For instance, Adams is noted as being six feet one inch tall and brown haired.) The compilation was made for use by TCG Belfast.

The Provisionals were at a distinct disadvantage in the twilight war, a disadvantage from which they would never recover. In the 1980s it would cost them heavily; indeed, to a certain extent it lost them the war. It stemmed from the fact that they never penetrated the security forces and intelligence-gathering agencies. They had no one on the inside to give them the kind of information that would allow them to identify undercover agents operating against them. The disadvantage is all the more apparent when the Provisionals' campaign is compared to the IRA's, conducted in 1919–21 under the command of Michael Collins. Collins's penetration of security force intelligence allowed him to mount a devastating counterstrike in Dublin on the morning of November 21, 1920. Fourteen undercover agents were killed, and the heart was ripped out of a major British intelligence-gathering operation.

There were a number of reasons for the Provisionals' weakness in this area. It was due partly to their failure early on to grasp the nature of Britain's commitment to Northern Ireland. Their mistaken notion from 1970 to 1975 that one big push would force the British to leave meant they made no long-term scheme to plant agents in the security forces, especially the RUC, who could later be activated as they rose in rank. Indeed, a sort of militaristic stupidity led them to do the opposite and to single out any Catholic for assassination who dared to join the RUC or UDR. They were also limited by the inherent sectarianism of Ulster society, which discouraged the vast majority of Catholics from joining the police or UDR and prevented them from rising to high-level positions within the civil service. Finally, because the Provisionals' support base was almost entirely working class if not lumpen proletariat, they found it hard to recruit the kind of educated, middle-class activist who might have been able to provide a way into the relevant social strata.

However, briefly in the late 1970s the Provisionals in Belfast overcame this handicap. They recruited an English-born RUC detective whose code name was "Fox." The RUC discovered his relationship with the enemy in the course of a surveillance operation in August 1979 that targeted the head of the IRA's internal security unit, known innocuously as the Civil Administration Team. Regardless of its name, there was nothing very "civil" about CAT. It was responsible for uncovering and interrogating suspected touts, usually by brutal means. Suspects had their heads submerged in tubs filled with water, or they were burned with cigarette butts. In 1979 the Special Branch recruited CAT member Peter Valente as an informer. He revealed that the head of CAT was in contact with a renegade policeman who had a list of ten informers working within the Provisionals, which he was prepared to sell for £200—that is, £20 a head.[19] "Fox" was apprehended in October 1979 and dismissed from the force, but at the insistence of MI5 and some senior police officers who feared a scandal, charges against him were never pressed. Several informers did not get off so easily. Included among them was Peter Valente, shot in November 1980. Valente may have lost his life as a result of the operation against Fox. It seems before he died he was tortured into giving up the names of other touts. In January 1981, Maurice Gilvary's body was found near Jonesborough in south Armagh, an area where suspected informers were frequently held for long periods of interrogation. The purge of informers left a few still operating, including "DJ," who would later play a crucial role in the undercover war.

· 2 ·

WHILE THE TWILIGHT war was hitting its stride, constitutional politics was in abeyance in Ulster, where power sharing had become a dead issue. But John Hume was intent on keeping it alive elsewhere. There was no better place than the world's most powerful nation where something of a revolution was occurring in relation to the Ulster problem, mainly thanks to the SDLP leader and the efforts of the Irish government. Hume went to Boston in 1976, where he struck up a friendship with Senator Thomas "Tip" O'Neill and Senator Edward Kennedy. Hume convinced O'Neill and Kennedy of the need for a political solution based on power sharing and opposition to the Provisional IRA.

The lure of Irish America had always been strong for all shades of Irish nationalism, who saw it as a potential ally. But for constitutional nationalists the dangers were also evident. The IRA exercised a powerful, if mostly sentimental, appeal among some Irish Americans who saw the conflict in Ulster as merely a continuation of the 1919–21 War of Independence. The Protestant dimension was usually ignored.[20] Senator Kennedy's earliest proclamations on Ulster in 1971 calling for a British withdrawal had smacked of Provisional IRA sentiments, to the horror of the Irish government. The year that Hume was in Boston, the Irish government became alarmed again when Democratic presidential candidate Jimmy Carter was approached by the Reverend Sean McManus of the Irish National Caucus, which Dublin believed to be a lobbying group for the Provisional IRA. Rev. Sean McManus was Ulster born and had attended Sean MacStiofain, the IRA chief of staff, during his hunger and thirst strike in late 1972. Carter had agreed to make human rights in Ulster an issue if elected. The human rights issue had always been a delicate one for Dublin to handle in the Irish-American context, where it was easily transformed into support for the Provisionals. Tutored by Hume and Irish government diplomats, Washington's heavyweight politicians, O'Neill, Kennedy, and Senator Patrick Moynihan of New York, immediately began a rescue mission to make sure that when Carter, the newly elected president, spoke on Ulster he was using the right script, not one crafted by a troublesome priest with unsettling connections to the Provisionals.[21]

Along with Senator Moynihan and New York State Governor Hugh Carey, O'Neill, now House Speaker, and Kennedy formed the Friends of Ireland. They began issuing Saint Patrick's Day statements that coupled demands for an agreed settlement with denunciations of those who supported the IRA's violent campaign. They also applied pressure on Carter to make a public statement on Ulster but one more in keeping with the ideas of Hume and the Irish government.

For most of the twentieth century, successive U.S. governments had accepted the British position that Northern Ireland was an internal British problem and the only contribution that the federal government could make was stopping weapons and money going to the IRA from its American backers. In spite of pressure from Irish America, over the years successive U.S. administrations practiced a studied noninterventionist policy on Ireland. The "special relationship" between the United Kingdom and the United States, cemented by World War II and the Cold War, seemed unassailable. When British diplomats learned of the moves to change this, they fought hard to prevent the president from saying anything about Ulster other than making the ritual condemnations of violence. But British diplomacy failed, suffering a major defeat on August 30, 1977, when for the first time in U.S. history a serving president, Jimmy Carter, broke one of the golden rules of Anglo-American diplomacy and made a public statement on Northern Ireland. It represented the first real triumph of Irish government diplomacy in the United States over the two forces that were aligned against it: the British embassy in Washington and the Provisional IRA's sympathizers, backers, and funders in organizations such as Irish Northern Aid, or NORAID, as it was commonly known.

President Carter began by recalling the contributions that Irish men and women had made to the United States. The president said,

> *It is natural that Americans are deeply concerned about the continuing conflict and violence in Northern Ireland. We know the overwhelming majority of the people there reject the bomb and the bullet. The United States wholeheartedly supports peaceful means for finding a just solution that involves both parts of the community of Northern Ireland, protects human rights and guarantees freedom from discrimination—a solution that the people of Northern Ireland as well as the Governments of Great Britain and Ireland can support. Violence cannot resolve Northern Ireland's problems; it only increases them and solves nothing.*[22]

President Carter said that the United States, while not wanting to impose a solution, would support a "form of government in Northern Ireland which will command widespread support throughout both parts of the community." In closing he promised:

> *In the event of such a settlement, the United States Government would be prepared to join with others to see how additional job-creating investment could be encouraged, to the benefit of all the people of Northern Ireland.*[23]

To most it seemed like an unremarkable and uncontroversial statement, but a chip was knocked off the "special relationship" with the United States that gave Britain global significance in the chilly postwar imperial twilight. The veiled references to power sharing were unwelcome at a time when the Labour government, now under the leadership of James Callaghan (Harold Wilson having resigned), increasingly relied on the Unionist vote in parliament to keep it in power. Callaghan had agreed to increase the number of seats Northern Ireland MPs held in Westminster from twelve to seventeen, knowing that most of them would go to Unionists. He did not need the ghost of power sharing to haunt this particular banquet. Carter's speech was, in fact, a landmark on the long road to putting the Ulster crisis solidly on the U.S. presidential agenda and taking the initiative away from maverick groups such as NORAID.

Irish Northern Aid, since its foundation in 1970, had striven to stir up anti-British sentiment in the United States and involve sympathetic congressmen in various gestures of "solidarity" for the Catholics of Northern Ireland. They were joined by other groups such as the Washington-based Irish National Caucus and the more traditional Ancient Order of Hibernians, the organizers of the Saint Patrick's Day parade.

Some Irish-American activists, whose Irish nationalism found a Bronx bar more congenial than the marbled corridors on the Hill, found other ways to tweak the lion's tail and irritate the Irish government at the same time. They approached Mario Biaggi, the congressman for east Queens and the Bronx; when he was a New York policeman, he had chalked up more fatal shootings than anyone in the force's history. Biaggi's chief connection to Ireland had been an Irish-American cop he once worked with who, he said, "told me all about it" in 1942 or 1943.[24] The aim was for the congressman to set up an ad hoc committee on Ireland. Biaggi agreed at once and recruited seventy-nine members within weeks.

Specifically, the ad hoc committee on Ireland was to press for congressional hearings on human rights violations in Northern Ireland and to look into such issues as the visa ban on Irish republicans, which prevented men like Ruairi O'Bradaigh and later Gerry Adams from entering the United States legally. Dublin saw the committee with a jaundiced eye—as another way of spreading IRA propaganda—and asked Tip O'Neill to police it. Biaggi's hearings never took place.[25]

Congressional maneuvers were a sideshow. In an unlikely concordance with the British, the Provisionals (while appreciative of any sympathetic propaganda) still saw the United States primarily in terms of an arms source. George Harrison remained in place to make sure they were not disappointed. For him, too, the real business was making sure the weapons were acquired and reached the right hands. Harrison had survived federal detection by staying away from NORAID. His only contact with the Provisional Army Council for most of the time was Eoin McNamee, who would arrive in New York regularly with a "shopping list" from GHQ. From the mid-1970s, Harrison's network was dispatching between two hundred and three hundred weapons a year, mainly Armalite rifles purloined from U.S. military bases. One of his most successful acquisitions came in the spring of 1977 when an Irish-American gangster, Eddy Connors from Philadelphia, approached him with an offer of six M-60 machine guns. Connors was linked to the Mafia, which in a joint raid with Irish-American gangsters stole the weapons from an armory in Danvers, Massachusetts, in 1976. Connors got them for Harrison at a bargain price.[26] They left New York in July 1977 and arrived in Ireland in September, not long after President Carter had made his historic Northern Ireland speech.[27] GHQ was always on the lookout for a weapon that would escalate the struggle and give them even a temporary advantage over the increasingly well protected forces of the Crown.

The M-60, the general-purpose machine gun of the U.S. army, was just that. Capable of firing six hundred rounds per minute and taking down a helicopter, it was even deadlier when trained on a foot patrol. It made its first appearance in January 1978 during a Bloody Sunday commemoration, when the Provisional IRA unveiled it. The M-60 claimed its first victims in Ulster four days before Christmas 1978 in Crossmaglen. As an army foot patrol was passing a parked van, its back door flew open, and the Provisionals inside raked the soldiers with machine-gun fire, killing three before speeding away. The following year, on October 28, an Active Service Unit (ASU) equipped with an M-60 ambushed a mobile patrol as it left the Springfield Road RUC station in west Belfast, claiming the lives of a policeman and a soldier. It was used in several attacks on helicopters and, on May 24, 1985, forced one to land after smashing its windshield.[28]

The Harrison network was running smoothly enough; its chief figures, after Harrison himself, were McNamee, "the Emissary" for the GHQ; Tom Falvey, who helped Harrison clean and store the weapons; and George De Meo, who acquired them. Harrison made a point of not going to NORAID sources for money. His network had its own resources, and occasionally McNamee brought money with him from the Provisionals in Ireland. (Harrison reckons that in his years as an IRA arms supplier he raised and spent about $1 million.) Things began to change, however, in the spring of 1978 with the arrival of Martin McGuinness and Ruairi O'Bradaigh in New York, the two men having slipped into the country illegally. They stayed at Harrison's apartment in Brooklyn in spite of the fact that there was on the premises a large arms haul getting ready to be shipped to Ireland. It might seem remarkable that the Provisionals' chief of staff should be prepared to take such a risk, but it is an indication of how confident the IRA was in the security of the Harrison network. Among the weapons were Armalites, some of the features of which Harrison demonstrated to his guests.

The McGuinness-O'Bradaigh visit was to further the Provisionals' restructuring plans. The organization was increasingly dominated by Ulstermen. Adams, Bell, and McGuinness were gradually taking over its military and political structures, and putting in place their own people—usually northerners. McGuinness was also concerned that Harrison was not actually a member of the IRA; he had had a dispute with the leadership linked to the death of a former Sinn Fein president, Paddy McLogan, in 1964, who had been a close friend.[29] The chief of staff suggested to Harrison that he officially become a member. Harrison refused, citing the McLogan affair. There the matter was left—or so it seemed. But in the year following the visit, the Provisional leadership moved others into place in America, including a former IRA member from north Belfast who had been in the United States since 1975 and who soon began making it generally known that he was the IRA "representative" in New York. According to Harrison, things began to go wrong. Weapons were not moved on schedule. "There were too many unnecessary telephone calls," he said. "The new people didn't have a grasp of the job."[30] Though he said he felt "something ominous in the air," he went ahead with another large haul, which was handled by the new IRA "representative" and shipped to Dublin in the fall of 1979. That was the beginning of the end. One of those involved made a telephone call to Dublin on a line that was tapped to notify GHQ that "the Frigidaire was on its way." The haul was seized on Dublin's dockside; it consisted of 150 weapons—two of them M-60s—and sixty thousand rounds of ammunition. Eighty percent of it came from Harrison. But worse was to follow.

"Markings weren't removed as they should have been," according to Harrison; this allowed the police to trace part of the shipment to George De Meo. De Meo was arrested, charged, and convicted of arms smuggling. However, De Meo soon came to an arrangement with the federal authorities. In return for having to serve only half his ten-year term, and in a minimum security prison, De Meo would give up the IRA's main arms supplier in the United States.

"I knew by 1979 that the old operation was gone," recalled Harrison. "It would have to be reorganized on a larger scale than before." Though he had misgivings, they were not about his old friend De Meo but about the mistakes that had been made in the last shipment. Harrison was considering getting out. "I had always thought of leaving them plentifully supplied before I left the scene," he said.[31] De Meo contacted him, saying that he would like to do something for him before he went to jail. Harrison agreed to meet to discuss it. When they did, De Meo was wired. He told Harrison that he would introduce him to someone who had access to 350 MAC-10 machine pistols and a quantity of AK-47s. That someone was "John White," otherwise known as John Winslow, an undercover FBI operator. Instead of clinching an arms deal that would leave the Provisionals "plentifully supplied," Harrison walked into a major FBI sting operation that netted Tom Falvey and three others: Danny Gormley, Paddy Mullins, and Michael Flannery, one of the founding fathers of Irish Northern Aid. (Because of the unexpectedness of the deal with White, Harrison was in need of cash fast and broke one of his cardinal rules about not approaching NORAID.) Harrison and Falvey were arrested on June 19, 1981, the others later. Harrison's arrest effectively meant the end of the IRA's most successful arms smuggling network.[32] Its demise had come about at a disastrous time for the Provisionals, who were trying to intensify their campaign. The struggle over Special Category status, abolished in March 1976, had escalated into a major hunger strike that would change the face of Northern Ireland politics.

• 3 •

THE STORY OF the Ulster conflict is riddled with ironies. But perhaps the supreme irony lies in the fact that the process that set out in March 1976 to criminalize the Provisionals within five years transformed them into a legitimate political force—and would eventually propel them to the threshold of the government of Northern Ireland itself.

No one, including the leadership of the republican movement, foresaw this when in September 1976, Ciaran Nugent, the first IRA man convicted under the new dispensation, refused to put on a prison uniform or otherwise be treated like an "ordinary criminal." If they wanted him to wear one, "they'd have to nail the clothes on my back," he declared. He wore a blanket instead. The authorities responded by punishing him with loss of remission and the removal of furniture from his cell so that he was forced to sleep on the floor. In spite of these hardships, the numbers of protesters steadily increased. More and more convicted Provisionals, along with members of the smaller INLA, draped themselves in blankets in rejection of the government's insistence that, being ordinary criminals, they should wear a prisoner's uniform. They became known as the blanket men. The protest escalated in 1978 when prisoners refused to leave their cells to empty their chamber pots, alleging excessive supervision and harassment from the prison staff. They stuffed their excrement through the cell windows. The wardens hurled it back in. The protesters then began smearing the cell walls with it. An Irish journalist visiting the Maze was taken to a cell where he witnessed a well-known north Belfast IRA man, Martin Meehan, decorating the walls of his cell by painting palm trees with bits of rubber foam dipped in excrement.[33] By 1978 over three hundred prisoners were involved in what was now called the Dirty Protest. At the beginning of August 1978, the protesters received an extraordinary publicity boost when Ireland's Cardinal Tomas O'Fiaich (a native of the strongly republican south Armagh) visited the Maze. What he saw horrified him. "One would hardly allow an animal to remain in such conditions, let alone a human being," he said a few days later. "The nearest approach to it that I have ever seen was the spectacle of hundreds of homeless people living in the sewer pipes of Calcutta. The stench and the filth in some of the cells with the remains of rotten food and human excreta scattered around the walls was almost unbearable." In the women's prison in Armagh, republican inmates became involved in a similar protest, and soon their cell walls were covered with excrement and menstrual blood.

Coincidentally, August 1978 was the tenth anniversary of the first civil rights march. It would have been unthinkable, in 1968, that a struggle begun on the issue of housing and equal voting rights for Catholics should have led to a situation where people lived surrounded by their own excrement. But it was one sign that the problem had long ago left the sphere of the rational, where compromise is possible, to reside on the plane of conflicting absolutes.

In spite of the rising tide of concern and the increased publicity, the British government refused to concede: Special Category status would not be reinstated. Indeed, the one quarter from which they were not coming under much pressure to do so was the republican movement itself. Sinn

Fein had been slow to mobilize support for the protest, even though Adams claims he had conveyed its importance to the party president, Ruairi O'Bradaigh.[34] Relatives Action Committees had been formed as early as 1976 to draw attention to the deteriorating situation in the prison, but the republican movement did not throw its weight behind them. In contrast, the INLA's political wing, the Irish Republican Socialist Party, had become active on the issue even before Special Category status was abolished. "Political prisoners' status must stay," its newspaper, *The Starry Plough,* had declared as early as December 1975. "The attempt to do away with their special category status is intended to portray all political prisoners as common criminals, psychopaths, intimidators for personal gain, devoid of any politics."

However, the Provisional leadership regarded the protest as a distraction from its main business—conducting the war. In an interview with a leading Dublin magazine published in August 1978, a spokesman for the Army Council did not mention the H-block issue once—one indication of its low priority. The Provisionals had launched a murder campaign against prison officers, beginning on April 8, 1976, when they gunned down thirty-six-year-old warden Pacelli Dillon outside his home in Carrickmore, County Tyrone. But the idea of taking political action on the streets in conjunction with the RACs was resisted. Throughout their history the Provisionals have shown a marked reluctance to get involved with any movement unless they could completely control it In the spring of 1979, Bernadette McAliskey entered the elections to the European parliament, making the prisoners' plight the single issue of her campaign. But even at this late date, not only did the Provisionals refuse to support her, but they actively campaigned against her, advocating a boycott. In spite of this opposition, McAliskey won over thirty thousand first-preference votes. The proof that the issue could attract substantial support strengthened the hand of those who, like Adams, wanted some means of broadening the republican struggle.

In late 1979 a Smash H-Block Committee was set up with the Provisionals' backing, but the first attempts to broaden its appeal foundered on their demand that all those involved must also support the IRA's armed struggle. This was later dropped, and the committee soon enlisted support from left-wing groups and some trade unionists, even attracting some attention from the Peace People. The campaign was based on the prisoners' five demands: to wear their own clothes, to refuse to do prison work, to receive extra visits and food parcels, to freely associate with members of their own organization within the jail, and the restoration of remission lost because of their protest. By then, however, a formidable obstacle had risen in the prisoners' path in the shape of the new British prime minister, Margaret Thatcher, who had earlier ousted the debilitated Labour government.

Even before Thatcher entered office, the Ulster conflict had bloodied her. On the afternoon of March 30, just after parliament was dissolved to prepare for the elections, Airey Neave, her close friend and adviser who had helped engineer her takeover of the Conservative Party, got into his car, which had been parked in the underground garage of the House of Commons. Neave, a fierce advocate of stern law-and-order policies, including greater use of the SAS, was designated to be her secretary of state for Northern Ireland. As he drove up the ramp toward the street, a bomb attached to the floor panel under the driver's seat exploded, severing both his legs. It took thirty minutes to cut him free from the mangled wreckage. He died eight minutes after reaching the hospital. The INLA claimed responsibility for what was one of the most daring assassinations in the history of the Troubles. The operation was the fruit of a true international terrorist conspiracy. The pink-colored explosives that killed Neave were made in the Soviet Union, part of a shipment that came from the PLO, which also regularly supplied INLA with mostly Soviet-made weapons via East Germany. The information that helped the two-man team penetrate the House of Commons disguised as workmen came from leftist Labour Party activists who believed that Neave and Thatcher were about to lead a right-wing backlash. They told INLA that security was slack around legitimate workmen engaged in renovations and that security cameras were not monitored carefully. The sixteen-ounce chunk of explosives used in the bomb was carried in a lunchbox and cost about $8.[35]

Thatcher, nicknamed the "Iron Lady" because of her reputation for refusing to compromise, was in no mood to listen to IRA and INLA prisoners' claims to be deserving of special treatment. She responded to arguments that the IRA and INLA were political offenders by stating, "A crime is a crime is a crime"; if the blanket men lived in their own filth, it was self-inflicted, and obedience to the law would easily remedy it. Unionists were delighted that at last they had found someone as intransigent as themselves. The fact that most Catholics viewed the prisoners as having a valid grievance went unheeded. Neither Thatcher nor the Unionists could grasp the simple truth that while Catholics might not approve of the Provisional IRA or INLA actions, at the same time they saw them as the result of a historical struggle that conferred on them a certain legitimacy.

The conflict over the prisoners' status starkly revealed the depth of the dichotomy between Nationalist and Unionist, as it did the extent of the incomprehension of the British government concerning the nature of the republican movement and the kind of support it could invoke at certain times among ordinary Catholics. It also highlighted the capacity of the Provisionals for behind-the-scenes maneuvering. At the height of the Smash H-Block campaign, when the IRSP, the Relatives Action Committees, and various other organizations were galvanizing support, the Provisionals opened up secret talks with the British government using a channel that had existed since the 1974–75 cease-fire. Some feared that the Provisionals were quite prepared to abandon the protest if they could get a separate deal for their own prisoners.

The secret talks came to nothing, and the protests dragged on inside the jails, counterpointed by the violence outside. In the most serious incident, on August 27, 1979, two Provisional IRA bombs killed eighteen soldiers, mostly members of 2 Para, near Warrenpoint, a beautiful seaside town in south Down; this was the highest number of fatalities experienced by the British army in any single incident in the long conflict. The first bomb, estimated at five hundred pounds, exploded in a hay wagon at 4:30 P.M. as a convoy of paras drove past. The second, a one-thousand-pound device, went off nearby twenty-nine minutes later as more troops arrived to investigate the first. Both were detonated by remote control from a few hundred yards away, across a narrow stretch of Carlingford Lough, which at that point separates Northern Ireland from the Irish republic. So intense was the second blast that the remains of one officer, Lieutenant Colonel David Blair, who was standing near it, were never recovered.[36]

That same day, a few hours earlier, another remote-controlled bomb claimed the life of Earl Louis Mountbatten, the seventy-nine-year-old uncle of the Queen, as his thirty-foot boat left the harbor of Mullaghmore near Sligo in the west of Ireland. Along with him died his fourteen-year-old grandson, Nicholas, and Paul Maxwell, another teenager who worked on the boat. Dowager Lady Bradbourne, eighty-two, who had also been on board, died later of her wounds.

The massacre of the soldiers provoked demands from the army that overall responsibility for fighting the Provisionals be returned to it, effectively ending the three-year-old policies of Ulsterization and criminalization. An appeal to do so was made directly to Thatcher when she arrived in the province shortly after the bombings. To make his point, a senior army officer threw down in front of the prime minister the metal epaulettes worn by Lieutenant Colonel Blair, killed at Warrenpoint, announcing melodramatically: "This is all that's left of one of my bravest officers."[37] Given the prime minister's reputation, it might be thought that she would be sympathetic to the army's demand. But instead she listened to the chief constable, Sir Kenneth Newman, who was adamant that the policies that gave the RUC the primary security role represented the best hope of defeating the Provisionals and allowing the army to eventually withdraw. He demanded one thousand extra policemen and a strengthening of the RUC's role. Thatcher agreed. If ever there was any doubt that Britain was conducting anything other than a holding operation in Ulster, this decision should have dispelled it.[38]

Meanwhile, Thatcher continued to meet the prisoners' challenge to "criminalization" with undiminished intransigence. If the British army could not budge her, then a collection of dirt-covered convicts draped in blankets certainly would not succeed. The H-block protests depended mainly on one tactic, marches, and they were beginning to lose support, breeding a sense of apathy and increasing futility. As the protest went into its fourth year, the prisoners began to talk about taking the ultimate step—the hunger strike. This, the traditional weapon of last resort in the armory of Irish republican prisoners, had been discussed as an option as early as 1978. The Army Council was reluctant to sanction it. Michael Gaughan had died in 1974 on a futile hunger strike in England trying to get authorities to accord him Special Category status, as had Frank Stagg two years later. Before that, MacStiofain's hunger and thirst strike had ended ignominiously. The only propitious precedent was that of Billy McKee, whose hunger strike in June 1972 had won the prisoners the concessions they were now fighting to restore. His example persuaded many of them that the tactic would work again.

Both Sinn Fein and the Provisional IRA leadership were afraid that a hunger strike would further divert resources away from the war effort and that in the end the prisoners would be defeated, thus discrediting the whole movement. But in spite of their opposition, the prisoners' leader, Brendan "The Dark" Hughes—who before his arrest had succeeded Ivor Bell as commanding officer of the Belfast IRA in 1974—announced that he and six other prisoners (including one member of INLA) would begin to refuse food on October 27, 1980. It lasted less than two months before coming to a confused end, with the prisoners believing that the British were prepared to make concessions, especially on the issue of clothes, and the British denying it. According to Adams, "There was a feeling of despondency in the air" following the ending of the strike.[39] The prisoners had been outmaneuvered, and the issues remained unresolved as Ulster entered its fifth year of an increasingly bitter prison protest.

A series of loyalist assassinations and attempted assassinations of leading republicans associated with the H-block protest deepened the gloom. The first to die, John Turnley, a member of the Irish Independence Party, was shot dead as he was going to attend a political meeting on June 4, 1980. Three weeks later the killer squads targeted Miriam Daly, a lecturer in economics at Queens University, Belfast, and a former chairperson of the IRSP. For several years she had been a prominent speaker on H-block platforms, along with her husband, Jim, who was also an academic and prominent republican activist. Her ten-year-old adopted daughter came home from school on the afternoon of June 26 to find her bound hand and foot, a fatal bullet wound in her head and a bloodstained cushion used to muffle the sound lying nearby. In the early hours of October 15, gunmen sledgehammered their way into the home of Ronnie Bunting, Jr., a Protestant republican, a founding member of INLA, and the son of Paisley's former sidekick. They raced up the stairs and reached the door of the bedroom where he was sleeping with his wife, Suzanne. The couple struggled to prevent them from getting into the bedroom, but the gunmen fired through a gap in the door. She fell back on the bed, shot in the hand. According to Mrs. Bunting, "The next moment two men were in the room and started shooting Ronnie. . . . They wore those green ribbed pullovers with suede patches on the shoulders and ski-type masks which covered their whole faces with only holes for eyes. . . . They were cool and calm—like animals—without fear—they had no smell of fear about them."[40] Before leaving, the gunmen shot dead Noel Lyttle, a guest in the Bunting home, as he slept in the next room. At the time of his death, Bunting was the commanding officer of the INLA in Belfast, the highest-ranking member of the republican movement to fall victim to loyalist assassins. His demise would have profound consequences for the organization.

Barely two weeks into 1981, three masked gunmen shot and seriously wounded veteran civil rights activist Bernadette McAliskey and her husband in their home in County Tyrone as they dressed their children for school. This time, however, the attackers were arrested as they left the scene of the crime by a squad of British soldiers who had been on patrol nearby. The assailants turned out to be UDA men.[41] The Provisional IRA responded to these attacks with a murderous assault on the stately home of a prominent Unionist family in Armagh, the Stronges. Eighty-six-year-old Norman Stronge had been Speaker in the Stormont parliament. He died along with his forty-eight-year-old son, James, in a hail of IRA bullets.

Inside the dung-smeared walls of H-block, minds were focusing on a different kind of struggle. A twenty-seven-year-old activist named Bobby Sands was now the commander of the IRA prisoners in the Maze. Forced out of his home in a loyalist area of north Belfast in 1972, Sands joined the Provisionals. He was not a very successful or lucky IRA member because his two brief periods of activity led to arrests. During his first term of imprisonment, from 1973 to 1976, he became friends with Gerry Adams when they shared the same hut. Just six months after his release, he was caught after a bombing attack on a furniture store and sentenced to fourteen years for possession of a handgun. This time he was subjected to the new "ordinary criminal" regime and fought it, going on the blanket, then joining in the excremental war with the prison authorities. In spite of the hardships and horrors, he found time to write poetry, ballads, and accounts of his prison life, mainly in the form of "coms": messages, stories, and poems inscribed on tiny scraps of toilet or cigarette paper with the care and deliberation that would do credit to a medieval monk. They were smuggled out of the prison, often secreted in the visitor's anus and sometimes in a female visitor's vagina. In contrast to the unconventional means by which they were conveyed to the world, Sands's writings, especially the verse, are full of conventional sentimentality; but his prose description of prison life, *One Day in My Life,* is graphic and disturbing.[42] The writings are a testimony to the romantic power the Irish republican tradition exercised on young men like Sands, with its mystification of sacrifice and ideal of martyrdom. It enabled them to endure the most obscene squalor and humiliating violations of their persons and, finally, to undergo an agonizing death. Perhaps had Margaret Thatcher or some of her advisers read them, the confrontation that followed would never have occurred.

Sands notified the Provisional leadership that he was going to begin another hunger strike on March 1, 1981, the fifth anniversary of the abolition of Special Category status. Unlike the last effort, prisoners would join it in stages. The next hunger striker, Francis Hughes, would join Sands on March 15, and he would be followed a week later by Ray McCreesh and Patsy O'Hara, with others joining after shorter intervals until the British conceded to their demands.

Adams made the Provisionals' position clear: "Bobby, we are tactically, strategically, physically and morally opposed to a hunger strike," he wrote to Sands.[43] A march took place on the Falls Road to support Sands, but the outside world paid little heed other than to condemn the action. The Catholic bishop of Derry, Cathal Daly, stated that a hunger strike was not morally justified. *The New York Times* reported the event in one paragraph.

Four days after Sands began his fast, Frank Maguire, the Independent Nationalist MP for Fermanagh–South Tyrone, died suddenly of a heart attack. The constituency had a Catholic majority, and an agreed Nationalist candidate had a very strong chance of winning it. Bernadette McAliskey announced she would run as an independent on the H-block issue but would step aside in favor of an H-block candidate. The idea was seized on by Daithi O'Conaill, who, at a special republican convention held in Monaghan in April, argued that Sands should stand. What better way to refute the government's propaganda that the prisoners were common criminals who had no support other than that from a minority of republican fanatics? Of course, defeat could knock the heart out of the whole H-block campaign and discredit the prisoners' demands. The local Sinn Fein activists opposed the idea, but O'Conaill prevailed. Sands was nominated. The Provisionals finally persuaded the two other Nationalist candidates to step aside, but one was still threatening to put his name forward just minutes away from the close of nominations.

Sinn Fein's electoral limbs were pretty stiff from not having run in an election for years, but the party learned on the job, and quickly. The hope that a Sands victory would not only score an important propaganda breakthrough for the republican movement but would also save his life motivated the party activists. They flooded into the constituency from all corners of Ireland to fight the campaign. On April 9 the results were announced: Sands topped the poll with 30,492 votes, beating the Unionist candidate, Harry West, by over 1,000 votes. On the fortieth day of his hunger strike, Bobby Sands, the convicted IRA gunman and bomber, had become a Westminster MP. The government's attempts to criminalize the republican movement had given it the kind of political recognition it had not enjoyed since 1955, the last time one of its members was elected to Westminster.

Adams, who had been campaigning hard for Sands in the constituency, heard the news on a car radio. "I was ecstatic," he said.[44] Many assumed that Thatcher would now concede; after all, the Provisionals had proved that they were not a bunch of isolated gunmen who held sway through terror, that they did represent a considerable body of opinion within the nationalist community. But the fact that Britain's criminalization policy was actually achieving the opposite of its intentions did not penetrate the prime minister's obduracy. Nor did the spread of the campaign in support of the hunger strikers—marches and protests mushroomed in New York, Boston, Chicago, and San Francisco, and as far away as Australia. Thatcher continued to say no to the five demands. Sands grew weaker. On May 5 at 1:17 A.M. the Right Honorable Robert Sands, MP, died. Sixty-six days without food had reduced him to a shriveled, waxen corpse.

When it was learned he had died, there was a brief but profound silence in the Catholic areas of Belfast. Then came the insistent clang of garbage-can lids on the pavement, a sort of bush telegraph spreading the news. Gangs of Catholic youths took to the streets, hijacking, burning, hurling rocks and gasoline bombs at the soldiers and police sent to contain them. A Protestant milkman and his son died when their milk van crashed after a mob hurled rocks at it in a Catholic district of north Belfast. The Provisionals struck at policemen and soldiers in an effort to show the government that the dying men inside the prison had a military organization outside able to revenge their sufferings. Five soldiers died in one land-mine blast in south Armagh on May 19. But by then another hunger striker, Francis Hughes, had died, and two more, Patsy O'Hara and Ray McCreesh, were on the verge of death. The crisis deepened, then leveled out on the dull plateau of repetition as another six hunger strikers died throughout the summer. As the futility of the protest became more and more apparent, relatives—often under pressure from the Catholic Church—started to intervene, taking their loved ones off the protest as soon as they lapsed into unconsciousness.

The hunger strike had begun in the spring. The last hunger striker died on August 20 as fall closed in. On October 3 the six remaining hunger strikers ended their fast, and the following day spokesmen for the prisoners declared the hunger strike had ended.[45] Within three days the new Northern Ireland secretary of state, James Prior, announced that prisoners would be allowed to wear their own clothes at all times and that 50 percent of lost remission would be restored. Eventually, everything the prisoners had asked for was granted. That leg of the criminalization policy had collapsed. The consequences of this failure would resound for years to come.

The protest offered two contrasting lessons. The first was that republicans and their supporters could be contained—at a security level. The H-block and hunger-strike riots were almost entirely confined to west Belfast and other nationalist areas, so that even at the height of the protests, life went on undisturbed in most of Belfast and throughout the rest of the province. The Provisionals' military campaign, though stepped up, still could not reach the level it had attained during most of the 1970s. During the entire seven-month crisis (March to October), the Provisional IRA and the INLA combined managed to kill thirty members of the army, UDR, and RUC—no more than they had been able to kill during the first seven months of 1977, at a time when the armed campaign was going into decline. However, the second lesson showed that the political impact of the hunger strike could not be so easily contained. In the May local elections, twenty-one members of the nationalist Irish Independence Party won seats, along with two IRSP members. Adams concluded that it was a grave mistake for Sinn Fein not to have contested them. It was a mistake the party would not make again. In June two IRA prisoners were elected to the Irish parliament. In August, when a by-election was held to replace Sands, Sinn Fein's Owen Carron, who had been his election agent, won his seat with an increased majority. Soon afterward, Sinn Fein announced that in the future it would contest all Northern Ireland elections.

At the Sinn Fein *ard fheis* in November 1981, the political wing of the movement was accorded unaccustomed respect. Danny Morrison, the editor of *An Phoblacht/Republican News* and later a prominent member of

CAT (the IRA's informer hunting squad), closed his speech by asking, "Who really believes that we can win the war through the ballot box? But will anyone here object if with a ballot paper in this hand and an Armalite in this hand, we take power in Ireland?"

Treating republicans like common criminals had turned them into politicians.

· FIVE ·

BULLETS AND BALLOTS

1981–1985

THE BALLOT BOX energized the Provisionals and left the moderate nationalists dismayed and afraid. John Hume observed that after the hunger strikes "there was no disguising the bleakness of the scene that confronted us in Northern Ireland."[1]

With the rise of Sinn Fein in 1981, the Irish political establishment confronted a political threat that it did not expect. For the moderate nationalists of the Social Democratic and Labor Party it could not have come at a worse moment. In Belfast, where Sinn Fein was at its greatest strength, the SDLP was at its weakest. Four years before the hunger strike crisis in 1977, one of the SDLP's founding members, Paddy Devlin, was forced out of the party for denouncing what he saw as its departure from socialist politics. In those days, Devlin, a feisty working-class Belfast man, had a large following in the Falls area. Gerry Fitt, the party leader, was also unhappy. After ten years of relentless violence, he believed the conflict was more intractable than ever, and he was unhappy with the direction the SDLP was taking. His despair came to a crisis point in September 1979, during the first papal visit to Ireland. Pope John Paul II preached in Drogheda on September 30, attracting a crowd of a quarter of a million. The Pope in an emotional moment got down on his knees and appealed to the IRA to halt its campaign. The IRA rejected the plea, convincing the volatile and unpredictable Fitt that the situation was hopeless.

His dissatisfaction with the SDLP came to a head shortly afterward when the government proposed a conference to discuss the future of

Northern Ireland, but one that would exclude from consideration the Irish dimension, or Northern Ireland's constitutional status. Fitt advocated that the party should join the conference regardless. However, Hume, who earlier in 1979 had won a massive vote in the elections to the European parliament, had already formulated the way forward as he saw it: Any solution had to go outside the parameters of Northern Ireland itself. Fitt resigned, accusing the party of sharing the same politics as the IRA.

Like Devlin, Fitt came from a trade union and labor background, very much rooted in the traditions of British working-class politics. The bright new world of European politics, where Hume felt most comfortable, was alien to him. He was bitter toward his former colleagues, whom he accused of turning the SDLP into another Nationalist Party. "The others were nationalists," he said. "While it was in my blood to be a Labour man—it was in their blood to be Nationalists. There is no Labour standing within the SDLP. It is not a Labour party and never was."[2] Hume replaced him. In fact, Hume had been the guiding force behind the party for some time. But Fitt's departure meant that there was no one in the SDLP with the kind of grit needed to survive in Belfast's two-fisted street politics. The majority of the party's councilors in the city were well-meaning middle-class Catholics too polite to spit in public.

The fact that Margaret Thatcher was prime minister did not help matters as far as constitutional nationalists were concerned. Hume reflected ruefully: "Politics, our hope, were never bleaker. The British government was dominated by someone who seemed to care little about the problem of Northern Ireland. Northern Ireland, Mrs. Thatcher said, was as British as Finchley. We hoped, at least for the sake of Finchley, that she was wrong. . . . We were again, what we have so often been for British politicians: either an embarrassing nuisance to be concealed from view if possible or a political football in which our fortunes were usually neglected."[3] However, in spite of this grim assessment, Irish Taoiseach Charles Haughey met with Thatcher for an Anglo-Irish summit in late 1980. Hume was encouraged that at last there might be some movement out of the stagnating swamp of political inertia that was Ulster.

At this summit the two leaders commissioned a series of studies to look at, among other things, the possibility of new institutional structures, economic measures, and ways of building mutual understanding between the two nations. This dovetailed well with Hume's belief that going outside Ulster and dealing with the relations between Britain and the Irish republic that underlay the crisis was the only way to solve it. But the hunger-strike crisis followed, and that "derailed the Anglo-Irish process," in the words of one SDLP member.[4] A year later came the war over the Malvinas, during which Haughey withdrew his government's support for European Union sanctions against Argentina, outraging the British. This chilled Anglo-Irish relations for some time.

In the meantime, dire economic developments deepened the political gloom in Ulster. Unemployment reached levels not experienced since the 1930s. In January 1982, figures showed that 113,000 people were out of work, representing 19.7 percent of the total adult population, the highest rate of unemployment in the United Kingdom. A month later Harland and Wolff shipyards, traditionally one of Belfast's major employers—and one that in the 1950s could boast twenty-two thousand workers on its books—announced that one thousand of the remaining seven thousand workers were to lose their jobs. On March 1, British Enkalon closed its plant in Antrim, throwing nearly one thousand people out of work. The company had been in Northern Ireland for decades, and as part of the artificial fibers industry was one of the "star performers" (in the words of one economist) in the reindustrialization of the Ulster economy, which had commenced under Terence O'Neill in the early 1960s. Unemployment climbed relentlessly throughout the year; by September 1982, 25 percent of the adult male population was registered as out of work.

It was not only the political violence that was affecting the province's economic fortunes. As a marginal economy, Ulster was disproportionately hurt by the international recessions of 1973 and 1979. Its traditional industries, shipbuilding and linen, were already weak and by the early 1980s had virtually collapsed. In 1981 only 30 percent of the workforce was employed in industry, compared to 62 percent in the service industries.[5] By 1985 there were more people out of work than were employed in the entire industrial sector. The only bright spot in the economy was the development of the security industry. Because of the political violence, there was a huge increase in the number of people employed in defense-related services and in the public administration needed to support them. It is estimated that some fifty-nine thousand people, the vast majority of them Protestants, were employed in this sector (not including those in the UDR and RUC). That is, by the 1980s the Provisional IRA was, at least indirectly, keeping more Protestants in jobs than Harland and Wolff.

While Ulster's economy continued to sink, it looked as if the British government was spending its time rearranging the political deck chairs. James Prior, who became secretary of state for the province in September 1981, launched his "rolling devolution" plans in early 1982. This envisioned the setting up of an assembly to which powers would be gradually devolved. The SDLP showed no enthusiasm for the plan. It was, in Hume's thinking, a purely internal solution that took no account of the broader context of the problem involving London and Dublin. Elections for the proposed seventy-eight-seat assembly took place in October 1982, and although the party ran candidates, it said they would not take their seats if elected. It meant, in effect, that Prior's plan was rolling nowhere. But the elections were notable in Northern Ireland's history as the first in which Sinn Fein put up candidates on a province-wide basis. The results stunned the Irish and British political establishments.

Sinn Fein won five seats and just over 10 percent of the vote; the SDLP won fourteen seats, representing 18.8 percent of the vote. In west Belfast, Gerry Adams was elected well ahead of his SDLP rival, Dr. Joe Hendron, an ominous sign for the party's organization in that area. Martin McGuinness, former chief of staff of the Provisionals, was elected in Derry. The Ulster Unionists began to beat back Paisley's challenge for the first time in years and took almost 30 percent of the vote and twenty-six seats, leaving Paisley's DUP with 23 percent and twenty-one seats. But this resurgence of "moderate" unionism was largely ignored as the spotlight rested on the drama within the Nationalist community. In a panic, some predicted that Sinn Fein was poised to overtake the SDLP. Others consoled themselves by affirming that the Provisional IRA's political wing was still exploiting a sympathy vote for the hunger strikers, which would soon fade. The events of the following year made this explanation look less tenable. In March 1983, Sinn Fein contested local elections in Northern Ireland for the first time in fifty years and won a seat on the Omagh district council in County Tyrone. Three months later, in the British general election, Gerry Adams was elected as MP for west Belfast, defeating veteran Gerry Fitt, who ran as an Independent candidate. In Mid-Ulster, Danny Morrison, the editor of *An Phoblacht* and coiner of the "ballot-paper in this hand and an Armalite in this hand" phrase, came within seventy-eight votes of giving Sinn Fein a second seat. Had Morrison won, the IRA's political wing would have had two MPs to the SDLP's single success, John Hume. It would have scored a devastating propaganda victory, allowing it to claim to have overthrown the SDLP in only its second full scale electoral campaign. As it was, Sinn Fein took 42 percent of the nationalist vote. Overall, the party increased its share of the vote to 13.4 percent (102,701 votes) from 10.1 percent, while the SDLP's share declined to 17.9 percent from 18.8 percent the previous year, though its actual vote rose somewhat compared to 1982.

Margaret Thatcher's obstinacy during the 1981 hunger strikes undoubtedly helped Sinn Fein in their electoral campaigns in the following two years. So did her insistence on removing references to closer Anglo-Irish relations in the proposals of her Northern Ireland Secretary of State, James Prior.[6] Prior himself did not help matters when he said his plans for the new assembly would tie Northern Ireland closer to the United Kingdom. Thatcher would write in her autobiography, *The Downing Street Years:* "My instincts are profoundly Unionist." In part, the Sinn Fein vote was in reaction to this sentiment. The question was, how high would electoral support for Sinn Fein go? Neither the SDLP nor the Irish government felt they could afford to wait around passively to find out.

· 2 ·

A POLITICAL MACHINE and a killing machine were now running in tandem. The most powerful weapon in the armory of the Provisional IRA was surprise. It was the single advantage that compensated for the Provisionals' actual military weakness when compared to the might of the British state. And the police had only one way to counteract it—through the gathering of intelligence. If they knew what the Provisional IRA and other groups were planning to do, they could prevent it. Whoever has intelligence about an operation can control it, at least in theory. During the early years of the twilight war when the RUC Special Branch was honing its intelligence-gathering skills, it became clear that in practice it was not so easy. There were problems in interpreting intelligence and in mounting effective responses to anticipated terrorist actions, and difficulties coordinating the different arms of the security forces. But results showed an overall decline in the levels of violence.

The year of the hunger strike, 1981, was a turning point in more ways than one in the Ulster conflict. It was the last year in which more than 100 people lost their lives as a result of the political violence (101 died that year, including the 10 hunger strikers). In 1982 the figure was 97. The following year it fell to 77. In 1984 and 1985 it stood at 64 and

54, respectively. That is, between 1981 and 1985 the yearly average was 78.6 deaths, compared to an average of 270.8 between 1971 and 1975. A marked feature of the Northern Ireland violence has always been the disparity between the numbers of military personnel killed and the number of civilians, with the latter far outnumbering the former. This disparity became even greater in the early to mid-1980s. In 1983, for example, of the 77 victims of the violence only 5 were serving members of the British army, and of those the Belfast IRA, which in the early 1970s had been the most active and dangerous part of the organization, accounted for only 2. The statistics were also affected by a sharp decline in the number of killings carried out by loyalists. In 1981 there were 9; in 1982, there were 8, in 1983 and 1984 there were 6, and in 1985 only 2.

While there were several reasons for the decline in violence, intelligence operations played a key role in bringing about this reduction, especially in Belfast, the cockpit of the conflict. The city was in the grip of the hunger strike crisis, and the Provisionals and INLA were doing all in their power to wreak havoc. But by early 1981 the RUC Special Branch had identified some of the city's top republican gunmen and operators—part of a new generation of activists who had grown up since the civil rights movement and whose childhood was overshadowed by the conflict. Among them were young men in their twenties such as Bobby Storey, Dermot Finucane, and Danny McCann, Provisional IRA members, and Gerard Steenson, who took over control of the INLA after the murder of Ronnie Bunting in 1980. Finucane came from a west Belfast republican family. Two of his brothers were also active Provisionals, and another, Patrick, was a well-known Belfast lawyer who specialized in defending IRA suspects. Storey had been active in the IRA since his teens, and although a suspect in several killings and bombings from 1973 onward, he always managed to slip through the police net. McCann, like Storey, already had a history of IRA involvement by the mid-1970s when he served several periods of imprisonment. He was convicted of possession of explosives in 1983, but on his release quickly became active again, both as a gunman and as the Belfast Brigade's explosives officer.

Often the key to catching the gunman was locating the arms dump where the guns were kept. An E4A surveillance operation in the spring of 1981 had uncovered a dump used by an Active Service Unit whose leading members were Finucane and Storey. The ASU had killed a police officer in

February 1981. Finucane was held and questioned about the murder but released in May. Later, police learned that he and his colleagues were planning to ambush an army patrol. By monitoring the arms dump over a period of weeks, they were able to keep track of the weapons when they were moved and then intercept the gunmen as they tried to escape following an attempted ambush on August 20. Storey, Finucane, and a third man were arrested near the scene of the attack in which a soldier was slightly wounded. All three were sentenced to eighteen years in jail. The removal of Storey and Finucane was a severe blow to the Belfast Brigade's operations in the west of the city.

The police enjoyed another important breakthrough that crippled several major Provisional operations in Belfast in 1981. Thanks to "DJ," the informer recruited in late 1979, they had identified the route the IRA used to get resupplies of explosives into Belfast. It ran from County Tyrone northeast through Antrim town, a mainly Protestant town near Lough Neagh, about thirty miles from the city. The Special Branch located the house in the town that was used as a temporary storage place. In July 1981 they tracked a large haul of explosives from Antrim to Belfast, where they swooped, netting three top members of the Belfast Provisional IRA and five hundred pounds of explosives. In September another attempt to resupply the Belfast units was frustrated when the police arrested a leading member of the Belfast Brigade, Anthony Cahill, and more bomb-making material was found.

However, forewarned was not always forearmed, as became apparent when the police tried to counter the rising threat from the Belfast INLA. In the emotional climate of the hunger strikes, INLA attracted more recruits, teenagers and young men from the Catholic ghettos who found its left-wing rhetoric attractive. They also found that the less stable INLA afforded them more opportunities to carry out operations than the more hierarchical Provisionals. As for Steenson, a fastidious young man with a murderous streak, the most important thing was the willingness to do the job.

"He looked like an off-duty policeman," one RUC Special Branch officer described him. Behind the well-groomed look and good manners, which he invariably displayed when stopped at checkpoints, lay a ruthless operator who was not only willing to take risks himself but could inspire others to follow him. Steenson had first come to police attention when he was a teenager in 1975. He murdered the Official IRA Belfast commander, Liam McMillen, and then spent four years in jail on an arms charge. He was released in April 1980.

He began killing again in December 1980, claiming two victims, one an off-duty UDR man and the other a member of the territorial army. By January 1981 the Special Branch had intelligence about Steenson coming from within the INLA. Yet, although E4A commanders knew in advance about INLA "hits," they failed to prevent a whole series of attacks that claimed the lives of several members of the security forces.[7]

One frustrating operation followed another. Meanwhile, INLA struck again and again, sometimes rivaling the Provisionals in the number of attacks mounted in Belfast. The most embarrassing failure of all came in September 1981. Information allowed the RUC to identify the next INLA target as a twenty-year-old off-duty UDR man named Mark Stockman who worked in Mackies, a predominantly Protestant engineering factory in west Belfast. Stockman was warned of the impending attack but agreed to follow his normal routine, safe in the knowledge that E4A and Specialist Support Units (police officers trained in the tactics of the Special Air Service) were primed to pounce in the streets surrounding the factory. At lunchtime, Stockman was playing a game of football outside the factory, as he did every day. Steenson and several other INLA members were spotted in a nearby street, and the police went after them. As they were pursuing Steenson, two gunmen walked up to Stockman and shot him dead. Two other RUC officers in a side street heard the shots and gave chase, opening fire on the gunmen. They missed, and the assassins escaped.[8] Several of Steenson's unit were arrested, but he got away. He had used himself as a decoy to distract the RUC who were covering Stockman. The repeated failure of the police to intercept Steenson led some high-ranking RUC officers to advocate the use of the more highly trained SAS in such situations. But the authorities remained reluctant to employ the firepower of the troop in built-up areas.

Steenson was not arrested until one of his colleagues turned "supergrass" and began naming names, in February 1982.

Although the security forces managed to contain the upsurge in republican violence during 1981, the Provisionals still remained very capable of brutal surprises. From 1981 on they carried out a series of attacks on prominent people, varying their targets from politicians to paramilitaries to leading legal figures.

The South Belfast Unionist MP, the Reverend Robert Bradford, had vehemently opposed any concessions to the hunger strikers. On November 14, 1981, two unknown IRA gunmen murdered him, along with Kenneth Campbell, the caretaker of the community center where the MP held constituency meetings. The police arrived just as the gunmen escaped, almost capturing them. The fact that the republican movement was now involved in the electoral process did not stop them from attacking its very basis.

Thanks to a surveillance operation code-named Furlong that targeted the Provisionals' intelligence-gathering cell in Belfast, police identified the next high-profile IRA target as Lenny Murphy, the most notorious loyalist killer in the history of the Troubles. Murphy, the head of the Shankill Butchers gang, had been released from prison in 1982 after serving six years for an arms offense. He quickly started up where had he left off, torturing and murdering a forty-eight-year-old Catholic, Joseph Donnegan, on October 24, 1982. The RUC learned that the Provisionals were planning to shoot him on the evening of November 11. Undercover officers tracked the IRA Active Service Unit into the Shankill Road, ready to strike as soon as the gunmen made their attempt, but due to British army activity in the area the Provisionals pulled out and the operation was abandoned. A decision was made to lift surveillance on the UVF leader. Five days later Murphy was visiting his girlfriend when Provisional IRA gunmen shot him dead. It was another frustrating setback in the shadowy war against the paramilitaries, this time caused by poor coordination between undercover operations and those of the regular security forces.

Operation Furlong, however, produced results. It had uncovered a strange alliance between the Provisional IRA and certain UDA men who were passing information to republicans about fellow loyalists. The commanding officer of the Belfast Brigade was meeting regularly with two well-known UDA men, Tommy McCreery and James Pratt Craig, in bars in downtown Belfast. Both McCreery and Craig had abandoned any pretense of being involved in paramilitary activities for anything other than personal gain. McCreery had been a close associate of UDA Vice-Chairman Tommy Herron and may well have been involved in his murder in September 1973. Craig, a former boxer turned UDA thug, had been released from jail in 1981 after serving a sentence for hijacking. He was a high-living criminal with a taste for leather and furs who had set up many lucrative rackets in Belfast. In return for money and other favors,

McCreery and Craig gave information to the Provisionals about fellow loyalists whom they regarded as underworld rivals. McCreery became involved in an attempt to murder an IRA informer in prison in 1983 by poisoning him with arsenic, which the Provisionals' Belfast commanding officer had provided. However, he was arrested before the deed was done.[9]

Operation Furlong was also crucial in uncovering a series of IRA plots against prominent legal figures in Northern Ireland between 1982 and 1983. In March 1982 gunmen tried to kill the lord chief justice, Lord Lowry, as he was visiting Queen's University in south Belfast. The university, located near the city's wealthy Malone Road district, was outside the normal area of operations of republican gunmen. Following the attack on Lowry it became evident that the Provisionals had a cell operating in the university itself. Thanks to Furlong, police learned about an assassination plot against a Catholic judge, fifty-five-year-old William Doyle. The Provisionals particularly targeted Catholic members of the judiciary, believing them to be traitors to the nationalist cause. Unfortunately, the information led the police to conclude that the killers would strike as the judge left his home. On Sunday, January 16, 1983, Judge Doyle went to mass as usual at a chapel not far from the university, having refused a police escort. He was shot dead as he left mass.[10]

The RUC believed that a university lecturer and two students were passing information to the head of the Belfast IRA, who was also the intelligence officer for the Northern Command. The lecturer allowed Doyle's killers use of a house on the elegant Malone Road, a few blocks from the scene of the shooting.

For their next prominent victim the Provisionals hatched a plot as brutal as it was elaborate. Their target was another Catholic judge, Judge Kelly. A milk truck would deliver a bomb to Kelly's home early in the morning. If the judge survived the blast, an ambulance coming behind the truck and driven by IRA men would arrive to "aid" the unfortunate man but instead would take him away to be finished off. One of the most prominent players in this grotesque scheme was Daniel McCann, the Belfast IRA's chief bomb maker. The Provisionals' plans unfolded over the summer of 1983. In June two IRA members, one of them a woman, Evelyn Glenholmes, rented an apartment in a village near the judge's home. Glenholmes was a suspect in several major PIRA operations in Ireland and in England. The RUC got ready to launch a counteroperation. However, the Provisionals did not strike for another two months. But when they did, the RUC had the trap ready.

As the unlikely convoy of milk truck, ambulance, and backup car made its way to the target on the morning of August 4, it "just happened" to run into a police checkpoint. The police stopped the truck to express their concern as to the stability of the milk crates. Much to the relief of the IRA man in the truck, after a cursory glance the police waved the vehicle on, only to stop it a second time to inspect it more carefully. When the officers tired of this little jest, they seized the bomb. Two of the Belfast IRA's top gunmen, Alex Murphy and Harry Fitzsimmons, in the ambulance disguised as medics, were arrested. McCann, meanwhile, was arrested at the home of the milk truck owner.[11]

The interception of the ASU had been aided by the RUC's uncovering and bugging a major Provisional IRA explosives dump in a building at the rear of a housing development in west Belfast. A device (named after a flower) had been installed that detected movement and alerted the police that bomb-making materials were being shifted. This led the police to uncover the Provisionals' major bomb-making factory, located in a nearby glass-making works. The factory was raided and four hundred pounds of explosives recovered, packed into cylinders, apparently intended for an attack on a south Belfast RUC station. Although another RUC success, subsequent events demonstrated some of the difficulties in fighting a twilight war in which the need for secrecy is paramount. Three men were arrested on the premises, two of them known to the police as active Provisionals who had been frequently observed in the factory and at the explosives dump. However, the courts later freed them. The problem for the police was that the twilight war was waged mostly in secret, its participants rarely if ever identified, and its connections to other events hardly ever made public. In the case of the bomb factory, this meant that the police could not reveal in court much of the evidence they possessed without exposing a valuable ongoing surveillance operation. Instead, they chose to keep that secret and continue monitoring the hideout. Further successes and arrests throughout 1983 compensated them for the fact that culprits walked free.

The RUC's military role, while increasingly effective against terrorism, frequently clashed with efforts to "normalize" its relation to the community. In 1982 a series of incidents highlighted this problem dramatically.

The task of running the RUC had fallen to Jack Hermon, a burly, tough-minded fifty-year-old Ulster man whose puritanical streak was alleviated only slightly by an appreciation of Bushmills whiskey. In January 1980 he replaced Sir Kenneth Newman as chief constable. Hermon, as one of the architects of the "Ulsterization" policy, could be relied on to see it implemented. He also boasted that he was keen to see the day dawn when the RUC could patrol the streets without needing flak jackets or weapons or a patrol of soldiers in tow. But the "Ulsterization" policy with which Hermon was so closely identified continued to frustrate that ambition. In 1982 it led to accusations that the RUC was little better than an Ulsterized version of the SAS; it also led to the exposing of features of the twilight war that the police would rather have kept secret.

Two separate events were involved, which nationalists claimed proved the police were pursuing a "shoot-to-kill" policy. The first had its genesis in a surveillance operation on a Provisional IRA explosives dump in a hay shed near Lurgan, County Armagh. In spite of its being covered, the Provisional IRA managed to retrieve the explosives and use it for a land mine that killed three RUC men on October 27, 1982. Fifteen days later, three unarmed members of the IRA, Eugene Toman, Sean Burns, and Gervaise McKerr, were shot dead. A Special Support Unit—a squad of heavily armed RUC men used to back up surveillance operations—was responsible. They claimed they had fired at the IRA men's car after it had crashed through a checkpoint, but forensic tests indicated the victims had been shot after their car came to a halt.

On November 24 undercover RUC men opened fire on the hut from where the explosives had been taken, killing a seventeen-year-old Catholic, Michael Tighe, who it soon emerged had no connection with the Provisional IRA. Along with a friend who survived the shooting, he had stumbled haplessly on a covert operation.

The next sequence of events involved the INLA. As one of the organization's most dangerous activists, Gerard Steenson, was going behind bars in February 1982, Dominic McGlinchey was being freed. McGlinchey had been a member of the Provisional IRA but switched to INLA while in jail in the Irish republic. He was a volatile character, cunning, manipulative, and violent, who had operated with such figures as Martin McGuinness and Francis Hughes, the south Derry IRA man who had died on a hunger strike shortly after Bobby Sands. He once boasted to an Irish reporter that he had murdered at least thirty people. The press nicknamed him "Mad Dog." In 1982 he became operations officer on INLA's GHQ staff. On December 6 of that year an INLA bomb, consisting of ten pounds of Frangex explosives stolen from a silver mine in the Irish republic, exploded at a pub and disco frequented by off-duty British soldiers from an army base in Ballykelly, County Derry. It killed seventeen people, eleven of them soldiers and four of them young women whom the INLA in a follow-up statement contemptuously referred to as "consorts." McGlinchey became the most wanted man in Ireland.

An informer told the RUC that McGlinchey was in Armagh in the company of Seamus Grew and Roddy Carroll, both active INLA members. Carroll had been involved in several operations with Steenson in 1981, and Grew came from a family of republican activists.[12] Grew and Carroll were shot dead after passing a checkpoint near Armagh on December 12. They were unarmed. Again, officers of the same Special Support Unit were involved, and again they advanced similar claims to those made after the shooting of McKerr, Toman, and Burns. They claimed that the suspects had run through a checkpoint. And yet again forensic evidence contradicted important aspects of the police version of events. Grew was shot four times from a distance of between thirty and thirty-five inches as he lay outside the car.

The three incidents provoked an outcry in the Catholic community. It prompted allegations that the RUC was following a "shoot-to-kill" policy and was involved in an elaborate cover-up to hide the truth of what happened. Pressure mounted on Chief Constable Jack Hermon to have the officers involved prosecuted on murder charges. An internal RUC investigation into the incidents led to a recommendation that one of the officers be charged with murder. Hermon firmly rejected it. He secretly argued that such a hearing would expose vital aspects of police undercover operations and put informers at risk. Meanwhile, the Northern Ireland director of public prosecutions ignored Hermon's objections. Four RUC men were charged with murder. Their acquittal in the spring of 1984 provoked another outcry and a demand for an outside investigation.[13] To the dismay and disgust of the Special Branch, the demand was met. John Stalker, deputy chief constable of Greater Manchester, was appointed to head the investigation.

Stalker arrived in Belfast in May 1984. Although he had spent most of his police life as a detective, he was despised within Special Branch circles because he did not have the kind of operational experience they thought was needed to comprehend the nature of the problem the RUC faced. One high-ranking Special Branch officer, when asked what he would do if he met Stalker, said, "I'd punch him." Jack Hermon was alleged to have said to him, "Remember, Mr. Stalker, you are in a jungle now."[14]

Their fears that Stalker would expose too much were borne out when very early on his inquiry disclosed that MI5 had bugged the hay shed in which explosives were hidden and Michael Tighe was shot dead. This was the first time that such details about MI5's role in Northern Ireland were made public. RUC resistance to the inquiry mounted. Stalker complained that files he wanted were missing or were handed over late. Nationalists saw this as evidence that the Special Branch was concealing evidence of a shoot-to-kill policy. In fact, the police reaction stemmed largely from the inherent reluctance of the Special Branch, a closely knit elite within the force, to share information with anyone, including other police departments and MI5.

Stalker was removed from the inquiry in May 1986 to face disciplinary charges relating to his relationship with a Manchester businessman, charges of which he was later acquitted. It was taken over by Colin Sampson, chief constable of the West Yorkshire police force, who also was put in charge of the investigation into Stalker. The report of the Sampson-Stalker investigation was never made public for reasons of "national security," but two high-ranking Special Branch officers involved in the 1982 shootings were suspended from duty pending further inquiries.

Stalker had some harsh words for the RUC, especially in connection with the shooting of Tighe and the attempt to cover it up, which he described as the act of a "police force out of control."[15] But he also said that he had found no evidence of a shoot-to-kill policy. Some RUC officers undoubtedly thought there should have been one. One Special Branch superintendent who played a leading role in the undercover war in the 1990s, when confronted with allegations that there was a shoot-to-kill policy, used to joke: "I wish." The truth was that in the vast majority of cases during the time the police surveillance teams had paramilitary activists under prolonged observation, or when police antiterrorist units intercepted paramilitary operations, there were no fatalities. As evidence, the statistics show that the RUC was responsible for only fifty-three deaths between 1969 and 1994, by far the lowest attributed to any of the organizations involved in the conflict and a tiny minority of the well over three thousand violent deaths that occurred during that period. Eighteen of those fifty-three were acknowledged as members of the IRA, INLA, UDA, or UVF.[16] The 1982 incidents were the exception to this rule. Had there been a shoot-to-kill policy then, there surely would have been far more deaths at police hands.

Because of the controversy surrounding the shootings and the inquiry, a decision was made to reduce the role of the police antiterrorist units in situations where they were forced to confront the IRA; instead, the Special Air Service's role was to be increased, provoking its own bitter allegations about a shoot-to-kill policy. Some RUC officers had advocated this all along. Not only is SAS training superior to that of the police, but soldiers do not have to live in the community where they are stationed and are returned to Britain after their tour of duty is finished. Any police officer who is exposed at a trial because of incidents such as those that occurred in late 1982 is placed in a grave situation and might become the target of paramilitaries thirsting for revenge.

There were other consequences of the "Stalker Affair," as it became known. INLA's Dominic "Mad Dog" McGlinchey went on a hunt to find the informer who had attempted to set him up in late 1982. Suspicion fell on Eric Dale, a forty-three-year-old republican who lived across the border in County Monaghan. On the night that Drew and Carroll were shot dead, Dale had been detailed to provide a car for them to ferry McGlinchey from the Irish republic into Northern Ireland. Dale failed to show up, getting drunk instead with a well-known republican, George Poyntz, who owned a pub in Castleblayney. The pub was a haunt for both the Provisional IRA and the INLA. On May 3, 1983, Dale was taken from his home and tortured for several days, during which a hot poker was thrust under his armpit. It was hardly surprising that he "confessed" to being an informer. He was "executed" and his body dumped in south Armagh. It was after this that George Poyntz suddenly disappeared, showing up later in Northern Ireland where it was revealed that he had been working for the police for many years. Republicans, including Bernadette McAliskey, were stunned. McAliskey had long known him and had stayed at his home on occasion.[17]

Shortly after the hunger strike ended, the Provisionals resumed their bombing campaign in Britain, killing a bomb disposal expert in Oxford Street, London, on October 26. In July 1982 a double bomb attack in Hyde Park killed eleven soldiers, including six bandsmen and five members of the regimental cavalry, along with their horses. One of the IRA's biggest propaganda coups came a year later. On Friday, September 23, 1983, the Special Branch learned that a jailbreak was "imminent." Unfortunately for them, the information was not precise enough to launch a counteroperation. Under the leadership of Bobby Storey and six others—Gerry Kelly (serving life for bombing London in 1973), Brendan "Bik" McFarlane, Gerry McDonnell, Padraig McKearney, Kieran Fleming, and Tony McAllister—the prisoners planned to take over an entire block of the supposedly escape-proof prison, H-7, which held 125 men.[18] The original breakout had been scheduled for September 18 but was postponed for one week. Thirty-eight Provisionals were chosen. Twenty-five of those picked were Belfast activists, and twenty-eight were serving life sentences for murder. Plans had been under way for a year, masterminded by Larry Marley, an Ardoyne IRA man, nicknamed the Wee Devil. He had broken out of different jails on two occasions and had a reputation as an escape artist. Because of his escape attempts, he earned another nickname: Papillon. But when the time came for Marley's most grandiose escape plan to be put into action, he stayed behind, having only two years left to serve in prison.

The thirty-eight Provisionals took command of H-7 on late Sunday afternoon, September 25. Some disguised themselves as prison officers and hijacked a food truck that took them to the main gate.[19] There, things went wrong, however, and nineteen were recaptured almost immediately. The others got away after a chaotic chase. The Army Council regarded it as a great success—it was the biggest breakout in the IRA's history. Many of those who remained free were among the organization's most valuable operators. They included Dermot Finucane, Gerry Kelly, and Gerry McDonnell from Belfast, and Padraig McKearney and Seamus McElwaine from counties Tyrone and Monaghan.[20]

The Provisionals came close to effecting an even more stunning propaganda blow against the state the following year. The hunger strikes had made Thatcher into the figure the republican movement hated most. In 1988, Gerry Adams said of her: "She will be remembered when even some of the names of the hunger strikers are forgotten. All the six- and seven-year-olds have the memory of Thatcher in their heads."[21] In 1984 the Provisionals devised a plot to kill her.

On September 15, 1984, a man named Roy Walsh checked into the Grand Hotel in Brighton on England's south coast. He stayed for three days in room 629 and was not much noticed, nor did anyone realize that the name he signed in under was that of a Provisional IRA man arrested and jailed in England in connection with the 1973 London bombings. Patrick Magee, the man's real name, was playing a little joke. Magee was a thirty-three-year-old Belfast IRA man who had taken part in one bombing campaign in England in 1978. He was wanted in connection with an arms find in England in 1983, along with another prominent IRA activist, Evelyn Glenholmes.

When Magee checked out on September 18, he left behind a bomb thickly wrapped in cellophane, weighing between twenty and thirty pounds, in the wall of the bathroom of room 629. It had a long-delay timer like the ones used in video recorders; it was set to explode at 2:54 A.M. on Friday, October 12. That day, Thatcher would be in the hotel along with most of her cabinet, attending the Conservative Party's annual conference.

On the morning of October 12, Jennifer Taylor, who was staying at the Grand Hotel with her husband, Eric, was falling asleep at around 2 A.M. "The next thing I remember is a loud bang. I was lifted upwards and then had the sensation of falling and falling. When I finished falling I opened my eyes believing I had been dreaming but I couldn't see anything. My eyes slowly cleared and I found myself sitting on the ground. I saw a wall and a light to my left about four feet away. There was debris all around me—a stainless steel sink, girders, bricks and water, and lots of smoke and dust."[22] Her husband was killed in his sleep, along with four others, including an MP, Sir Anthony Berry. One woman who died, Mrs. Jeanne Shattock, was preparing to take a bath in room 628 and was cut to pieces with shards of tile. The blast brought a massive chimney crashing through the twenty-eight rooms below, narrowly missing Mrs. Thatcher, who emerged shaken but uninjured.

The Provisionals quickly claimed responsibility for the attempted assassination. They ended their statement with a warning: "Today, we were unlucky, but remember, we only have to be lucky once—you will have to be lucky always. Give Ireland peace and there will be no war."[23]

The RUC's top priority was to catch the Brighton bomber. A fingerprint found on the hotel registration card identified Magee as the man who had checked into room 629 on September 15. The problem was finding him.

In May 1985, the RUC Special Branch in Belfast learned two things: one, that the IRA was planning another series of bomb attacks in Britain, and two, that it wanted to smuggle someone, identity unknown, into Britain. A leading member of the Belfast IRA was involved in making the arrangements. On June 20 he met up with an "unknown," who after some confusion the police identified as Peter Sherry from Dungannon, a prominent member of Sinn Fein and the commander of the East Tyrone Provisional IRA, one of the most violent of the IRA's brigades. Sherry was known as a marksman and was suspected of involvement in many murders and attempted murders.

Undercover police officers followed him by boat. Sherry was tracked to the Carlisle railway station where the police watched as a man approached him. They recognized him as Patrick Magee, the Brighton bomber. Sherry and Magee took the train to Glasgow, Scotland. The Brighton bomber was later trapped in a house by twenty-two police officers, most of them armed. When it was raided, they found Magee, Sherry, and Gerry McDonnell, the Maze escapee, who was commander of the IRA's bombing operation in England. Along with him were two young women, Martina Anderson, a former beauty queen from Derry, and Ella O'Dwyer, a middle-class student from Dublin. McDonnell was found with a set of plans to bomb eleven seaside resorts and the Hotel Rubens near Buckingham Palace in London. Like the Grand Hotel bomb, they had long-delay timers. The first was due to explode in over a month, on July 29 at 1 P.M.

All were convicted of conspiring to cause explosions, and Magee was also convicted of the murders of five people at the Grand Hotel. He was sentenced to eight life sentences. The judge commented: "You intended to wipe out a large part of the government, and you very nearly did."[24] The Provisionals took that as an unintended compliment. But the arrest of Magee, Sherry, and McDonnell was a demoralizing blow and a bad setback for the IRA's bombing campaign in England.

The occasional "spectacular" operation, such as the "great escape" or the Brighton bombing, could not disguise the fact that many crucial operations were being intercepted, and as a result the level of violence was dropping considerably. Sectarian attacks by the UDA and UVF fell significantly between 1981 and 1985, and the nature of their targets changed somewhat. While the majority of the victims were still ordinary Catholics, often picked at random, the UDA and UVF began to have some success in targeting members of the republican movement. One of the most notable attacks came in February 1981 when a lone UVF gunman broke into the home of IRA man James Burns and shot him dead. Burns, a close ally of Adams, had been the quartermaster for the Northern Command. As Sinn Fein became more active, it provided loyalists with ready targets. Two members of the party were shot dead in 1982 and another in 1984. Loyalists almost pulled off their own "spectacular" on March 14, 1984. As Gerry Adams and several colleagues drove through central Belfast, three UDA gunmen pulled alongside their vehicle and sprayed it with bullets. The Provisional leader was in the front passenger seat. He felt the thumps as four of the twenty rounds that smashed into the car hit him. "So this is what it's like," he thought. Everyone in the car was wounded. Adams was surprised to find he was still alive when the shooting stopped.[25] Undercover RUC men chased the gunmen who ran into another car driven by an off-duty UDR man.[26] All three were arrested. One of them was accidentally shot by a colleague and bleeding badly.

Between 1982 and 1986 violence went into a sharp decline. The successes of undercover police operations were not the only cause. Police began to "turn" paramilitaries. Known as "supergrasses," after their arrests they agreed to give evidence against their former colleagues in return for leniency and financial rewards. Although paramilitaries had been "turned" before, it was not until 1982 that it became an important weapon in the war against terrorism.[27] For the next few years it became the main weapon. Altogether there were some thirty supergrasses between 1981 and 1983, leading to the arrests of three hundred people, most of them from Belfast. It was as many as were held after the first internment swoops. A special wing of Crumlin Road prison, where suspects were incarcerated pending trial, was set aside to accommodate the supergrasses. Rumors spread about the privileges they enjoyed, including access to drink, drugs, and women. The defendants appeared en masse in the dock, which led civil rights and pro-republican groups to denounce the trials as "show trials." There were several mass convictions. The most successful supergrasses, in terms of sheer numbers of arrests, were Christopher Black, a member of the North Belfast Provisional IRA, and Harry Kirkpatrick, a petty criminal and henchman of Gerard Steenson, the INLA leader. Black's testimony led to the conviction of thirty-eight people, and Kirkpatrick's convicted twenty-four, including Steenson, who received a life sentence after the judge declared him an "enemy of society."[28] According to police, thanks to Black's confessions only four active IRA men were left in north Belfast. The statements of two loyalist supergrasses, Joseph Bennett and William "Budgie" Allen, led to the arrests of many UVF men.

Thirteen supergrasses retracted their evidence before trial. Meanwhile, there was genuine disquiet among civil rights groups and lawyers about convictions obtained solely on the word of a convicted criminal, without any corroborating evidence. The judgments handed down thanks to the evidence of the other supergrasses did not hold. By December 1986 nearly all the convictions, including those in the Black and Kirkpatrick cases, had been overturned on appeal.

Although the use of such evidence gave genuine cause for unease, its crippling impact on the paramilitary organizations was undeniable, as the decline in violence indicates.

While the twilight war was being waged behind the scenes, the political struggle for the hearts and minds of the Nationalist voters took on a sudden urgency. Sinn Fein's challenge to the SDLP would prove more of a spur to the Irish and British governments than the IRA's faltering campaign. It convinced them to launch the most daring political initiative that Northern Ireland had seen in over a decade.

· 3 ·

FOLLOWING THE assembly elections in 1982, the SDLP sought support in the Irish republic for establishing a Council of Ireland on which all parties—barring those committed to violence—could discuss the issue of Ulster and how to find a way of incorporating Unionist identity into a new Ireland. This idea soon blossomed into the New Ireland Forum, with the backing of recently elected Irish Taoiseach Dr. Garret Fitzgerald. The aim was to produce proposals to encourage the British to reopen the Anglo-Irish process, which Hume held was the key to resolving the conflict. It was in reality an attempt to counteract the growth of Sinn Fein, as Fitzgerald admits. "I had come to the conclusion," he wrote in his autobiography, *All in a Life,* "that I must now give priority to heading off the growth of support for the IRA in Northern Ireland by seeking a new understanding with the British government." In the aftermath of Adams's victory in the June 1983 general election, Fitzgerald went to Thatcher to impress upon her the urgency of the situation.

"I had a meeting with Dr. Fitzgerald at the European Council at Stuttgart in June 1983," wrote the British prime minister. "I shared the worry he expressed about the erosion of SDLP support by Sinn Fein. However uninspiring SDLP politicians might be—at least since the departure of the courageous Gerry Fitt—they were the minority's main representative and an alternative to the IRA. They had to be wooed."[29] It would prove to be a very stormy courtship, with the SDLP often playing the role of the scorned suitor. But because it was a courtship based on political expediency, it would have a happy outcome.

The Unionists refused to take part in the proceedings of the New Ireland Forum, though two party members of the younger generation, Chris and Michael McGimpsey, with a more liberal, intellectual background, did make the journey south to give the northern Protestant angle and later claimed that what they said was ignored.[30] Protestants were, as ever, skeptical about the participants' claims to be forging a new, "pluralist" Ireland, where their identity and traditions would have a place. Their skepticism was heightened due to the fact that the forum's deliberations were going on against the background of the Irish republic's abortion referendum, which brought to the surface the deeply conservative strain of Catholicism in Irish life. An overwhelming majority voted in September 1983 to enshrine the state's antiabortion law as part of the constitution, reinforcing Protestant fears that Rome still ruled south of the border.

The New Ireland Forum produced a series of study papers and a report in May 1984. It criticized British government policy in Northern Ireland as being one merely of "crisis management" and sounded a note of desperation: "The situation is daily growing more dangerous. Constitutional politics are on trial and unless there is action soon to create a framework in which constitutional politics can work, the drift into more extensive civil conflict is in danger of becoming irreversible."[31]

It was for the most part unsurprising in its conclusions. They posed three different solutions to the Ulster crisis: a unitary state, joint rule from Dublin and London, and a federal/confederal structure. The preferred option was, of course, the first. But the report's emphasis on it tended to distract attention from the fact that constitutional Nationalists were prepared to accept joint authority—a compromise of their historic aim.

However, Thatcher's response made the matter academic. The report was presented to her at the Anglo-Irish conference in November 1984. The timing was, to say the least, unpropitious, being just over a month after the Provisional IRA, also in pursuit of a unitary state, almost murdered her and her entire cabinet. At a press conference with Fitzgerald, the Iron Lady lived up to her reputation as she responded to the three options: "A united Ireland was one solution. That is out. A second solution was confederation of the two states. That is out. A third solution was joint authority. That is out. That is a derogation from sovereignty." Fitzgerald called her reaction "gratuitously offensive."[32] It would not have helped matters had he been aware that at the time Thatcher was privately discussing the possibility of another solution, repartition, and the moving of hundreds of thousands of Catholics from Northern Ireland into the south, which has been called a form of "ethnic cleansing without the bloodshed."[33] It was one more indication of her alarmingly uncertain grasp of Ulster realities.

Thatcher's reaction to the New Ireland Forum report became known as the "out, out, out" speech. It was a humiliating blow to the efforts of the constitutional Nationalists to offer a convincing response to Sinn Fein. However, because of John Hume and the Irish government's patient cultivation of American support, other resources were at hand to set Anglo-Irish relations back on course. Thatcher was due to visit Washington in the wake of her "out, out, out" remarks. She was scheduled to speak before the joint houses of Congress in February 1985. Hume's congressional watchdog, Speaker Thomas "Tip" O'Neill, forewarned Thatcher that her reaction to the forum report made it difficult for him to offer her such a platform. At the same time the Irish utilized an even more powerful channel.

President Ronald Reagan was a close ally of Thatcher's and emulated her brand of free-market economics. In return for her practical and ideological support, Reagan relentlessly hounded IRA supporters in the United States and initiated a series of extradition hearings against IRA men who had fled to the United States.[34] In early 1985 he was persuaded to step into the Anglo-Irish dispute by one of his advisers, Bill Clark, who was a close friend of the former Irish ambassador to Washington, Sean Donlon. Donlon had returned to Ireland in 1981 to become the secretary of the Department of Foreign Affairs but had kept up contacts with his friends in the administration to make sure they were informed of developments in the Irish question. Reagan called Thatcher about the matter and later praised the New Ireland Forum's work as "courageous and forthright." When Thatcher came to Washington in December, Reagan raised the Northern Ireland issue and "stressed the need for progress and the need for all parties concerned to take steps which will contribute to a peaceful resolution of the existing problems."[35] From then on, Thatcher sounded a much more conciliatory note and when speaking before Congress was fulsome in her praise of Garret Fitzgerald and his efforts to reach a settlement.

Within months the British and Irish governments were locked in secret negotiations as rumors spread about a new Ulster initiative. Just what shape it would take was a matter of wild speculation throughout the summer of 1985. Joint authority was the favorite guess, and indeed it was in line with the Irish government's own expectations. Although it fell far short of this, when it was revealed in November 1985, the Anglo-Irish Agreement proved to be a landmark in Ulster history.

It accommodated many of the ideas that Hume had long been seeking to establish as working principles in the search for a solution. There was a formal recognition of the right of the majority to remain part of the United Kingdom as long as they wished. The agreement set up an intergovernmental conference to meet on a regular basis and deal with a range of matters relating to politics, security, and the administration of justice. It gave the Irish government a direct role in Northern Ireland for the first time as guarantor of Northern Irish nationalists' rights. To exercise this function, an Irish secretariat was to be set up in Maryfield, just outside Belfast, staffed by Irish civil servants. It established parity of esteem between Protestant and Catholic traditions. And it provided for a devolved government on the basis of "widespread agreement within Northern Ireland"—which was shorthand for power sharing. It contained as well a transatlantic dimension, with President Reagan and Tip O'Neill issuing a joint statement on the day the agreement was signed, promising U.S. financial support for the areas most affected by the violence.

When the Anglo-Irish Agreement was signed on November 15, 1985, the SDLP and the Irish government regarded it as a triumph. According to Hume it was not a solution to the Ulster crisis but the framework in which such a solution could be worked out. He wrote later: "When history is written, the Anglo-Irish Agreement will be seen to have been the first major step in the current peace process."[36]

The agreement presented problems for both Unionists and republicans. The Unionists had not taken part in the negotiations that led up to the accord and were deeply perturbed at what they saw as a weakening of the British parliament's claim to sovereignty over Northern Ireland. Britain's link now depended on the will of the majority within the northern Irish state, not on any active desire on the part of Britain as a sovereign power to maintain that link. However, it was simply making explicit what had been the case for a long time. Over the years British politicians would occasionally let the truth slip out, as the first Labour Party Northern Ireland secretary of state, Merlyn Rees, did when he once said, "We have not the faintest desire to stay in Ireland and the quicker we are out the better."[37] Now, an international agreement formalized that position.

During a two-day debate on the agreement in the House of Commons at the end of November, Ulster Unionist Party leader James Molyneaux predicted, "The agreement will not bring peace, but a sword. . . . I have to say honestly and truthfully that in the forty years in public life I have never known what I can only describe as a universal cold fury which some of us have thus far managed to contain."[38] Unionists launched an "Ulster Says No" campaign to try to overturn the agreement as they had the Sunningdale Agreement in 1974, holding monster protest rallies.

The republican response was more uncertain. They denounced the agreement as "copper-fastening partition" and emphasized its security aspect, which promised greater cooperation between the RUC and the Irish police. Yet they realized that the recognition of the Irish government's relation to northern Irish nationalists was a real step forward. Sinn Fein began to claim that if any benefits accrued from the agreement, it was because of the IRA and Sinn Fein, since fear of republican militancy had forced Britain to make this concession. But the agreement's assertion that the link between Northern Ireland and Britain depended on the popular will was as much anathema to Sinn Fein as it was to Unionists. It contradicted the republican claim that British imperialism maintained Ulster. On this rested the whole justification for their armed campaign.

Adams had been elected president of the party in 1983, in the euphoria surrounding the party's electoral success, ousting the old guard of O'Bradaigh and O'Conaill. Both the military and political wings were now in the hands of northerners. But by the time the Anglo-Irish Agreement was signed, that euphoria was fast disappearing. The party had received a setback in 1984, during the European parliamentary elections, when its candidate, Danny Morrison, came in far behind John Hume, receiving 91,476 votes to Hume's 151,399. The next year Ruairi O'Bradaigh's prediction that Sinn Fein would overtake the SDLP at the local level proved to be overly optimistic when the party won 59 seats on local councils to the SDLP's 101. Republican leaders were beginning to accept that as long as the Provisionals were engaged in a violent campaign, there was going to be a limit to the amount of political support that their party could expect. For the first time Sinn Fein leaders began to criticize, at least obliquely, IRA actions, calling for a "controlled" and "disciplined" use of force. Following the setbacks of 1984 and 1985, the criticisms became more frequent. Warned Adams: "There is a number of people who, while they voted for us in June 1983, may not have been able to tolerate some aspects of IRA operations in which civilians were killed or injured."

In August 1985, at the very moment that republican leaders were reevaluating their attitude toward political violence, a huge shipment of weapons arrived from Libya. It was the first, but it would not be the last. The Provisional IRA was now better armed than at any time in its history.

· SIX ·

QADDAFI'S GIFT

1985–1990

INTERNATIONAL EVENTS are not usually seen as helping to shape the Ulster crisis, which of all the world's trouble spots is usually regarded as among the most local and immune from outside influence. The right-wing rhetoric of the Thatcher-Reagan era, with its talk of international terrorist conspiracies, was singularly inappropriate when viewed from the market towns of east Tyrone or the alleyways of Belfast, where people needed to go no further than the next field or street to explain the sources of their conflict. However, the Cold War and the situation in the Middle East had a direct impact on what happened in Ulster, most profoundly in 1985 when the Libyan dictator Colonel Qaddafi's intervention may well have changed the course of the crisis.

The Middle East and eastern bloc were already playing a role in the conflict. The INLA had received much of its weapons and explosives from the Al Fatah wing of the PLO. PLO officers trained INLA activists in the Bekaa Valley in Lebanon, as they did members of the Provisional IRA. In the 1980s, PLO safe houses in Prague and East Berlin were made available to the INLA as it arranged for arms shipments via Eastern Europe through Paris to Ireland.[1]

In 1972, Libya supplied the Provisionals with a shipment of RPG-7 rockets, a deal that Joe Cahill had help arrange. A subsequent attempt to ship arms from Tripoli in March 1973 failed, with Cahill, then chief of staff, caught red-handed on board the ship with a huge arms haul. Another effort failed four years later.

As relations between the United States, Great Britain, and Libya deteriorated throughout the mid-1980s, an offer came from the Libyan president, Colonel Qaddafi, that would dwarf all previous Arab contributions to Irish republicans. A Libyan contact approached a member of the INLA Army Council to arrange a meeting with him in Malta. When the INLA leader arrived, the Libyan said he had an arms offer to make. "How much?" the Irishman asked. "How big a ship do you have?" the contact replied. He was talking in tons. There was so much being offered that INLA had to refuse; it simply could not have absorbed it all.

In the meantime, Libya was spreading its largesse elsewhere. Between August 1985 and September 1986, Qaddafi shipped approximately 150 tons of weapons and explosives to the Provisional IRA in Ireland. There were four shipments. The first arrived in August, the second in October of that year. Following the U.S. bombing of Tripoli in April 1986, there were two more—one in July and the other in September. The United States used British air bases to launch its strikes, so Qaddafi decided to punish Thatcher, Reagan's closest ally. "The Arabs were ready to give you anything. You could have gotten anything you wanted then," according to a high-ranking INLA member.

Another shipment of 150 tons on the *Eksund* was dispatched in October 1987, but this one was intercepted by French authorities off the coast of Brittany on November 1.[2]

The police estimated that the Provisionals received more than a thousand AK-47 rifles, a million rounds of ammunition, a dozen surface-to-air missiles, large quantities of handguns, Russian-made heavy machine guns, and four tons of Semtex plastic explosives. Colorless, odorless, and malleable, Semtex can be molded into almost any shape, from a bar of soap to a box of chocolates; it would soon figure prominently in the IRA's bombing campaign. A piece of republican graffiti that appeared on a wall near the Falls Road declared with hate-filled Belfast humor: "IRA Recent Survey Shows Semtex Is Killing More Germs Than Vortex . . . Ha Ha." (Vortex is a well-known household drain cleaner.)

When the size of the shipment became known, a frightened Irish government minister said that the IRA now threatened "the very existence of the state." The huge influx of weapons, the largest the IRA had ever received, affected the organization at every level. According to one Belfast Provisional IRA man, "After the Libyan arms came in, volunteers were handed an AK-47 for a job that usually required only a pistol and told they could have 100 pounds of Semtex for bombs."[3] At a political level it prolonged the dual strategy of ballot and bullet and led the Army Council to believe the IRA could score a significant military breakthrough that would end the political deadlock. At this time a new chief of staff took over—Kevin McKenna from Tyrone. The RUC claimed he was active in the border areas from the 1970s, and they linked him to twenty murders. According to a senior republican, McKenna was given carte blanche to conduct the war.[4]

The Provisionals were not only better equipped than ever, thanks to Qaddafi, but they also developed their own do-it-yourself terrorist technology. In the mid-1980s they constructed a mortar capable of hurling a forty-pound bomb over the protective walls of security bases and RUC stations. On February 28, 1985, a mortar attack on the Newry police station in south Down struck a busy canteen and killed nine constables, two of them women, the largest loss of life the RUC ever suffered in one incident. One of the ASUs involved came from south Armagh, which had a reputation for harboring the IRA's most effective units.

The well-armed ASUs launched a series of attacks on small, isolated RUC stations in a campaign concentrated mainly in east Tyrone. They hoped to duplicate the IRA's successes in the 1919–21 War of Independence when they forced the police to abandon their garrisons in nationalist areas of the Irish countryside. East Tyrone seems an unlikely setting for a brutal conflict that was part civil war, part political terrorism. It is a rural patchwork of Catholic and Protestant districts, mostly small farms and dull market towns, a featureless landscape bounded on its northern side by the Sperrin Mountains and on the east by the flat expanse of Lough Neagh, the biggest lake in the British Isles.

In December 1985, Provisionals killed two RUC men at a base in Ballygawley, County Tyrone, entering the station with a flamethrower and destroying everything they came across. They then left a bomb that devastated the building. An ASU consisting of up to thirty-five men demolished another at the Birches, near Portadown, using a mechanical digger loaded with a bomb to crash through the building's defenses. It was one of sixteen bases hit in a period of just over a year, at a cost to the British government of £150 million (about $230 million). Only one was ever reopened. As part of this campaign, the Provisionals murdered building contractors who repaired the damaged buildings. Seamus McAvoy, a successful County Tyrone businessman who lived in a middle-class area of Dublin, was the first to be targeted. He was shot dead outside his home on August 20, 1985. His crime: He supplied portacabins to the police.[5] On November 21, six days after the Anglo-Irish Agreement was signed, the Provisionals shot dead Kurt Konig, a German building contractor, at his home in Derry. Within days of his death it was revealed that some three hundred building workers were laid off work because their firms were refusing to carry out jobs on behalf of the security forces due to threats made against them. In east Tyrone the campaign against building contractors took on a particularly vicious character. Late on the night of April 21, 1987, IRA gunmen burst into the home of Harold Henry, who with his brother, James, ran a building firm that specialized in doing repair work for the police and army. Five IRA men dragged him outside in his stocking feet, put him up against a wall, and shot him in the head.[6]

A few days later the South Armagh Provisionals exploded a huge bomb near the main road across the border as seventy-four-year-old Chief Justice Maurice Gibson and his sixty-seven-year-old wife, Cecily, drove past on their way from Dublin to Belfast. (It was Gibson who had congratulated an RUC officer involved in a controversial shoot-to-kill incident in 1982 on his marksmanship.) The assassination put further pressure on the RUC to do something to counter the upsurge in Provisional IRA violence.

An opportunity came when police received information from a complex surveillance operation that the Provisionals were planning another "spectacular" like the one that had destroyed the Ballygawley and Birches RUC bases. Their target was a small RUC station in Loughgall, just across the Armagh border. The information came from a surveillance operation directed at Jim Lynagh. At thirty-one years old, Lynagh was the Provisional IRA's commander in charge of all cross-border operations in the Monaghan-Armagh region. A former Sinn Fein councilor, he was known to the local Irish police as the "Executioner."[7] The RUC connected him with about a dozen murders. Loughgall had little or no security significance, but in terms of loyalist mythology it was the holiest of holies. In 1795 the Orange Order was founded there to counter rising republican militancy. Loyalists would view a successful IRA attack in Loughgall as a desecration. To counter it, a complex operation code-named Judy was mounted, involving undercover soldiers, surveillance police, UDR, and heavily armed RUC Headquarters Mobile Support Units (HMSUs). The Special Branch superintendent in overall charge was Frank Murray. The forty-two-year-old Murray (who died of cancer in March 1996) was badly wounded by the IRA the decade before, losing an arm, a leg, and an eye in a booby-trap bomb attack. His hatred of the Provisionals was legendary.

Four cut-off groups of SAS men were placed outside the station, hidden in the hedges, and one group inside, along with three policemen who had volunteered to man the station to make it look normal. There were other observation groups and surveillance units covering all approaches to the area. HMSU patrols were hiding in hedgerows in a lane just outside the village to block any attempted escape by the ASU. Amazingly, the Provisionals failed to detect any of the considerable amount of security forces' activity in the area all that day.

It was a well-laid trap, and at around 7:20 P.M. on the evening of May 8 the Provisionals' eight-man ASU, clad in blue coveralls and balaclavas, drove right into it. The ASU arrived in a blue Hiace van, scouting the village before coming to a halt near the entrance to the station. Two gunmen got out, walked up the road a little, and began firing at the target. A mechanical digger with a bomb in the bucket came rumbling down the road, turned, and crashed through the high wire fence surrounding the station. One of the two Provisionals in the digger's cabin lit the bomb's fuse. The device, between three hundred and four hundred pounds, exploded, turning one side of the station into a pile of rubble and lifting off the roof. Other members of the ASU began scrambling out of the van, intending to rake the damaged building with automatic fire. Jim Lynagh was accompanied by Paddy Kelly, the commanding officer of the East Tyrone Provisionals; Paddy McKearney, who had escaped from the Maze in 1983; and Declan Arthurs and Eugene Kelly. Suddenly they were enfiladed with heavy fire. In the words of one officer who was there, they were "totally shocked at such a reception."[8] The SAS poured a sustained fuselage from two general-purpose machine guns, Heckler and Koch high-velocity rifles, and Browning pistols. Fire came from the side of the road, the station itself, and a nearby wood.

The machine guns hit the driver of the van, Seamus Donnelly, and blew off his head. Kelly returned fire and was into his second magazine before he was riddled, near the door of the van. Lynagh and McKearney climbed back into the van for cover, but it was futile because its walls were perforated with bullets on all sides. When one of them moved suddenly, wounded and dying, an SAS soldier finished him off with a final shot (though at the inquest, not held until May 1995, the soldier described it as a "warning shot"). Arthurs and Eugene Kelly were killed trying to find cover at the side of the van. Tony Gormley, one of the two men in the digger, shouted, "I'm a Special Branch source." But this did not save him. He died alongside the others, still holding what appeared to be a detonator in his hand. Not far away, two brothers, Anthony and Oliver Hughes, also dressed in coveralls, drove into the ambush. Anthony was killed and his brother seriously wounded. Another innocent bystander, a Guinness sales representative, stumbled into the jaws of death and found himself being chased toward a nearby house where an SAS trooper was about to shoot him but hesitated because the suspect was respectably dressed. His suit saved his life.

The exact number of shots fired in the few minutes of hell that was Loughgall has never been satisfactorily established. The official figure of 678, of which 78 were from IRA guns, seems rather conservative considering that one soldier alone used up 125 rounds from a belt-fed machine gun.[9] A police officer who was at the scene noted that the bodies looked like sieves. The weapons recovered from the dead men were forensically tested and shown to have been used in a string of seven murders, including that of Harold Henry a few weeks earlier, and twelve attempted murders.

It was the single biggest loss that the IRA suffered since the 1919–22 period and the RUC's most successful blow against the Provisionals. Three of their top operators—Kelly, Lynagh, and McKearney—were dead and the entire ASU annihilated. At the funerals of the dead men, who soon became known as the Loughgall Martyrs, Gerry Adams delivered an oration, using the rhetorical trick of turning defeats into victories: "Loughgall will become a tombstone for British policy in Ireland and a bloody milestone in the struggle for freedom, justice and peace."

The battle for east Tyrone was far from over, and the Provisionals would enact bloody reprisals. In August 1988 a British army bus carrying soldiers back to their base took a route through Ballygawley to Omagh, nicknamed by the SAS "Bomb Alley." The RUC warned the Ministry of Defense never to allow the security forces to use it. SAS units avoided it even if it meant crossing the Irish border, an illegality that the authorities ignored. On

August 20 the bus full of troops was blown to bits just outside Ballygawley, and eight men were killed. Ten days later the SAS struck back, killing two brothers, Gerard and Martin Harte, and Brian Mullin as they tried to murder an off-duty UDR man near Carrickmore in County Tyrone.[10] One of the IRA men had the top of his head blown off, a phenomenon the SAS refer to with grisly wit as a "flip-top terrorist." Mullin reportedly had been questioned about the British army bus bombing, as had Martin Harte. His brother, Gerard, was believed to be the commanding officer of the local Provisionals.

Between 1983 and 1992, the Provisionals in east Tyrone lost thirty-four men, of whom the SAS killed twenty-five. The UVF, which was also active in the area, killed four in two separate shootings in 1989 and 1991. In the end, the East Tyrone Provisional IRA was, in the words of one of its activists, effectively "wiped out."

For the Provisionals, the "final push" was off to a bad start. It was not only their own members who paid the price. On November 8, 1987, a remote-controlled bomb exploded prematurely at a Memorial Day service in Enniskillen, County Fermanagh. Eleven people were killed. The IRA's explanation that a British army radio signal detonated the device only gave comfort to its hard-core supporters. Most people, Catholic and Protestant, were appalled. For Sinn Fein and its president, Gerry Adams, it was an especially bitter blow, effectively nullifying their efforts to build some electoral base in the twenty-six counties. The leadership was beginning to realize the cost that the bullet was exacting from the ballot as the dual strategy started to break down. The republican cause had not been helped, either, by a bloodbath earlier in the year when feuding factions of the INLA turned their guns on each other, leaving twelve people dead within a few weeks, including Gerard Steenson, the organization's foremost gunman.[11] Much of this internecine violence took place south of the border, further convincing the southern electorate to have nothing to do with Ulster and its problems. The Enniskillen massacre only confirmed the growing feeling that the Ulster crisis was intractable.

• 2 •

LONG BEFORE the Enniskillen massacre, Gerry Adams believed that the Provisionals had to broaden their base of support if their struggle was to succeed. By the mid-1980s the former barman was the dominant figure in the organization, both in Belfast and nationwide. While a member of the Army Council, Adams was probably not involved directly in the operational side of the movement. Perhaps it is for this reason that Special Branch surveillance on him was less than might have been expected, given his stature. At any rate, he was in a position to impose his vision on the course the Provisionals should take. He had already helped guide it through a whole series of transformations, honed down its terrorist structure, and built up its political machine. In 1986 he and his supporters asked the Provisionals to take a major step away from traditional republican thinking and recognize the Irish parliament.

The nonrecognition policy dated back to the 1921 treaty that had partitioned Ireland. Republicans rejected the treaty and the institutions that flowed from it, and barred any of their members from taking their seats if elected to either the Stormont parliament near Belfast or the Dail. Unhappiness with such a strict line led Eamonn DeValera to resign from Sinn Fein, of which he was president, in 1926, and establish a new party, Fianna Fail. It was a dispute about the same matter that had led the IRA to split in 1969 into Official and Provisional wings. In the mid-1980s the issue reemerged yet again. Adams and his supporters were arguing that Sinn Fein's refusal to recognize the Dail meant that it would be permanently isolated in the twenty-six counties, unable to tap into the hidden reserves of nationalism that he believed existed there, especially among Fianna Fail supporters. In effect, Adams was following the line Seamus Costello had expounded in the late 1960s, that abstentionism was a tactic, not a principle. (Indeed, Adams later maintained that even though he opted to go with the Provisional wing in 1969, his decision was not based on the new group's attitude to abstentionism.) Traditionalists like O'Bradaigh countered that to recognize the legitimacy of the Irish state was to go down the road to constitutional nationalism; the Provisionals would end up like DeValera and the Official IRA before them—just another moderately radical political party.

The IRA held an army convention in September, the first in over a decade, and voted to endorse the change of course. In November, Sinn Fein followed suit at its *ard fheis*. Martin McGuinness gave the keynote speech. He was blunt: "We must accept the reality that sixty-five years of republican struggle, republican sacrifice and rhetoric have signally failed to convince the majority of people in the twenty-six counties that the republican movement has any relevance to them," he said. "By ignoring that reality we remain alone and isolated on the high altar of abstentionism, divorced from the people." McGuinness appealed to the traditionalists: "If you allow yourselves to be led out of this hall today, the only place you will be going is home. Don't go, my friends; we will lead you to the Republic." A bitter debate ensued that ended in a reprise of the 1970 *ard fheis*. O'Bradaigh and O'Conaill walked out with about one hundred supporters—whom one commentator has described as a "geriatric minority"—and founded their own party, Republican Sinn Fein.[12]

The split did not greatly affect the Provisionals. The founding members of the Provisionals, most of whom were strong advocates of abstentionism, were nearly all gone by then. MacStiofain never attained any status within the movement after his failed hunger strike in 1972. O'Conaill and O'Bradaigh had lost credibility because of their handling of the 1974–75 cease-fire. The Provisionals' longest-serving chief of staff, Seamus Twomey, on his release from prison in 1982, worked on Sinn Fein's electoral efforts in the south but eventually became disillusioned and left the movement. Billy McKee, the former Belfast leader who was in favor of abstentionism, had already resigned from the IRA because of a dispute over the kidnapping of a prominent Irish businessman.[13] Only Joe Cahill remained of the old guard, still playing a key role on the Provisional Army Council. But he was ready and willing to adapt to the new outlook of the younger generation. Crucially, the Adams-McGuinness line had strong support north of the border, where the traditional republican quarrel about the status of the Dail had less resonance than among republicans in the south. It was also a recognition that regardless of what republicans might say about a "British-imposed" Dail, the people of the twenty-six counties accepted the Dail as their parliament, and they showed this in election after election. Any party that did not take account of this was doomed to political irrelevancy. Recognition of the Dail also represented an admission on the leadership's part that the republican struggle was about the northern state and was not aimed at the Republic of Ireland. In that sense, the ending of the policy of abstentionism was the last stage in the Ulsterization of the republican movement and its struggle.

Behind the scenes, the Provisional IRA warned O'Conaill and O'Bradaigh that if they tried to split the IRA by daring to set up another republican "army," they would be shot. In spite of this threat, within a few years O'Conaill was at the head of a new Army Council, recognized by republican purists as the legitimate inheritor of the 1916 revolutionaries. It would take eight years for it to emerge under the name Continuity IRA and challenge the Provisional IRA for the mantle of violent republicanism.

In New York the new group won the support of the old IRA gunrunner George Harrison, who along with another member of his network, Tom Falvey, issued a statement denouncing the Provisionals' change of course. It declared, "We reaffirm our support to those who stand solidly behind the traditional Republican policy of abstention or boycott of all British-imposed institutions of servility and replace, not reform them, with Republican institutions of liberty and freedom."

Some saw the change as a harbinger of things to come. If abstentionism can be sacrificed to political expediency, using the argument that it was blocking Sinn Fein's progress, why not that other previously untouchable principle, the "right" of the IRA to use violence to achieve a united Ireland? It was not long after the 1986 decision that one leading Provisional, Danny Morrison, admitted publicly that if indeed it could be demonstrated that the armed campaign was standing in the way of political progress and there was a viable alternative, the IRA would halt its violence.[14]

· 3 ·

BELFAST REMAINED the key to the Provisionals' armed campaign. If that campaign was to continue to pose a threat to British rule, it was essential that the IRA demonstrate its ability to operate in the capital, against either so-called economic targets or members of the security forces. But from the mid-1980s, operational problems mounted. Attacks against on-duty members of the army and police fell drastically. The RUC, having uncovered the route from Tyrone that was used to ferry explosives into the city, successfully contained the Provisionals' bombing campaign. Over a period of two years, until June 1985, the IRA managed to detonate only one large bomb in the city center. Occasionally they succeeded elsewhere only because of police ineptitude. The most outstanding example of this occurred in December 1986 and led to the complete destruction of a police station.

The episode began when the RUC discovered that the Provisionals were using a rather unconventional place to store explosives: a mortuary. An army surveillance unit (known as a Det) was dispatched to cover it. However, the senior officer in charge of the operation concluded that the explosives were unlikely to be moved soon and made no plans to set up checkpoints as a precaution should the IRA decide it needed the material. Shortly afterward, the army surveillance team watched helplessly as the IRA moved the explosives from the dump and drove off to a safe house where the bomb was constructed. Two hours later, bombers forced the driver of a school bus to park it, packed with the explosives, outside the Lisburn Road RUC station in south Belfast. The bomb exploded with a thud that was heard for ten miles, igniting a gas main that burned for two days, consuming what remained of the shattered station. Seven hundred homes in the nearby streets were damaged in the blast, which caused millions of pounds' worth of damage. "It couldn't be our explosives," the senior officer stated. He was told it was. Another lamented that the failure was "one of the biggest acts of incompetence by Belfast TCG." No explosives were ever recovered from the mortuary.

However, the Provisionals could not always rely on police mistakes. Another major bombing blitz against Belfast was planned for the summer of 1987. The bomb-making material was being brought from a farm near Omagh in County Tyrone via their usual route, but this time in a horse box with a false bottom. When the police stopped it, they discovered twenty-seven hundred pounds of explosives hidden there. It was one of the largest finds ever made, and it thwarted the IRA's summer offensive.

Both the UVF and the UDA were facing their own difficulties by the mid-1980s. Unionism was facing a grave crisis as a result of the Anglo-Irish Agreement. Thousands of Protestants demonstrated in protest in Belfast and elsewhere as part of the "Ulster Says No" campaign. There were coordinated attacks on the RUC and their families in Protestant areas. By the summer of 1986, over five hundred RUC homes had been attacked, and Jack Hermon, the chief constable, was making plans to evacuate thousands of policemen and their families to England. For Protestants it was the most serious crisis since 1974, but unlike then, neither the UDA nor the UVF was playing a leading role in the attempts to frustrate Britain's plans. As a result, their support declined.

When looked at closely, the Troubles dissolve into a series of local conflicts in areas where, as in east Tyrone, the distribution of Catholics and

Protestants is a kind of patchwork. North Belfast is another. At the beginning of 1986 a mini-war erupted there that was a continuation of the old and bloody battle between north Belfast republicans and local loyalists, which had been going on since 1969.

Beginning in January 1986 the UVF carried out a series of sectarian murders of Catholics in the area, bringing an end to the period of inactivity that had lasted throughout most of the previous year. John Bingham, the UVF's north Belfast commander, was the man responsible. He had a long history of involvement in the UVF, going back to the early 1970s. For a while he was associated with Lenny Murphy, the leader of the Shankill Butchers gang, a man whom Bingham admired greatly. On the night of September 14, 1986, an IRA ASU sledgehammered its way into his home, shot the lock off the security gate that barred the way to the bedrooms, dragged him from where he was cowering, and shot him dead in front of his wife and child. The Provisionals had killed him at home in a calculated display of bravado, showing loyalists that they could penetrate the very heart of Protestant areas. In the days following Bingham's death, two Catholics were murdered at random. But the UVF plotted a more deliberate revenge.

Larry Marley, the man behind the IRA escape in 1983, was released from prison in November 1985. Soon he was ferrying explosives from Tyrone, working on the Toomebridge-to-Belfast stretch, sometimes driving up to three hundred pounds at a time to a dump in Ardoyne. Although watched, he managed to avoid arrest over a period of some eighteen months, during which he was also linked to a garage where the Provisionals were making mortars. But on April 2, 1987, two UVF men disguised as RUC officers shot him dead at his home, settling the score for the loss of Bingham. Marley's death was a severe blow to the Provisionals in Belfast, and the turnout at his funeral (around six thousand people) was the largest seen since the deaths of the hunger strikers.[15] More shootings followed, as the Provisionals revenged themselves, killing William Marchand, a lesser UVF figure.

However, this time the tit-for-tat threatened to take a more serious turn when the UVF targeted Gerry Adams. At the time, Adams was fighting to retain his west Belfast parliamentary seat in the 1987 British general election. The UVF planned to assassinate him on May 20. Police surveillance teams were forewarned and ready. But for reasons unknown, the UVF called off the attack at the last minute. If it had succeeded, it would have provoked a bloodbath.

The other main loyalist organization, the UDA, emerged from the doldrums of the mid-1980s with its own political program in a document called *Common Sense*. It emerged out of a rethink the UDA undertook in the late 1970s involving principally Andy Tyrie, Glenn Barr, who was a UDA spokesman during the 1974 action against the power-sharing executive, and John McMichael. In 1986, McMichael took over the running of the UFF. Somewhat paradoxically, given his links to sectarian violence, McMichael recognized there was a need to accord a role to Ulster Catholics in any settlement. *Common Sense* advocated a new constitution for Northern Ireland, with protection for human rights and a system of devolved government that would include power sharing. The fact that McMichael could organize a campaign of sectarian violence and at the same time advocate closer cooperation with the SDLP was symptomatic of the confusion within loyalist ranks.

Common Sense impressed Hume as a sign that ten years after being largely responsible for bringing down the first power-sharing government, the most militant wing of loyalism now accepted the need for power sharing. The UDA's efforts, however, did not impress the Provisionals. They hatched plans to murder one of the document's authors. The first plan was to shoot McMichael in the parking lot near the bar he ran in central Lisburn, a small town south of Belfast. That scheme came to nothing, but the Provisionals did not give up. Three days before Christmas 1987, the year *Common Sense* was published, the Belfast Brigade's explosives officer, Danny McCann, booby-trapped McMichael's car. The Semtex bomb killed the UDA chief as he left home. He was thirty-eight years old. His son, Gary, would later take up his father's political ambitions and become a major figure in the peace process.

The murder of McMichael shook up the UDA and helped bring about the end of the long career of its supreme chairman, Andy Tyrie. Tyrie had run the organization since 1973, his reputation resting on the pivotal role he played as the man who brought down the power-sharing government in 1974. After the UDA's 1977 "strike" failed disastrously, Tyrie said, "As far as loyalist paramilitary organizations are concerned, they will never be the same again—until there's a crisis situation. All we can do is hold on to a good nucleus of men and build an organization, wait for the opportunity and ride the waves again."[16] The opportunity came in 1985, with Unionist outrage at the Anglo-Irish Agreement. But the UDA failed to "ride the waves again."

In the meantime, corruption and racketeering were flourishing. The most prominent racketeer was Jim Craig, McCreery's associate and a close friend of Tyrie. Craig was burly, flamboyant, and ruthless. By 1984 he was running seventy-two protection rackets.[17] When asked how he disciplined his men, he replied, "I've got this big fuckin' hammer and I've told them that if anybody gives me trouble I'll break their fuckin' fingers."[18] After McMichael's murder, McCreery and Craig came under suspicion when someone noticed that their loyalist rivals had a tendency to get murdered by republicans—beginning with Lenny Murphy. A younger generation of UDA men were getting impatient with the old guard. Tyrie's relationship with Craig damaged his credibility with them. Following McMichael's murder, Tyrie's standing was weakened even more by another blow in January 1988. A Lebanese–South African connection had provided loyalist organizations with a large arms shipment. Davy Payne, a close colleague of Tyrie's from the 1970s, was put in charge of delivering the UDA's share of the weapons. E4A had Payne and one of his colleagues under close watch. The arms smugglers met with Tyrie on January 7 to discuss their plans. The following day, as Payne drove the weapons to the city, he was stopped and arrested at a checkpoint, along with the arms haul—fifty AK-47 rifles, fifty 9-millimeter pistols, 150 Russian grenades, plus eleven thousand rounds of ammunition.[19] The police uncovered a second arms supply on February 3, destined for the UVF, which included rocket launchers. However, a third supply got through and was eventually divided up between the UDA and UVF.

One morning not long thereafter, Tyrie found a retirement present from his UDA colleagues, not in the form of a gold watch and chain but of a bomb attached to the underside of his car. The vote of no confidence taken by the organization's ruling body, the Inner Council, was a formality, and he resigned in March 1988. Seven months later the UDA murdered Craig as he played pool in a bar in east Belfast. His fellow conspirator McCreery disappeared from Northern Ireland.

Under Tyrie the UDA declined from around twenty-six thousand members to "well under 10,000."[20] With his departure, younger activists soon took control, eager for the UDA to return to its violent habits of the early

1970s. They had their way. The UDA would increase the level of its violence until it was killing more people than the Provisionals.

• 4 •

AS SINN FEIN sought a way out of the political impasse, a series of meetings began between John Hume and Gerry Adams. The two were brought together by Father Alex Reid, a west Belfast priest whom Sinn Fein trusted in spite of his opposition to violence. Adams and Hume first met in January 1988 and were later joined in their deliberations by other representatives of their parties. Hume's aim was to impress upon Adams his view that Britain's role in Northern Ireland had fundamentally changed and that there was no justification for the armed campaign. The Anglo-Irish Agreement hinged on consent, and the British government had accepted that if the majority wanted a United Ireland, then it would effect the legislation necessary to bring it about. In other words, Britain was now "neutral" on the question of a United Ireland. He argued that the task was to persuade the Unionists that a United Ireland was to their benefit. This could not be achieved through terrorism. Hume envisaged a process that would include representatives from all parties with a mandate, convened under the auspices of the British and Irish governments. But it could take place only if violence ended. He told Adams that if the IRA called a cease-fire, it would change the situation drastically and open up all sorts of political opportunities for Nationalists.

Dishearteningly for Hume, Adams replied that there was no chance of a cease-fire. His arguments were based on the standard republican analysis that the Anglo-Irish Agreement's primary function was to consolidate British rule in Ireland by co-opting the Irish government to help it maintain control. Britain, republicans still insisted, was the problem. It had strategic concerns about preventing "another Cuba" from appearing. However, no one other than the extreme right wing of the Conservative Party took seriously Sinn Fein's aspirations for a Cuban-style revolutionary socialist republic. The party's subsequent development showed that not even Sinn Fein took them seriously.

In the exchange, republicans found it more and more difficult to explain their view that somehow Britain was strengthening its hold over Northern Ireland by diluting its sovereign claims, which was one of the effects of the agreement.

The broad political establishment did not welcome the first Hume-Adams dialogue. Within the SDLP itself there were some members who feared that in the aftermath of the Enniskillen massacre the dialogue was helping the republican movement repair its public image. Sinn Fein would benefit politically because Hume was seen to take them seriously. The Unionists were outraged and accused the SDLP leader of throwing a political lifeline to terrorists. The Irish government, too, was uneasy. But for Hume it was of paramount importance to find a way of bringing the republican movement into the political process. He knew there could be no settlement with the IRA still active.

As their talks progressed, the two developed a level of trust. "When I first started talking to Adams," Hume recalled, "I found him to be totally straightforward in what he said to me, and we built a strong personal trust in one another, even though we had different opinions on many matters. It was this mutual regard and trust that was crucial to our success."[21] The first Hume-Adams initiative was stillborn. The "success" would not come for another six years.

• 5 •

THE PROVISIONAL IRA, more and more restricted in its ability to carry out operations in Belfast and throughout Ulster generally, constantly sought other fronts in which to extend its campaign. It carried out a handful of attacks in Europe from the late 1970s, claiming several lives, including that of the British ambassador to the Netherlands, Sir Richard Sykes, and his nineteen-year-old Dutch valet, Krel Straub. But European operations did not seriously get under way until the late 1980s. In 1987 a bomb exploded outside a British army base in West Germany. The following year, the Provisionals planned a major operation in Gibraltar—using its new supplies of Semtex. The bomb maker in charge of the operation was Danny McCann, the Belfast Brigade's explosives officer.

It was a foolish choice. McCann was well known to the Special Branch as an active republican and under steady surveillance. In July 1987 he was involved in a scheme to blow up a boat that was used by off-duty British soldiers in the seaside town of Bangor, County Down, but it fell through. A month later McCann, along with Sean Savage, gave E4A surveillance teams the slip long enough to murder two Special Branch officers in a bar in the docks area of Belfast. In December McCann assassinated UDA chief

John McMichael. But surveillance was stepped up, and it led to the revelation of the Provisionals' Gibraltar plans, which also involved Savage and two women, Mairead Farrell, who had served time for a bombing attack in the 1970s, and a woman who is currently a prominent member of Sinn Fein. The ASU moved south to a safe house in the west of Ireland before leaving to carry out their operation in Gibraltar.

The quartet wanted to plant a huge car bomb not far from a changing-of-the-guard ceremony. On March 5, SAS men followed the second woman as she did a "recce" of the target area before going into a nearby chapel to light a candle. The next day, as Farrell, Savage, and McCann walked away from a parked car, near where the ceremony was due to take place, the SAS struck, shooting dead all three. The fourth—the woman who was seen in the chapel—escaped.

The killings outraged many people. Catholics condemned them as cold-blooded murder and argued that the three could have been arrested. Anger increased when it was discovered that the parked car did not have any explosives. However, on March 8, two days after the shootings, a car linked to the ASU was found in a lock-up garage in Marbella, just across the Spanish border; it contained detonating equipment and 140 pounds of Semtex, the biggest Semtex bomb ever uncovered in the history of the Troubles. Had it exploded, it would have caused horrendous casualties.

McCann, Savage, and Farrell all came from west Belfast, where thousands gathered as a mark of respect when their bodies were returned. Their deaths set off a chain reaction of violence. At the funeral on March 15, Michael Stone, a UDA gunman, attacked the mourners in the cemetery, hurling grenades and firing wildly, creating pandemonium in an assault that killed three people. Four days later, at the funeral of one of Stone's victims, two off-duty British officers drove into the funeral cortege and in panic mounted the pavement, then reversed. The mob quickly surrounded their car, thinking another loyalist or SAS attack was imminent, and dragged the men away to a nearby football field where they were stripped and brutally beaten. The bloodied and almost naked captives were bundled into a taxi and driven to an empty field where they were dragged out and shot in the head. A British army helicopter videoed the whole horrifying spectacle from between 500 and 1,500 feet above, including the final scene: the dark form of a priest standing over the corpse of one of the dead who lay stretched out, stripped and blood-covered on the grimy, rubble-strewn vacant lot.[22] There was almost universal disgust at the mob killings, and west Belfast became for some the heart of darkness. But for west Belfast the response of the mob was the visceral reaction of an embattled community driven to desperation by decades of violence.

In 1988 the Provisional IRA leadership gave itself a timetable of about two years to show whether or not the armed campaign was capable of breaking the stalemate.[23] A bombing in June that killed six soldiers and another that August that claimed the lives of eight prompted Thatcher to consider the reintroduction of internment without trial, which the IRA would have regarded as a propaganda victory, whatever its military ramifications. The prime minister was dissuaded only with some effort from taking this retrograde step. There were attacks in the Netherlands in which three off-duty members of the RAF were killed. And on August 1, for the first time in almost five years, an IRA bomb went off in Britain, killing a soldier and wounding nine in an attack on a barracks in north London.

Instead of internment, the government banned Sinn Fein representatives from being interviewed on radio and television. The ban also applied to spokespersons for the UDA and Republican Sinn Fein. The government also announced it was curtailing the right to silence. Northern Ireland Secretary of State Tom King said that the courts would now be allowed to give "whatever weight they think proper" to a suspect's refusal to answer questions.[24] Civil liberties groups were outraged at this erosion of the judicial principle of innocent until proven guilty. It was actually unpopular even with the government ministers who took the measure in order to "divert" Thatcher from reintroducing internment.[25] The army also launched a massive sweep through Catholic areas of the province, searching 700,000 vehicles and 1,100 buildings, and on occasion using pneumatic drills to dig up the floors of houses as they tried to unearth the Libyan arms shipments.[26]

The Provisionals saw these and other measures as proof of growing British desperation. Danny Morrison, the Sinn Fein spokesman and editor of *An Phoblacht,* was in a seemingly confident mood when he claimed:

> *There is a recognition that we can break the will of the British government to remain in Ireland. There's a tremendous sense of confidence within the nationalist community and particularly*

> *that section of it which owes its allegiance to the republican movement. . . . Next year, August 1989 will be the 20th anniversary of the open deployment of British troops on the streets here. . . . That represents twenty years of British military and political failures to stabilize the North in British interests.*

When asked if he still thought that the IRA had a hope of defeating the British, he answered:

> *I know there is. I wouldn't be involved in a struggle if there was nothing but the prospect of a glorious failure . . . the struggle goes on. And we sniff in our nostrils the smell of success.*[27]

Morrison, a self-confident and shrewd propagandist, was aware of the obverse of his argument—that almost twenty years of IRA violence had failed to dislodge Britain, which seemed in fact to have regained enough control of the situation to restore a sense of normality. This was noticeable to a visitor to Belfast in late 1988. The downtown area was bustling, the shops were brightly lit and busy with shoppers, and traffic poured down the roads, where army checkpoints were just another irritation for rush-hour commuters. Of course, the more normal the city seemed, the greater the propaganda benefits the Provisionals could derive from disruptive bombings that "proved" that this normality was a sham.

Their campaign was being waged at an increasing political cost, which in the cold calculations of the propaganda war were measured in civilian lives lost, most of them Catholic. In a period of nine months in 1988, the IRA killed eighteen in botched operations. It wiped out an entire family—Robin Hanna, forty-four; his wife, Maureen, also forty-four; and their six-year-old son, David—in a huge bomb blast that disintegrated them and their car not far from where Chief Justice Gibson and his wife were murdered in 1987. The car they had been driving was mistaken for that of the actual target, another high-ranking judge. On the Falls Road itself a sixty-year-old woman, Elizabeth Hamill, and a twenty-four-year-old man, Eamon Gilroy, were killed when an IRA bomb went off prematurely near the public baths. Adams was spending more and more of his time fending off questions about what the Provisionals chose to call "mistakes" and trying to give a rationale for continuing a campaign that was taking such a toll. He called the sequence of civilian deaths an "unfortunate coincidence of tragic accidents," reiterating an "appeal" to the IRA "to pursue the armed struggle in such a way that it helps either to broaden the base or doesn't obstruct the broader aims of the movement." He said it would have to "put its house in order." But the "accidents" continued and claimed the lives of three Derry Catholics who triggered a booby-trap bomb placed in a neighbor's apartment in an elaborate plot to lure troops or RUC men to their deaths.

The political toll on Sinn Fein was more obvious in the Irish republic. In a general election in February 1989, the party's vote collapsed. It polled a poor 1.2 percent of the vote.[28] It was a bitter blow to the leadership's hopes of breaking out of the political ghetto. The strategy of the Provisionals, as evolved under Adams, of building a broad nationalist front was unable to overcome the reluctance of southern Irish voters to put their trust in a movement responsible for atrocities such as the Enniskillen massacre. The conclusion was obvious: The armed campaign was the chief obstacle to political success in the Irish republic. To analyze the obvious is difficult enough, but to face up to the consequences of that analysis—that the armed campaign would have to end sooner rather than later—was something that in 1989 the Provisional Army Council was unable to do.

The year 1989 provided lots of opportunity for reflection on these and other matters relating to the Troubles as the twentieth anniversary approached of the introduction of British troops to the streets of Derry and Belfast. It marked the longest uninterrupted period of conflict that Ulster—and Ireland—had sustained in centuries. In September the Northern Ireland political magazine *Fortnight* marked the anniversary with a front cover that reflected the general mood of deep pessimism. AND NOW FOR THE NEXT TWENTY YEARS, it proclaimed, illustrating the sentiment with a photograph of a boy wearing a balaclava and carrying an automatic rifle almost as large as himself. His proud parents were political inertia and political murder, and he was striding into the future with alarming confidence.

The issue contained an open letter from Gerry Adams to Margaret Thatcher, a "wee 20-years-on-note," as he described it with a rather self-conscious attempt at folksy bravado. It proclaimed the mood of west Belfast as being as defiant as ever as it entered "the 21st year of this phase of British military rule." He wrote of the "happy and confident aura" among local Nationalists as they celebrated the annual West Belfast

Festival with poetry, music, and dancing. "In a way I think we were like marathon runners who hit and cleared the wall and discovered to our surprise that we have lots of stamina left. It was fitting therefore that we celebrate 20 years of resistance with such joy and good humour." The letter ended: "Until then, take care. You'll be hearing from us again," a somewhat sinister note considering that Adams's organization had tried to murder her.

The British had already heard from the Provisionals during the anniversary year, but it was not a message set to the refrain of an Irish tune. In March they claimed the lives of the two highest-ranking RUC officers to die in the Troubles; in July they detonated a one-thousand-pound car bomb outside the High Court in central Belfast; and at the end of September a time bomb killed eleven soldiers in a barracks in Deal, County Kent, England—the worst loss of life for the army since 1979.

An even more drastic lapse in British security occurred when the Provisional IRA was given an unprecedented opportunity to assassinate members of the Royal family, including Her Majesty the Queen, Prince Philip, and Prince Charles. In the summer of 1990 a member of the IRA working in England was hired as a food supervisor in Green Park, a banqueting hall near the Mall in London that was often used as a venue by the Royal family. He got the job after going through two MI5 security checks. Although active in the IRA for several years, he had never been arrested, nor had any member of his family.

Before important events, Scotland Yard gave the staff security briefings. Police officers instructed the bemused IRA man in how to detect bombs and recognize a detonator. Since he had already been involved in several bombing operations himself, it was quite unnecessary. The four-man ASU to which he belonged had been operating in England for about a year; it had carried out a series of attacks, including an attempt on the life of Sir Anthony Farrar-Hockley, commander of land forces in Northern Ireland between 1970 and 1972. It would later bomb Victoria Railway Station in London, killing a passerby.

Part of his job was to help set up the tables for the banquet. He was able to look at the schedule of upcoming events for that summer, complete with lists of those attending, which included Her Majesty the Queen and Prince Philip. Prince Charles was being honored on another occasion, and there were events involving leading members of the British government, including Michael Portillo, a cabinet minister. In September there was to be a conference on international terrorism.

Realizing the potential to strike a terrible blow at the heart of the British state, he returned to Northern Ireland for a weekend, pretending it was for a sister's birthday. He took with him a list of possible targets, at the top of which was the Queen and Prince Philip. The Provisionals' intelligence chief at Northern Command told him it was "too hot" for them to handle. He would have to cross the border to speak directly to the GHQ staff. A meeting was arranged in Dundalk. After showing the GHQ representative the target list, he was promptly told that the Royal family was a "no-no." They were not regarded as legitimate targets.[29] But the Provisional leadership was interested in the conference on international terrorism scheduled for September 27 because it would involve, among others, Professor Paul Wilkinson, who had acted at times as an adviser to the Thatcher government. Also attending would be high-ranking officers from Italian, French, and German police forces, as well as the RUC, Scotland Yard, and the London Metropolitan Police. The bomb, consisting of four pounds of Semtex, was smuggled into the banquet hall in a lunch box and placed under the lectern. It was timed to go off at 10:30 A.M. when Wilkinson was due to speak. However, it was located and defused.[30] But it was a propaganda victory for the Provisionals and a tremendous political embarrassment for the government, which put half a million pounds' ransom on the head of the former Green Park table setter.

Not long after *Fortnight* carried Adams's jokey and defiant epistle to Mrs. Thatcher, a very different view emerged of the republican position and its prospects from a source within the Belfast IRA. It was contained in a secret "comm" smuggled out of Crumlin Road prison in early 1990. The comm was written on a tiny piece of cigarette paper and directed to a veteran republican requesting assistance for an escape attempt, a previous one having failed. The sender, a high-ranking member of the Provisionals' Belfast Brigade, approached the veteran rather than go through the brigade itself because a "number of significant R.U.C. 'successes' in Belfast and elsewhere recently i.e. the abortive Crum prison break, the arrest of Morrison & co plus a number of abortive op[s] like ours. Our conclusion is the B.B may well be compromised."[31] The comm goes on to ask for stun guns, wigs, and a simple means for making a facial disguise. But it is the closing words that are interesting:

> *Hoping that this talk of bringing the armed struggle to a conclusion that McGuinness and co. are talking about bears fruit as I've thrown the hands up on at least two occasions. But I've an awful feeling this war is set for at least another decade. Whether we have the ability to break out of the containment the Brits are imposing on the war I think is crucial to the ultimate success/failure of the conflict. At the present I'm not optimistic of our ability to do so. You would not believe the change in attitude and resolve of the Northern nationalist community regarding their commitment to the war.*

The comm contains none of the hollow bravado of Adams's letter, a pose for public consumption. The reality was that after twenty years the Provisionals were being contained, and their support base was wearying of the endless violence. An especially vicious series of operations in late October using human car bombs suggested the desperate lengths to which the Provisionals were prepared to go to break out of the containment being imposed on them. On three different occasions the IRA strapped men into bomb-laden vehicles. One of them, Patrick Gillespie, a forty-two-year-old Catholic who worked in the canteen of a British army base in Derry, was forced to drive to a checkpoint on the Donegal border a few miles from the city. As Gillespie neared the checkpoint in the early hours of October 24, the Provisionals armed the bomb by remote control. Four minutes later, as the soldiers approached, the one-thousand-pound device exploded, blowing him to bits along with five soldiers. His body was never found. Another soldier died in a similar attack in south Down, but the driver managed to escape with a broken leg. In a third attack, the bomb failed to explode. Even in a society where the language of condemnation was by now exhausted and horror had grown monotonous, the manner of Mr. Gillespie's death made decent people shudder.

The fact that the Derry Provisionals were responsible for this atrocity did not discourage the British government from secretly opening up direct contacts with Martin McGuinness, their overall commander, at around the very time it took place. They used a line of communication that dated back to the cease-fire negotiations of 1974–75 and was used during the hunger strikes in 1980–81. When the approaches were made, beginning in mid-1990, McGuinness was a member of the Provisional Army Council and head of the IRA's Northern Command. "We thought that this was only an opening approach aimed at picking up on the bad situation between us since the hunger strikes, and we received some general and occasional oral briefings on the British position during this time," wrote McGuinness.[32] However, the contacts would prove to be the opening moves in a complex endgame, soon involving Adams, Hume, the Irish government, and the U.S. administration. These moves would eventually bring a halt to the twenty-five-year-old IRA campaign and set the stage for the most ambitious attempt so far to settle the Ulster crisis.

PART III

THE PERILOUS PATH TO PEACE

· SEVEN ·

THE TWILIGHT OF THE ARMED CAMPAIGN

1990–1994

FEW GUESSED as the new decade dawned that the end of the Provisional IRA's long war against Ulster was in sight. The tradition of physical force that had endured for two centuries within Irish republicanism was in its last days. But if anything, the opposite seemed to be happening. With a dramatic series of bombings, the Provisionals broke out of the containment the British were imposing on them.

Bombing Britain, the IRA believed, was the key to keeping pressure on the British government. The Army Council gave Kevin McKenna, the Provisionals' chief of staff, the go-ahead to put all the resources he could command into English operations and create "mayhem," according to a veteran republican activist.[1]

In the 1990s, all operations in Britain were under the control of the South Armagh Provisionals. South Armagh was regarded as a safe base because so far it had been impervious to penetration from the intelligence services, which were making inroads elsewhere, especially in Belfast. Matériel was supplied from south Armagh, and all volunteers involved in the British campaign, whether from Derry or Belfast or Dublin, were placed under the authority of the commanding officer of the South Armagh IRA. Those chosen to join the overseas ASUs were usually Provisionals with no security trace on them, such as the volunteer involved in the Green Park plot.[2] When their period of "active service" in Britain was finished, they were brought back to south Armagh or its environs (often Dundalk or County Monaghan) for debriefing.

In February 1991 an IRA mortar shell landed in the back garden of 10 Downing Street during a cabinet meeting to discuss the Gulf War. The same unit that was responsible for this affront to British security was also involved in a firebomb campaign on the London subway system that caused massive disruptions in the weeks leading up to Christmas. But the most massive strike came over a year later, on April 10, 1992. A bomb consisting of one ton of explosives constructed in south Armagh and smuggled into England exploded in the Baltic Exchange, the financial heart of London, killing three people and causing £750 million worth of damage. A second bomb went off the same day next to an overpass in the north of the city. A report in *The Belfast Telegraph* later revealed that the Baltic Exchange bomb cost more in insurance claims than all the bombs that had exploded—some ten thousand of them—in Northern Ireland between 1969 and 1992.

The Provisionals' renewed bombing campaign in Northern Ireland was also proving costly to the government. In 1991 a series of large car bombs in Banbridge, County Down; Kilrea, County Derry; Craigavon, County Armagh; and Belfast—where two went off within two weeks in the city center in December—forced the government to freeze public spending in certain areas in order to drain off sufficient funds to pay the £2 million in damage that the IRA's attacks had inflicted on housing. But the bombing that caused the most outrage occurred on November 2 when the Provisionals left a twenty-pound Semtex device inside the military wing of Musgrave Park Hospital in south Belfast, killing two army medics and injuring several children in a nearby civilian ward. Demands for the reintroduction of internment grew louder, mainly from the Unionist Party. But there was also some support from within the army for the measure. An unnamed high-ranking security source told the London *Independent on Sunday* that without the reintroduction of internment, the police and army had no hope of beating the IRA.[3]

The government did not give in to internment demands, partly because not long after the gloomy prognosis was being aired in the *Independent on Sunday,* the Special Branch in Belfast recruited a major source within the IRA leadership. Internment was not needed. But the government was also reluctant to use it because it feared the political backlash. Chiefly, it did not want to upset the delicate, preliminary approaches being made in secret toward the IRA. So the public response to the rising wave of violence was to dispatch several hundred extra troops to patrol Northern Ireland's increasingly edgy capital and put fourteen hundred members of the UDR on full-time duty.

The hospital incident highlighted the increasingly contradictory position in which Adams was finding himself as he struggled to marry the armed campaign with ordinary politics as west Belfast's MP. The day after the IRA bombed the hospital, Adams made two statements. In the first he refused to condemn the bomb attack, saying that the hospital was a "British military installation." In the second he criticized a proposal to take Belfast's leading hospital, the Royal Victoria, which was in his constituency, out of Britain's National Health Scheme and turn it into a trust-funded institution. He said such a move "would be bad for the hospital, bad for workers, but particularly bad for patients." He claimed that "patient care will be severely affected." He made this statement just after television news viewers witnessed pictures of rescue workers digging children from the rubble of the devastated ward; even as he spoke, doctors from Musgrave Park Hospital were forced to cancel operations because of the bomb. The juxtaposition was a study in contradictions so startling as to make an observer wonder if the republican movement had lost its grip on reality. There is no more serious way of affecting patient care at a hospital than by planting a bomb in it. But the political absurdity and the cost of the armed campaign were already obvious to the aparatchiks of Sinn Fein. The party no longer celebrated the IRA's terrorism with an Armalite in one hand and a ballot paper in the other; now its spokesmen more often than not said they could neither "condone nor condemn" it. Increasingly cornered apologists, they employed the evasive vocabulary of people who realize they are defending the indefensible. "Understanding" the reasons for the violence was often the best they could do.

A prominent Sinn Fein spokesman in Belfast, Richard McAuley, was unusually direct about the party's and the republican movement's dilemma: "We're not going to realize our full potential as long as the war is going on in the North and as long as Sinn Fein is presented the way it is with regard to armed struggle and violence. I think that is a reality that perhaps we weren't conscious or aware of back in the early '80s when we first got involved in electoral politics."[4]

The winter of 1991 was a gloomy one for Ulster. Headlines in the local papers screamed of a return to the dark days of the early 1970s when death squads stalked the streets, killing at random. There was good reason for this fear. The murder rate began to climb again, mainly thanks to a resurgence in loyalist assassinations. In the space of a few days in mid-November a forty-year-old Catholic woman and her sixteen-year-old daughter were burned alive after loyalist gasoline bombers attacked their home in a Protestant district; the Provisionals shot dead four Protestants; and the UVF killed three workers (two Catholics and, by accident, one Protestant, for which they apologized) as they left a factory near Lurgan, County Armagh. The UDA was also active again under the control of Joe English, a little pit bull terrier of a man. Behind him a pack of young bloods growled menacingly, hot to revenge themselves for republican attacks.

Nineteen ninety-one was the first year in which loyalist groups ran neck and neck with republicans in the grim race of death known as the Troubles. Of the ninety-eight political murders in Northern Ireland, loyalists were responsible for forty-one—almost 50 percent. During the late 1980s, loyalist groups had been responsible for about 25 percent of the deaths. But from 1992 to 1994, loyalists established themselves as Ulster's most prolific killers. Sinn Fein councilors and party members were increasingly targeted; between May and September the UDA murdered four leading members of the party. On one of the rare occasions when loyalists managed to successfully target an actual republican operator, a UVF hit squad murdered Martin O'Prey, an ex-INLA gunman. (O'Prey was once active with Gerard Steenson but had since joined another splinter group.)

The safest thing to be in Ulster in the 1990s was a member of the security forces because fewer and fewer of them fell victim to republican groups. Only nine soldiers and policemen died violently in Ulster in 1992, representing just 10 percent of all victims.[5]

The reemergence of the loyalist threat was linked to several developments. The old leadership of Tyrie was overthrown at the same time that a resupply of weapons and explosives fell into the hands of the UDA and UVF. Behind the scenes another factor came into play. One of the British army's top agents within the UDA, a forty-four-year-old former British soldier named Brian Nelson, had been exposed and brought to trial.

Nelson's arrest in 1990 was the result of another inquiry into the RUC after allegations that the police force was colluding with loyalist groups. Police files on suspected republicans had gone missing, turning up in the hands of loyalist killers. When the UDA murdered Loughlin Maginn on August 25, 1989, they justified it by producing an RUC file identifying him as a republican. The crisis occurred just as Sir John Hermon, who successfully brought the RUC through the Stalker affair, was retiring and his replacement, Sir Hugh Annesley, was taking up his post. Annesley, a Dublin-born Protestant, was a quiet-spoken, cautious, and low-key diplomat, in contrast to his predecessor. When an investigation into the leaks was announced, the new chief constable was determined to make sure it did not get bogged down in controversy as had the Stalker inquiry. An English police officer, John Stevens, selected by Annesley himself, was put in charge of the inquiry.

The Special Branch was not happy that for the second time in five years its most sensitive area of operations—the compilation and handling of intelligence—would be exposed to an outsider. Stalker's investigation had made public vital aspects of how the RUC fought the twilight war. The Special Branch was afraid of a repeat performance. Their fears were not misplaced. Stevens's inquiry cleared the police of charges of collusion. For the most part, the files that were leaked had passed through the hands of UDR members, many of whom were found to have loyalist associations. The inquiry undoubtedly helped convince the government to dissolve the UDR, which it did in 1992, merging it with the Royal Irish Rangers.[6]

Police fears about damage to intelligence operations were heightened when, in early 1992, Nelson was brought to trial on charges of murder and conspiracy to murder, as a result of the Stevens inquiry. Most sensationally, it was revealed that Nelson's handlers in British army intelligence did not act on information he gave them concerning three murder plots. One of those killed as a result was Patrick Finucane, a well-known Belfast lawyer from a prominent republican family. (His brother, Dermot, who escaped from the Maze in 1983, was head of the Provisionals' Southern Command.) Finucane routinely defended paramilitaries, especially republicans. It was alleged that while the RUC was interrogating loyalist suspects, the detectives would say things like "Now that Finucane, he's a real IRA man," with the clear suggestion that he should be shot.

During Nelson's trial it was claimed that he had been involved in gathering intelligence about Finucane for the UDA. On February 12, 1989, UDA gunmen broke into the Finucane home and shot him dead in his kitchen in front of his family.

Allegations of cover-up and collusion once more hit the intelligence community. The RUC defended itself, insisting that the army did not pass on the information needed to prevent the planned murder. In spite of the setting up of the TCGs, rivalry between the various intelligence-gathering wings of the security forces was still endemic. It is feasible that army intelligence officers deliberately withheld information from the RUC Special Branch in order to protect their agent. The RUC itself has frequently withheld information from other agencies, including BOX (MI5) if it thought that it might compromise one of its operations or agents. (In fact, this rivalry would lead to a crisis between the Special Branch and MI5 in 1994.)

Murder charges against Nelson were dropped, and he was sentenced to ten years for conspiracy to murder. But the case left a cloud hanging over both the RUC and army intelligence concerning the handling of information and the relationship that its agents have with the terrorists they are supposed to be thwarting.[7] As with cases involving IRA informers, it exposed the uncomfortable fact that in order to maintain their cover within paramilitary groups, people working for the security forces often had to commit crimes.

The exposure of Nelson severed the flow of information from one important source about UDA activities, and as loyalist killings increased, Ken Maginnis, the UUP spokesman on security, blamed the government. In a speech at the party's 1991 conference, he accused the government of "being responsible for a great deal of the terrorism in Northern Ireland." He alleged that the Stevens inquiry "blew the identity of people who were providing the Royal Ulster Constabulary with information" about loyalist gangs.[8] Maginnis, who was himself the target of several IRA assassination plots, was a former UDR man with close contacts in the security forces; no doubt he was reflecting the feeling of police and army officers that once more politics was allowed to take priority over security concerns.

Recruitment to both the UDA and UVF increased. Continued anger at the Anglo-Irish Agreement, frustration at the security forces' failure to defeat the IRA, and a rise in Protestant working-class unemployment in Belfast contributed to what some were calling Protestant "alienation" from the state they once saw as their own. The UDA became active again in areas such as east and south Belfast where it had been relatively quiet since the 1970s.

On January 17, 1992, near a crossroads called Teebane in east Tyrone, the Provisional IRA bombed a busload of Protestant building workers, employed by the Henry Brothers company to work on security force bases. The six hundred pounds of explosive killed eight workers (ages twenty-two to sixty-one), scattering body parts over several fields, where the mutilated lay screaming in pain in the winter darkness. The young turks of the UDA swore revenge. Just after lunchtime on February 5, a small crowd gathered in a betting shop on the Lower Ormeau Road in south Belfast, a once-Protestant district that was now Catholic. It was the scene of many sectarian killings, including the bombing of the Rose and Crown pub, next door to the betting shop, which left six Catholics dead on May 2, 1974. As the bettors were watching a race, two UDA gunmen walked into the shop, armed with a rifle and handgun, and opened fire. In the small space, the dead and wounded fell on top of each other. "It was horrifying," said an ambulance driver who arrived at the scene shortly after the shooting. "There were bodies all over. . . . It was so bad we could hardly get into the place." Another witness said tersely, "It was like a butcher's shop." Five people lay dead and nine seriously wounded. The dead ranged in age from a fifteen-year-old boy to an old-age pensioner of sixty-six. When the RUC arrived to cordon off the area, the grieving and sometimes hysterical relatives greeted them with hostility. "Bastards," one screamed, and another shouted, "I hope one hundred of you are blown to bits by the IRA tonight."[9]

The UDA issued a claim of responsibility under its nom de guerre UFF and said, "Remember Teebane," and threatened more to come. By February 16, thirty-one people had been killed, compared with three for the same period in 1991. An off-duty RUC man went berserk and shot dead three people in the Sinn Fein headquarters in west Belfast, and the SAS ambushed and wiped out a four-man IRA ASU near Coalisland, County Tyrone, after it attacked the local RUC station. Little did anyone realize at the time, but these four would be the last victims of the SAS in Ulster.

For the first time since 1976 the British government called a security conference with the heads of the four major parties in Northern Ireland, but it produced nothing other than the perennial demands from Unionists for more security and from nationalists that the UDA, still legal, should be outlawed. Six hundred extra troops were sent to the province.

The government, however, finally took the step that many nationalists had been calling for for over twenty years: It banned the UDA on August 10, 1992. By this time the group had killed around five hundred people (the exact figure is impossible to estimate), and over one hundred of its members were in jail serving life sentences for murder. Yet as late as 1988 a Northern Ireland office briefing paper, prepared for foreign correspondents, could say of the UDA: "There is no evidence that it is engaged in organizing terrorist attacks."[10] The government's reluctance to acknowledge the real nature of the UDA may have been the result of its wish to keep the world's attention focused on the Provisional IRA as the cause of the conflict. Or it may have thought that as a legal organization, the UDA could be more easily persuaded to go in a political direction, which it at times gave hints of doing. There was also a fear that driving the UDA underground would remove the more "moderate" leaders and replace them with young hotheads. By 1992 this had already happened, and the authorities perhaps concluded they had nothing to lose.

Ban or no ban, the killings continued until, by the year's end, ninety-one new names (including six victims in England) had been added to the Ulster Troubles' death list—seventy-nine of them civilians.

After almost a quarter of a century of violence, despair had turned the face of Ulster into a mask of resignation contorted at times by rage.

· 2 ·

POLITICS HAD NOT gone away, however. Both behind the scenes and in public, minds were focused as never before on finding a way to end the political stalemate.

In 1989, Peter Brooke became secretary of state for Northern Ireland. Brooke, an affable upper-class sort with a slight speech defect, seemed far too good-natured to make an impression on the calloused hide of Ulster politics. He was a lover of cricket; whatever might be said about Ulster politics, it was definitely *not* cricket. He soon provoked a reaction from the Unionists, who suspected he was a typical English softy, bland and gutless. In November 1989, one hundred days after he took office, he declared during a television interview that the IRA could not be beaten. "The first factor is that I would recognize," he said, "that in terms of the late twentieth-century terrorist, organized as well as the Provisional IRA have become, that it is difficult to envisage the defeat of such a force." A policy of containment allows normal life to go on, he mused, and meanwhile it might spark off among the terrorists a debate as to whether or not "the game had ceased to be worth the candle." He added that if violence did end, then the government would be "flexible and imaginative" in its response.[11] Brooke was reiterating what many of his predecessors had come to accept as a given fact of life about the Ulster situation—the policy of "an acceptable level of violence," as Reginald Maudling had put it almost twenty years earlier. Predictably, Brooke's broad hint about what would follow if the IRA gave up the Armalite entirely and embraced the ballot box exclusively provoked outrage from the Unionist community. But among the republicans it aroused cautious curiosity.

The British had reopened their secret channel of communication with the Provisional leadership, and in October 1990 the government's contact with the republican movement met with Martin McGuinness to tell him that a new contact would reactivate the "long-standing line of communication."[12] Just over a month later, after a leadership challenge, John Major replaced the Provisionals' old nemesis, Margaret Thatcher, as leader of the Conservative Party and prime minister of the government.

Thatcher had been Conservative leader since 1975 and prime minister since 1979. In that time she managed to alienate both communities—the Unionists because of the Anglo-Irish Agreement, and the Nationalists because of the hunger strikes—thus achieving a rare status in Ulster: Unionists hated her almost as much as Nationalists.

With the arrival of the more mild-mannered Englishmen, Major and Brooke, on the political scene, two separate political processes were initiated. In public, Brooke began a series of meetings with the four main parties—the SDLP, the UUP, the DUP, and the Alliance Party—in what most thought was a hopeless effort to reach a new constitutional settlement for Ulster. In secret, the government stepped up its contacts with the Provisional IRA. The aim of these contacts was to convince the Provisionals to end their armed campaign. A few days before Brooke was to make an important speech—indeed, it has since been seen as a watershed—the British secretly forwarded a copy of it to Sinn Fein. In the speech, given on November 9, 1990, Brooke declared that partition was "an acknowledgment of reality, not an assertion of national self-interest." Britain had no "selfish strategic or economic interest in Northern Ireland; our role is to help, enable and encourage." The British would not stand in the way of Irish unity if it came about with the consent of the people of Northern Ireland. Hume had long argued that the Anglo-Irish Agreement of 1985 showed that Britain was now "neutral" on the question of Irish unity. In discussions with Hume in 1988, Adams had demanded "proof." Brooke's speech, which was written after consultation with Hume, was an attempt to meet that demand.

The Provisionals wanted more than words. They asked that Britain abandon its support for what they called the Unionist "veto" over a united Ireland and begin the task of persuading Ulster's recalcitrant Protestants that unity was to their benefit. In Sinn Fein's view, it was unacceptable that the Unionists, referred to as a "minority" within the island of Ireland, should be allowed to hold such power over the country's future. The very fact that republicans engaged with the British at this level suggested that they were starting to accept Hume's analysis that Britain was no longer an imperial power aggressively defending its last colony but was, in fact, stuck there and was willing to disentangle itself if circumstances were right. In itself this represented a significant change in Sinn Fein's position. As significant as Brooke's speech and the republican response to it was the fact that the British had secretly shown it to Sinn Fein in advance. This was a gesture of trust, made at a time when the official statements from the government continued to denounce Sinn Fein and the IRA as terrorists.

Hume's influence was seen not only in Brooke's "no selfish interest" speech but within the structure of the Brooke talks themselves. The SDLP leader had long argued that the Northern Ireland problem could only be dealt with by taking into account three different strands or sets of relationships: the relationship between Catholics and Protestants, the relationship between Dublin and Belfast, and the relationship between Ireland and Britain. The crisis was a product of all three. If the Gordian knot of Ulster was to be untied, then it had to be picked apart one strand at a time. So Brooke's approach had three strands: Strand One would deal with relations between Northern Ireland's two communities, Strand Two with relations between Belfast and Dublin, and Strand Three with the relations of Dublin, Belfast, and London.

Between April 1991 and April 1992, the talks stumbled along. There were problems right from the start. The Unionists were going into the talks in the hope of finding a replacement for the hated Anglo-Irish Agreement, which their years of protest and boycott had failed to remove. The SDLP was taking part in the talks to strengthen the agreement, especially its Irish, cross-border dimension. In the end, only Strand One made any headway, with the four main parties discussing the form of any new devolved government for Northern Ireland.

As the process went on, it became apparent that Hume did not seem to be fully engaged in the negotiations. He disliked the emphasis on Strand One, fearing that it would push the talks toward an internal, Northern Ireland–only settlement, anathema to his thinking since the early 1970s. He was also afraid that the British would try to appease the Unionists by building up Strand One at the expense of the other relationships. But underlying this was a deeper and more fundamental concern about the viability of the whole process: The talks lacked a key player—the republican movement. Hume believed that unless Sinn Fein, the Provisionals' representatives, were included, then the process could not succeed in bringing peace and stability. The Unionists were prepared to offer considerable concessions to the SDLP—a power-sharing government, a Bill of Rights, and recognition of the Irish dimension. But Hume stalled, even though others in the SDLP were willing to cut a deal. As a result, the process collapsed in November 1992. The UUP has ever since remained bitter about what they saw as Hume's undermining of the Brooke talks. But for Hume the stakes were much higher than just finding a way of accommodating constitutional nationalism and unionism. By late 1992 he had already begun in secret a new round of contacts with Sinn Fein in the hope of ending the historical conflict forever.

While Sinn Fein was not part of the 1991–92 talks, they were engaged in their own talks with the British—a sort of Strand Four that London kept secret. The government made sure that the republican movement was kept abreast of developments. Its representative told Sinn Fein in April 1991 that the loyalist groups were about to call a temporary cease-fire to coincide with the beginning of the Brooke talks. He forewarned republicans of an upcoming Brooke speech in October that year, and in early 1992 promised them a copy of the British prime minister's scheduled address to Scottish Conservatives. In a long (undated) message from the government, it was recommended to the secretary of state that if the Provisionals decided to declare a Christmas cease-fire, then "we should prepare to respond very quickly." It spoke of the possibility of the need to take a "far-reaching political decision" in such an event.[13] The British kept the Provisionals fully informed as to the progress or lack of it that the Brooke talks were making throughout 1992, their representative usually expressing pessimism.

On October 26, 1992, the government allowed Sinn Fein to preview a speech that the new secretary of state, Sir Patrick Mayhew, was to make, but not until December 16. In it he said that if there was an end to the IRA campaign, then troops would be withdrawn and Sinn Fein would be included in the talks process. Republicanism would be able to "seek a role in the peaceful political life of the community." Communications between London and the Provisionals were stepped up in early 1993. On January 12 the government's representative assured the Provisionals that given the political risks the government was taking in contacting them, "they should be in no doubt that this indicates their seriousness in the whole thing. The conflict had been going on for too long. He said that the British government were not serious in 1974/75 but they were now."[14] For the Provisional leadership this admission about the events surrounding the previous, failed cease-fire was hardly news, since Adams and McGuinness had come to that conclusion seventeen years earlier. But it seemed significant that the British government's representative was ready to admit it.

He also stressed that "there was a conviction by senior civil servants that talks had to start. . . . It could not be done without a major gesture from republicans. They realized that an IRA cease-fire was a non-starter. He voiced his view that a suspension—an easing off—would start the ball rolling in a significant way. That republicans would be convinced in that time that armed struggle was not necessary any longer." On March 19, 1993, the British sent a nine-paragraph document to the Provisionals that outlined the conditions for their involvement in an "inclusive" peace process. When it spoke of the need for a "healing process" and the recognition that "no one has a monopoly of suffering," it actually used the same language as Hume and Adams. Paragraph four stated: "If violence had been genuinely brought to an end, whether or not the fact had been announced, then progressive entry into dialogue could take place." Such a process would not have a predetermined outcome, but if a united Ireland was agreed on, with the consent of the people of Northern Ireland, then the British government would "bring forward legislation to implement the will of the people here."[15]

A growing sense of urgency marks the subsequent communications. The Brooke talks' three-strand format had by then collapsed, and the new secretary of state, Sir Patrick Mayhew, was planning to meet with the parties bilaterally—a means that would allow Sinn Fein to enter the process more easily. The British representative told the Provisionals on March 23 that a recent speech by McGuinness "had triggered government action. Mayhew had tried marginalization, defeating the IRA, etc. That's gone. . . . Mayhew is now determined. He wants Sinn Fein to play a part not because he likes Sinn Fein but because it cannot work without them. Any settlement not involving all of the people North and South won't work. A North/South settlement that won't frighten unionists. The final solution is union. It's going to happen anyway. The historical train—Europe—determines that. We are committed to Europe. Unionists will have to change. This island will be as one."[16]

The government sought to reassure the Provisionals that there would be "no cheating involved" and referred again to the 1974–75 cessation and the failed negotiations between the IRA and the British during which, it was admitted, the government had deliberately set out to "con" the republicans, and succeeded. The representative said the government had authorized him to tell Sinn Fein that if agreement on ending the violence was reached at "six o'clock," then "clearance for meetings at the level of delegations would be forthcoming by one minute past six."

In spite of what they were hearing from the government's secret representative, who at times sounded like John Hume, the Provisionals moved cautiously. There was a noticeable decline in Provisional IRA activity in Ulster, but on April 24, 1993, they successfully exploded another huge bomb in the center of London, killing a press photographer who entered the evacuated area after it was cleared. The explosion caused hundreds of millions of pounds' worth of damage. At the beginning of May the Army Council sanctioned a two-week cessation of violence.[17] It was a gesture of goodwill to the British, and it gave them an opportunity to follow through on their previous statement that in the event of violence ending, they would respond rapidly.

The secret notification of the May stoppage was accompanied by an outline of Sinn Fein's basis for entering into dialogue with the British. It recognized "the concerns and perceived concerns" of the Unionists about an "Irish national democracy" but resorted to the traditional republican analysis that the cause of the continued instability in Ireland was Britain's defense of partition. Before there would be any hope of peace, "this must be addressed," the notification stated. Paragraph nine recognized "the most urgent issue facing the people of Ireland and Britain" was "the need for a genuine peace process which sets equality, justice and political stability as its objectives and has as its means, dialogue and all-embracing negotiations in the context of democratic principles. In attempting to progress towards that position we are prepared to be as reasonable and flexible as possible.

"In this context, we are willing to seriously consider any proposal which genuinely aims to set such a process in train and to take the accompanying political risks involved."[18]

Accordingly, the armed campaign was brought to a halt on May 11 for two weeks, one of the longest cessations in the history of the conflict. But despite the promise of immediate clearance for further talks, it wasn't until five days later that the Provisionals were told that the "May 10 position" had been accepted and that "a new draft British paper had been formulated" that would be put to John Major "at a special meeting on Tuesday 18 May in Downing Street." The British were becoming much less open with their documents at this stage and refused to hand over a draft of the new position to Sinn Fein. Meanwhile, the British contact man went off on a walking vacation. When he returned on May 24, he told the Provisionals that he was "absolutely disgusted" at the government's lack of action.

At the May 18 government meeting there was consternation among some ministers at the prospect of entering into dialogue with the Provisionals. Kenneth Clark, who was Major's chancellor of the exchequer, said it was "much too risky at the present time with the government under siege and if republicans were sincere about their intentions then the Prime Minister should hasten slowly to adopt such a radical departure from their previous publicly successful anti-terrorist line."[19] Mayhew also expressed "reservations" and vacillated between accepting the two-week cessation as sufficient and calling for a longer cease-fire. Major dithered and began working on a new plan which demanded that the Provisionals call a longer cessation. On June 3 a message to the Provisionals said that the government was working on another plan which because it was "radical . . . needed careful crafting." It was a far different response from the promised "one minute past six" clearance for delegate meetings that the British had promised in their March 23 communication.

The British representative expressed his "depression and anger . . . at our failure to respond to your brave and straightforward offer" of May 10.

Further communications continued throughout the summer, but the secret peace process was now mortally wounded, mainly thanks to Major's prevarications. During the summer, his government was clinging to power and became more and more dependent on the support of Ulster Unionists in Westminster, which made it even harder for him to risk any daring initiative such as opening talks with the Provisionals. At the same time, the revelation that John Hume and Gerry Adams had reached an accord in an "Irish peace initiative" began to eclipse other efforts—overt and covert—to launch a peace process. The prospect that after seventy years the two wings of Irish Nationalism, representing the constitutional and physical force traditions, were on the verge of reconciliation appeared now as the best hope that history's deadweight would finally be thrown off and progress made toward a lasting peace.[20]

The secret communications between Sinn Fein and the British government after 1992 occasionally referred to the "Irish initiative" without elaboration. In fact, by late 1992 there were effectively four sets of exploratory talks going on in Ulster, only one of which—the Brooke-Mayhew talks—was being held in the open. The other three, involving Sinn Fein and the British government, Sinn Fein and Hume, and Martin Mansergh, an envoy from Fianna Fail leader Albert Reynolds, who met with Sinn Fein leaders from 1988 to 1994, were all secret.[21]

After the fall of 1992, Hume was in contact with Mitchel McLaughlin, a high-ranking member of Sinn Fein in Derry, exploring the possibility of more thorough talks with the aim of reaching an understanding between the two parties. It was an ambitious goal; the republican movement had long castigated the SDLP as the "Stoop-Down-Low Party." In Derry, Hume's home was regularly daubed with slogans proclaiming "TRAITOR HUME." In 1987 young members of the Provisionals fired shotguns at the windows, attempting to smash the glass to enable them to hurl gasoline bombs into the downstairs rooms. The reinforced glass withstood the shots, but the attackers hurled their bombs anyway. The house went up in flames, and John Hume's wife and youngest daughter were lucky to escape with their lives. Hume himself was at a conference at the time.[22]

The historical roots of the animosity between them were deep. Republicans regarded the SDLP the way they did Fianna Fail in the Irish republic—as collaborators who had come to terms with British imperialism in order to forward their own selfish interests. As long as Sinn Fein saw itself as a revolutionary socialist party whose "cutting edge" was the Provisional IRA, able to take power in Ireland, then this attitude would remain. But from the late 1980s onward, Sinn Fein spokesmen moderated their criticisms of the SDLP. Sinn Fein's view of the republican movement's prospects began to change, thanks to continuing difficulties with the armed campaign and a sense of the party's growing isolation.

This sense was heightened in April 1992 when Adams lost his west Belfast seat to Dr. Joe Hendron of the SDLP in a British general election. Following a bitter campaign, Adams lost by a margin of just 589 votes. Hendron, a persevering but not very inspiring candidate, won the support of some Shankill Road Protestants, among whom he canvassed. This apparently proved crucial to the outcome. The Sinn Fein president and his supporters were outraged. Their reaction revealed not only anger but a feeling almost of persecution. Richard McAuley, Sinn Fein spokesman, declared: "Joe Hendron went to the electorate with a ballot paper in one hand and a loyalist death squad in the other." Adams himself reacted with anger and said that "the seat has been stolen from people of West Belfast. I am sure it will not be long until they get it back."[23] The implications of this went beyond the usual terms of electoral politics to identify the supporters of Sinn Fein as "the people" of the constituency, as if SDLP supporters who live there are somehow not really part of west Belfast. It was also a reflection of Sinn Fein's increasing anxiety that the electoral tide was decisively turning against it. In other constituencies there was a swing against Sinn Fein and toward the SDLP. Sinn Fein's overall share of the vote was reduced to 10 percent, compared to the SDLP's 23.5 percent. In Fermanagh–South Tyrone, a shrine of republican mythology as the seat formerly held by hunger striker Bobby Sands, the SDLP overtook Sinn Fein and became the largest nationalist party.

By ending its policy of abstentionism in the south, Sinn Fein had changed its attitude toward Fianna Fail's role in the settlement of the conflict; from 1988 it had begun to modify its approach to the SDLP. After the 1992 loss, it accelerated this change of course. Contacts with Hume were resumed in secret so that by late 1992, Sinn Fein could refer confidently to an "Irish" peace initiative in its secret communications with the British government.

The Mitchel McLaughlin–John Hume talks came to the attention of the RUC when they were investigating a Sinn Fein wiretap on Hume's telephone in December 1992. They were of sufficient interest to the authorities that the RUC Special Branch got permission from the government to tap Hume's telephone in January 1993. A report was drawn up and presented to Mayhew about the developing contacts between the SDLP leader and high-ranking Sinn Fein officials. Its contents led Mayhew to ask if Hume's antipathy to the Provisionals was sincere.[24]

Hume's contacts with Sinn Fein were finally revealed on April 10, 1993, when Adams was seen visiting his house in Derry, walking in through the door that six years earlier the Provisional IRA had firebombed. On April 24 the two issued a joint statement. It recognized the need for "national reconciliation" based on the

> *peaceful accommodation of the differences between the people of Britain and Ireland and the Irish people themselves.*
>
> *In striving for that end, we accept that an internal settlement is not a solution because it obviously does not deal with all the relationships at the heart of the problem.*
>
> *We accept that the Irish people as a whole have a right to national self-determination. This is a view shared by a majority of the people of this island, though not by all its people.*
>
> *The exercise of self-determination is a matter for agreement between the people of Ireland. It is the search for that agreement and the means of achieving it on which we will be concentrating.*
>
> *We are mindful that not all the people of Ireland share that view or agree on how to give meaningful expression to it. Indeed, we do not disguise the different views held by our own parties. . . . We have told each other that we see the task of reaching agreement on a peaceful and democratic accord for all on this island as our primary challenge.*[25]

The statement's language was more Hume than Adams, more SDLP than Sinn Fein. Its thesis accepted that a section of the Irish people—the Protestants—do not share the goals of Irish nationalists and that agreement had to be achieved on how to reach reconciliation with them. There is no hint of the traditional republican analysis of the role Britain has played in Irish history nor of the demand that Britain declare its intention to withdraw, which the IRA and its spokesmen insisted over the years was the key to bringing the armed campaign to an end.

The joint statement was the most dramatic indication so far of the tremendous transformation that was taking place within the Provisional movement—or at least within its upper echelons. It represented not only the beginning of the reconciliation of the two wings of Irish nationalism, constitutional and physical force, but effectively marked the ideological defeat of Provisional republicanism—the last significant exponents of the physical force tradition—and the beginning of its absorption into the wider spectrum of constitutional nationalist tradition, which had marginalized the IRA and Sinn Fein in the southern Irish state in the 1920s and 1930s.

A signal of the changing status of Sinn Fein was given in June 1993 when the Irish president, Mary Robinson, shook hands with Adams during a visit to west Belfast.

Hume and Adams continued to meet throughout the summer of 1993. On September 25 they issued a second statement, claiming that

> *our discussions, aimed at the creation of a peace process which would involve all parties, have made considerable progress. We agreed to forward a report on the position reached to date to Dublin for consideration. . . . We are convinced from our discussions that a process can be designed to lead to agreement among the divided people of this island, which will provide a solid basis for peace. Such a process would obviously also be designed to ensure that any new agreement that might emerge respects the diversity of our different traditions and earns their allegiance and respect.*

Just over a week later, the Provisional Army Council announced that it welcomed the Hume-Adams initiative. "If the political will exists or can be created," the IRA statement said, "it could provide the basis for peace. We, our volunteers and our supporters, have a vested interest in seeking a just and lasting peace in Ireland. Our objectives which include the right of the Irish people to national self-determination are well known. Our commitment remains steadfast."[26]

This was the most conciliatory statement from the IRA to date. Four days later, on October 7, Hume briefed the Irish government on his meetings and discussions with Adams and Sinn Fein. He reiterated his belief that the principles that he and the Sinn Fein leader had agreed to—contained in their April statement—could provide the basis for a peaceful settlement to the Ulster crisis. Later, the results of the Hume-Adams discussions were presented to John Major. But efforts to get both the Irish and British governments to endorse them failed throughout the fall of 1993.

The British told Dublin that "as long as Adams' fingerprints were on it," they couldn't touch the Irish peace initiative. With consummate hypocrisy, the London government was rejecting the initiative on the grounds that it involved negotiating with terrorists while it itself was still involved in secret talks with the Provisional IRA's leadership.

"I don't think they are going to run," Major commented at one point when asked about the Hume-Adams proposals. Albert Reynolds, whose shrewdness was born of years working as a provincial entrepreneur, now led the Irish government. Alarmed, he told Hume to stop "playing up" the Hume-Adams proposals. The Irish were engaged with the British in trying to devise their own proposals and found Hume's constant reiteration of what he declared was a recipe for peace embarrassing and unhelpful. In the meantime, both Dublin and London put pressure on the Provisional IRA to end its campaign. "We want to hear from the Provisional IRA that they are going to repudiate violence," said Major. "By that I don't mean a short-term cease-fire to be casually tossed away at the first opportunity. I mean the clearest possible indication that they have decided . . . to give up violence for good."[27]

The Provisionals' campaign produced another crisis in the peace process when on October 23 a bomb attack aimed at the UDA headquarters above a fish store on the Shankill Road went wrong. The bomb exploded prematurely inside the shop, killing the bomber and nine Protestants, including four women and two children, and injuring hundreds. It was a Saturday afternoon, the busiest time on the road.

There was a wave of loyalist retaliatory killings. Hume, who had staked his whole career on convincing the Provisionals to give up violence, had a nervous collapse and was hospitalized, suffering from exhaustion. It was perhaps the bleakest moment of the peace process and one of the grimmest since the conflict began. A week after the bombing, on a gray, sunless afternoon, one of the victims, seven-year-old Leanne Murray, was being buried. The bomber, Thomas Begley, a semiliterate twenty-three-year-old from Ardoyne in north Belfast, had grown up a short distance from the street where Leanne lived. As her small white coffin came slowly along the Shankill Road, Begley's funeral cortege crossed its path less than a hundred yards farther down. Gangs of youths who followed the Begley procession jeered and shouted obscenities at the Protestant mourners. How could the delicate hope for peace survive such hatreds? It seemed to have been buried in the rubble of the Shankill bomb, never to be exhumed. However, it would prove a hardier flower than most expected.

Oddly enough, it was nourished by the revelations, which appeared not long after the Shankill bombing, that for years the British government had been in secret contact with the IRA. Unionists were appalled, of course, but the reaction in the British parliament was less critical than many had predicted. The tale of secret IRA–British government diplomacy allowed the Dublin and London governments to address the Hume-Adams proposals more directly. Irish civil servants "rejigged" them, incorporating some of the proposals and jettisoning others. One of the civil servants, Fergus Finlay, brought them north where he showed them to the Reverend Roy Magee, who had been trying to persuade the UDA and UVF to call a cease-fire, and Gusty Spence, the former UVF leader. Spence had served more than seventeen years for the murder of Peter Ward and had been released in 1984. During his prison years he had been transformed from a sectarian thug into a rather thoughtful, tolerant man, anxious to find a way out of the endless cycle of violence. Magee and Spence suggested some additions to the draft. After a further period of intense working and reworking, it was presented to an expectant public on December 15, 1993, as the Downing Street Declaration.

It stated, "The ending of divisions can come about only through the agreement and co-operation of the people, North and South, representing both traditions in Ireland." The declaration committed both governments to "foster agreement and reconciliation, leading to a new political framework founded on consent and encompassing arrangements within Northern Ireland, for the whole island, and between these islands." Once more Britain reiterated that it had "no selfish strategic or economic interest in Northern Ireland." The statement declared that Britain's "primary interest" was "to see peace, stability and reconciliation established by agreement among all the people who inhabit the island, and they will work together with the Irish government to achieve such an agreement, which will embrace the totality of relationships." Further, Britain acknowledged that "it is for the people of the island of Ireland alone, by agreement between the two parts respectively, to exercise their right of self-determination on the basis of consent, freely and concurrently given, North and South, to bring about a united Ireland, if that is their wish."[28]

The declaration qualified the Hume-Adams reference to Irish self-determination by including the provision that the people of the north and the south were to exercise it separately, thus protecting the current wish of the Northern Ireland majority to remain within the United Kingdom; and it ditched the Sinn Fein demand that Britain act in the role of a "persuader" of the Unionists to join a unitary state. To further placate Protestants, it included paragraphs (at the suggestion of Spence and Magee) committing the Irish government "in the event of an overall settlement" to change the Irish constitution, removing territorial claims over Northern Ireland and removing any "elements in the democratic life and organization of the Irish state" that could be viewed as a "real and substantial threat" to the Protestant way of life. There was also a provision for the setting up of an institution that would give recognition to the "links between the people of Britain and Ireland as part of the totality of relationships." It opened the door to negotiation with all democratically mandated parties "which establish a commitment to exclusively peaceful methods and which have shown that they abide by the democratic process."

It was immediately clear to Unionists of all shades that this would include Sinn Fein. Coming so soon after the Shankill bombing, it outraged some Protestants, especially as Adams had been seen carrying the coffin of Begley, the IRA bomber, as it left his Ardoyne home. Yet the mainstream Ulster Unionist Party was restrained in its response and greeted the declaration with guarded acceptance. Others did not. "You have sold Ulster to buy off the fiendish republican scum and you are prepared to do this notorious deed with such speed that time is not even given for the Christian burial of their latest victim," Paisley wrote to Major after the declaration was published.[29] After thirty years of such fulminations, no one was surprised at Paisley's reaction. People were far more interested in seeing how Sinn Fein and the Provisional IRA would respond.

The Provisionals had rejected the Sunningdale Agreement outright in 1973. They had condemned, sometimes stridently, the Anglo-Irish Agreement twelve years later—but with some qualifications that left room for recognition that it indeed contained progressive elements. When confronted with the Downing Street Declaration, the Provisionals hesitated. The IRA had endorsed the Hume-Adams proposals as providing a basis for peace, but the declaration abandoned important parts of that initiative. Six days after the declaration, Adams held a press conference at which he criticized the Irish-British initiative for "its lack of mechanisms" and "its lack of a clear process." He said, "It needs to be clarified." Major rejected his appeal and said he would not enter into a dialogue with the republican movement about the declaration.

The Provisionals were trapped. The Downing Street Declaration was clearly insufficient for them to declare a cease-fire. But they could not reject it out of hand unless they were prepared to risk alienating their newfound constitutional nationalist allies in the SDLP and the Irish government. They continued to press for "clarification" while at the same time muting criticism of it. "More significantly, they did not encourage community groups or prominent personalities, such as Bernadette McAliskey, to identify the declaration for what in fact it was"[30]—a historic compromise of traditional republican goals or, some would say, an abandonment of those goals.

Among the political figures who supported the declaration as providing the basis for a permanent settlement of the Ulster conflict was America's new Democratic president, Bill Clinton, in office less than a year. While trying to win the Democratic nomination, Clinton attended a forum on Irish issues held in New York City in April 1992. During the discussion with Irish-American journalists and activists, including Martin Galvin, the prominent NORAID spokesman, Clinton more or less committed himself that if elected president, he would appoint a peace envoy to Northern Ireland and grant Gerry Adams a visa to come to the United States. Cynics dismissed Clinton's avowals as being no more reliable than the promises of a drunk. When Adams's application for a visa was rejected in May 1993, and talk about the peace envoy shelved, many British reporters in the United States chortled that once more the "special relationship" between the United Kingdom and the United States had triumphed over the gang of sentimental Irish Americans—the Irish lobby—which was pressing Clinton to put Ulster high on his administration's agenda. They declared victory too soon. The battle to place Northern Ireland on the U.S. agenda had hardly begun, as became clear that fall.

In September 1993, Bruce Morrison, a former congressman and Clinton confidant, led a delegation of Irish Americans to Belfast on a fact-finding mission. They were followed in late November by New Jersey lawyer Edmund Lynch, who was campaigning to have the visa ban on Adams lifted. On December 14, back in Washington, Lynch had a "confidential" meeting with Jane Holl, the director of European affairs on the National Security Council.[31] Holl told Lynch that Clinton would reconsider the visa ban if Adams was invited to the United States, which he was in January 1994. In spite of fierce opposition from the British government, Clinton lifted the ban and let Adams into the United States, where he received a rapturous reception during a weekend visit to New York. For Adams it was an impressive display of Irish-American power. In conjunction with the Irish government and the SDLP it would constitute a powerful pan-nationalist front that could wrest concessions from Britain. But before it could be fully harnessed, he knew the armed campaign would have to be brought to a close.

· 3 ·

BY EARLY 1994 two factors were pushing the Provisionals to end the armed campaign. The first was internal: the dynamic of their engagement in the peace process, which created expectations within the broad nationalist community that were becoming ever more difficult to disappoint. The second was external: the pressure from the security forces' intelligence services, which was crippling the ability of the IRA to conduct its operations, especially in Belfast. The truth was that by 1994 the RUC Special Branch and its allies in BOX were winning the twilight war.

Accurate intelligence built up through both human and technical sources allowed the RUC to acquire a detailed knowledge of the membership and structure of the Provisional IRA leadership. The organization's upper echelons were gradually penetrated. The seven-man Army Council was known and included one old hand, Joe Cahill, a founding member of the organization, along with Gerry Adams, Martin McGuinness, Gerry Kelly, Thomas "Slab" Murphy, Kevin McKenna, and Paddy Doherty. Belfast men (Kelly, Adams, Cahill) dominated the governing body.

Under the Army Council was ranged the PIRA's general headquarters, headed by Kevin McKenna as chief of staff. His two deputy chiefs of staff were Adams and McGuinness. The GHQ had ten departments: operations, intelligence, adjutant general, quartermaster general, training, finance, overseas operations, overseas liaison, engineering, and GHQ staff officers. Among the most important of these were the posts of quartermaster general, held by Micky McKevitt, which controlled the arms dumps; intelligence, headed by Belfast man Martin Lynch; operations, controlled by "Slab" Murphy; engineering, where new terrorist technology was developed and which was headed by Patrick "Val" Lynch and another man; and finance, with three officers, including Joe Cahill and a Belfast woman.

There were two separate commands, Northern and Southern. By late 1993, Martin McGuinness headed the first and Dermot Finucane (the Maze escapee) the second. Among Northern Command's officers were "Big John" Magee, a former British soldier from Belfast who was head of the Civil Administration Team (the tout hunters dedicated to rooting out informers and agents within IRA ranks), and Sean "Spike" Murray, a member of the Belfast Brigade who was a cousin of Danny McCann, shot dead in Gibraltar.

Successful surveillance and intelligence gathering cost the Belfast Brigade two of its chief bomb makers within a few months of each other. The first was arrested on January 11, 1992, with fifteen hundred pounds of explosives, and the second on July 23 while holding a bomb-making class. After that, the IRA's campaign using large car bombs against so-called commercial targets in the city center went into decline. (There were only two such explosions between July 1992 and May 1993.) A source, cited as "senior Special Branch," told a Belfast newspaper that "the IRA in Belfast is now facing operational difficulties because of a shortage of skilled activists in bomb making and other areas."[32] Meanwhile, sniping attacks against the security forces were rare in Belfast. When on August 2, twenty-four-year-old Damian Shackleton was shot dead in north Belfast, he was the first British soldier to die at the hands of an IRA sniper in Belfast in four years.[33] As of August 1992, the IRA had managed to kill only two soldiers and a policewoman. According to *The Irish Times* of August 13, 1992, it reflected "the lowest level of activity since the IRA campaign began in 1971."

The Provisionals were relying more and more on the do-it-yourself technology of small bombs made out of explosives packed into coffee jars and hurled like improvised grenades over the walls of RUC stations or at passing patrols. They inflicted injuries but hardly ever caused fatalities among the security forces.[34] The GHQ's engineering department developed a potentially more devastating weapon, the so-called Mark 15 mortar, or "barracks buster," as the Provisionals called it. It was unveiled in early 1993. It was sixteen inches in diameter and capable of hurling between three hundred and four hundred pounds of explosives over a sixty-foot fence or wall at a range of 150 yards. It was used in February 1993 to severely damage the Bessbrook RUC base in south Armagh, after several earlier attacks on other security installations failed. A subsequent attack on the Crossmaglen security base injured several soldiers. A civilian worker died when the barracks buster struck the RUC army base in Keady, County Armagh, on March 5, 1993. But the device, though menacing, was not enough to enable the Provisionals to regain the military initiative. It was never used in Belfast, the cockpit of the conflict.

If the Provisionals saw Belfast as the key to continuing the war, then they still saw London as the key to winning it—that is, instrumental in wearing down the British government's commitment to Ulster. For a long time the police had little or no successes in stopping IRA attacks in Britain. In 1992 the RUC's chief constable, Hugh Annesley, warned that there was a "void that is yet to be filled" concerning information on the IRA "mainland" ASUs.[35] But shortly after the Baltic Exchange bomb in April, the police arrested James Canning, a thirty-seven-year-old Scot, and uncovered a substantial arms and explosives dump in a garage in west London. He was linked to twelve bombings and later sentenced to thirty years' imprisonment. But small bombs continued to explode in London throughout the rest of 1992. There were five attacks between June and October. Between October 7 and October 12, there were eight, one of which killed a man in a pub in Covent Garden. However, shortly afterward a haul of Semtex, weighing seventy pounds, was found in a tea chest in a shop in east London. In November police thwarted two attempts to explode one-thousand-pound car bombs near the center of London. One of the targets was London's tallest building at Canary Wharf in the docklands area of the city.

The Provisional IRA remained defiant. In an interview with *The Guardian* on February 12, 1993, an IRA spokesman said that only "fortuitous luck" had been behind the success of the British police. The statistics he trotted out seemed to support him. In 1992 the organization exploded forty-six bombs in Britain, "causing 1,200 million pounds worth of damage, the collapse of insurance cover and the introduction of armed roadblocks in London. There were 1,000 occasions when commuter traffic and businesses ground to a halt" creating a "crisis in the heart of the British capital which has demonstrated that so long as interference in Irish affairs continues, then the consequences of that conflict will spill over and be visited on the national territory of the occupier." He also denied that there was any debate going on within the leadership about the continuation of the armed campaign. "Our discussions revolve around the best means of prosecuting the war," he said.

Luck was undoubtedly involved in many arrests. But the police were also helped by the fact that beginning in 1992 the Provisionals departed from their precaution of using for the English operations only "lily white" volunteers. In June 1992, English police arrested Paul "Dingus" Magee after he shot two constables who stopped him and another IRA man at a routine road check. One of the constables died. Magee was a well-known Provisional from the Ballymurphy area of west Belfast who was first jailed in 1971 for possessing explosives. He was arrested again in 1980 after a gun battle in north Belfast in which an SAS captain was killed.[36] He escaped a year later from the Crumlin Road jail and went on the run in the Irish republic before heading for England.

In 1993 two other well-known "players," Rab Fryers and Phelim Hamill, became involved in the English operations. Fryers had already been arrested in connection with a mortar-making factory in Belfast in the mid-1980s and was known for his republican sympathies, which he did little to keep secret in pubs and clubs. Thanks to telephone taps, the Special Branch was able to keep track of Fryers's movements around Britain. He was finally arrested in London on July 14, 1993, after the surveillance unit thought he was about to plant a bomb. Hamill was a different character entirely. He was an academic, but the police had him under suspicion since 1983 for links with an IRA ASU that was involved in a series of killings and attempted killings of legal figures near Queen's University, Belfast. Six months after Fryers's arrest, Hamill accepted a university job in Britain, a posting that some suspected was deliberately arranged in order to lure him to England where it was hoped he would lead the police to other IRA ASUs. Although this part of the plot failed, perhaps due to premature action on the part of the English police, when he was apprehended, he had in his possession a small arsenal, including Semtex, plus a list of 274 names of possible targets.

The Provisionals' main command center in south Armagh for English bombing attacks still continued to function. In April 1993 it successfully organized the huge bomb attack in Bishopsgate, London. At the beginning of 1994, shortly after Adams returned from his triumphant trip to New York, it was behind a series of mortar-bomb attacks on Heathrow Airport. None of the mortars was armed, however, and the incident was regarded as more of a demonstration of the IRA's continued ability to carry out such operations than a serious attempt to do damage. As it turned out, it was the last time in this phase of the struggle that they would succeed in demonstrating that ability. The RUC Special Branch preempted their next major bombing attempt, on July 12, 1994, when the police intercepted a truck as it came off a boat from Warrenpoint, County Down, at Southport on the English coast. It possessed a secret compartment packed with nearly a ton of explosives. The truck had originated in south Armagh. The cease-fire was only a matter of weeks away, and the Provisionals had intended this huge bomb to show they were quitting the battlefield from a position of strength, not weakness. Its interception was another demoralizing blow to the Army Council.

The eight months prior to the Southport bust had been bad ones for the Provisionals in Belfast. The UDA and UVF were on the rampage, especially in the north of the city, traditionally their favorite hunting ground. Three Catholics were murdered in August, including Sean Lavery, the son of a popular Sinn Fein councilor. Of the ten murders that occurred over the following days, only two were the responsibility of the Provisionals. The killings were largely the work of the Shankill Road UDA, C company, which in the early 1970s John White had helped mold into a feared murder machine. In 1993 it was under the command of Johnny Adair, a twenty-nine-year-old killer who, when once asked by a Catholic reporter if he had ever had a Catholic in his car before, replied "only a dead one."[37] The blundered bombing attack on the Shankill Road fish store was a desperate attempt to strike back at Adair, who the IRA thought was attending a meeting in a room above the shop. Loyalists went on a rampage and murdered another thirteen people, seven in one attack on a pub in County Derry, between October 24 and 31.

Adams was angry that the Shankill massacre had ruined his peace strategy. Under stress, he blew up, something of a rare event, shouting abuse at several high-ranking members of the Belfast Brigade.

In February 1994 the Provisionals suffered a further setback in Belfast when the RUC, disguised as building workers, intercepted one of their top ASUs as it made ready to assassinate Superintendent Derek Martindale, who had been in charge of the RUC's antifraud squad, C-13. Among the three IRA men arrested was David Adams, a cousin of the Sinn Fein leader, and a high-ranking member of the Belfast Brigade, who was badly beaten during the arrest and had his leg broken.

The failure of this assassination, which had been planned for almost six months, was a severe blow to the Provisionals. It caused a row between the Belfast Brigade and GHQ, which was convinced that a high-ranking informer had penetrated the Belfast organization, thoroughly compromising it. The tout hunt began. What the Provisionals did not realize was that the plot to assassinate Martindale was uncovered by a small unit in the Special Branch known as E9. Set up in 1988, it had only fifty members and was under the command of Superintendent Ian Phoenix, a fifty-one-year-old veteran of the RUC who had been in the force since 1970. In 1971 he was a young constable serving in the Springfield Road RUC station when the Provisionals hurled a fifty-pound bomb into it. Phoenix was blown off his feet by the explosion that killed an army sergeant. A Special Branch officer from 1979, he had reorganized E4A surveillance units and served on TCG South and then at RUC headquarters in Belfast. As the officer in charge of E9 from September 1992, he was responsible for many breakthroughs against the Protestant paramilitaries and the Provisionals, including the interception of the bombing mission of Hamill and Fryers in England and the seizure of the one-ton blockbuster bomb destined for London and intended to allow the Provisionals to go out with a bang.[38]

It is certain that these setbacks, coupled with the mounting political pressure on Sinn Fein, pushed the Provisional IRA to end the armed campaign. The Army Council discussed the idea of a permanent halt to the campaign in November 1993 but decided on a Christmas cease-fire lasting seventy-two hours and "not a second more." The resistance to halting the armed campaign was immense. It meant going against the most deeply embedded republican belief: the necessity of armed force to break the British link with Ireland. Even as the IRA leadership debated the issue, Martin McGuinness declared in January 1994 that the IRA would not halt its campaign short of the British giving a commitment to withdrawal. In countless assertions over the years, the IRA leadership made it absolutely clear that the campaign would go on until there was such a declaration. Among the more notable expressions of undying devotion to physical force was McGuinness's emotional speech during the 1986 debate on whether or not to recognize the Dail. He forcefully emphasized the movement's commitment to violence: "Our position is clear and it will never, never, never change," he declared. "The war against British rule must continue until freedom is achieved."[39] He shouted, "Shame, shame, shame," at the O'Bradaigh faction opposed to granting recognition to the Dail, for suggesting—correctly, as it turned out—that this would eventually lead the Provisionals down the path to revisionism and constitutionalism, as it had the Officials.

The same year (1986) Adams stated that "if at any time Sinn Fein decide to disown armed struggle they won't have me as a member."[40] As late as 1993, the IRA leadership was still sounding bellicose, as the interview granted to *The Guardian* in February that year showed. The spokesman boasted of the group's new terrorist technology and asserted the war would go on until Britain declared its intention to withdraw. "Unfortunately for us, the British are slow learners. But we are patient teachers," he concluded menacingly.

A year later things changed drastically. The situation the Army Council confronted in 1994 was critical. After twenty-five years of guerrilla war, in east Tyrone the Provisionals were effectively wiped out, Derry was more or less inactive, and the campaign in Britain was broken. And now Belfast was compromised. By the summer of 1994, according to Special Branch sources, 80 percent of all IRA operations in the city were either intercepted or aborted. Meanwhile, loyalist death squads were butchering Catholics with renewed ferocity. Although the Provisionals managed to carry out several successful revenge attacks against the UDA, they knew it was but a temporary measure.[41] South Armagh still remained defiant, but the IRA leadership realized that the twilight war could not be won through occasional sniper attacks or bombing ambushes along the border.

On August 31, 1994, the IRA issued a statement: "In order to enhance the democratic peace process and underline our definitive commitment to its success the leadership of Oglaigh na hEireann [Irish Republican Army] have decided that as of midnight 31 August, there will be a complete cessation of military operations. All our units have been instructed accordingly."[42]

On October 13 the loyalist paramilitaries followed in their wake. Gusty Spence, the founding member of the UVF, twenty-eight years later helped pen the loyalists' cease-fire announcement of October 13, 1994. The

Provisionals' statement was dry and formal, giving no hint that they felt they had been wrong. But Spence infused the loyalists' declaration with something of his own sadness and regret because of the suffering he and others like him had inflicted in the decades of violence. Part of it read:

> *In the genuine hope that this peace will be permanent, we take the opportunity to pay homage to all our fighters, commandos and volunteers who have paid the supreme sacrifice. They did not die in vain. The union is safe. . . . In all sincerity, we offer to the loved ones of all innocent victims over the past 25 years, abject and true remorse. No words of ours will compensate for the intolerable suffering they have undergone during this conflict.*
>
> *Let us firmly resolve to respect our differing views of freedom, culture, and aspiration, and never again permit our political circumstances to degenerate into bloody warfare.*

In 1966, Spence brought the gun back into Ulster politics; 3,351 deaths later, hope triumphed over history.[43]

· EIGHT ·

TO FORSAKE ARMS

1994–1998

THE NORTHERN IRELAND peace process was based on the failure of violent republicanism to achieve its aims. The Provisional IRA never admitted defeat, nor did the authorities ever utter that word, preferring the evasive language of conflict-resolution studies in which there are no winners and no losers. But all the euphemisms in the dictionary could not evade the fact that the IRA's violence failed to drive the British from Northern Ireland. Nor did it even secure a declaration of intent to withdraw.

Among most Nationalists it was not interpreted as a defeat for republicanism. On the contrary, in west Belfast the mood was celebratory. Many assumed that the Provisionals must have secured some major concession from Britain for them to have halted a campaign that their leaders swore over and over again would not end until their goals were achieved. Many in the Protestant community assumed the same thing. Even after the loyalist groups declared their own cease-fires, there was no rush to embrace the new situation. Instead, Protestants remained cautious and mistrustful, their free-floating paranoia ready to crystallize around any particle of suspicion that the perfidious English were once more doing a deal behind their backs. "The rank and file unionists are still wondering what the hell the IRA have been given," commented James Molyneaux, the UUP leader. Change always made the Unionists insecure. For twenty-five years IRA violence gave them justification for their intransigence and meant that their own moral and political position was not scrutinized too closely. At times their spokesmen almost seemed to regret the passing of the Troubles, when the menace was easy to identify. For them the new terrain of peace was full of potential traps. Britain, too, reacted warily. The British prime minister expressed skepticism and asked why, if the IRA was serious about ending its violence, it had not included the word "permanent" in its cease-fire declaration.

In Dublin and Washington, however, things moved swiftly. On September 6, 1994, the Irish taoiseach, Albert Reynolds, John Hume, and Gerry Adams met on the steps of Government House in Dublin. The three shook hands in public, a gesture of reconciliation between constitutional nationalism and violent republicanism that had taken seventy years to achieve. A month later, on a tour of the United States, Adams took a telephone call from Vice President Al Gore. Anthony Lake, Clinton's national security adviser, wrote to inform Adams that the administration was lifting its ban on meetings with Sinn Fein. An invitation to the White House was just months away. Within weeks of being declared, the Provisionals' cease-fire reunited the different wings of nationalism and secured the backing of the most powerful nation in the world. That was the easy part.

There was still the matter of Northern Ireland's 900,000 or so Protestants. Between them and the IRA lay a sea of blood. Those who had waded in it already seemed more willing to undertake the journey across than the conventional politicians of Unionism. At the end of October, Gusty Spence, the founder of the modern UVF and the man whose gunfire raised the curtain on the modern Troubles, led a delegation of loyalist paramilitary spokesmen to America. They followed in the footsteps of Sinn Fein as guests of the National Committee on American Foreign Policy. Among the delegation was Gary McMichael, whose father, John McMichael, was murdered by the IRA in late 1987, and Billy Hutchinson, a former UVF member who had served time in jail for his part in the murder of two Catholics in 1974. Spence, Hutchinson, and Davy Ervine represented the UVF-linked Progressive Unionist Party; McMichael and David Adams, the Ulster Democratic Party, which spoke for the UDA. The loyalists were not accorded anything like the reception Adams had received on his first visit to the city eight months earlier. As far as Irish Americans were concerned, they were an unknown quantity. For most, the Reverend Ian Paisley represented loyalism. If anything filtered through the almost complete absence of U.S. media coverage of loyalist actions, it was the Sinn Fein propaganda that portrayed them as the puppets of the British government and its security forces.

"Loyalist opinion can now be heard in the United States," McMichael declared on arrival in New York. The delegation soon made clear where they stood politically. "I am just going to talk from the heart," said Ervine, throwing away his notes. "Nationality is a state of mind. I am British. I will always be British. And I have always been British."[1] The UDA and UVF representatives insisted that the only reason their organizations called a cease-fire was that they were convinced a deal had not been made with the IRA behind the scenes and that, as they put it, "the Union with Great Britain was safe." This was the total opposite of the line that Sinn Fein was expounding. It was trying to reassure its supporters that the IRA ended its armed struggle because conditions were ripe to make political progress toward a United Ireland. However, there were two things that both loyalists and republicans agreed on and that Ervine stressed: the first was the need to free the "political" prisoners; the second was that there would be no paramilitary disarmament until a political settlement was reached on which all sides could agree.

To cement this agreement, Belfast IRA leaders met with UDA and UVF representatives in a south Belfast hotel three days before Christmas. An informal pact was made. The paramilitaries would present a united front on the release of their prisoners, disarmament, and the need for "inclusive talks." They vowed to oppose any attempt to make disarmament—or decommissioning, as it soon came to be known—a precondition for the entry of their political representatives into negotiations.

Christmas 1994 was the first in twenty-five years that Ulster people dared look to the future with hope. The clamp of security that had held Belfast and other towns in its grip began to ease. The shops thronged with customers; traffic poured into the city center; people stayed out late and did not rush home before darkness fell. Along the roads of north Belfast, for decades the favorite hunting ground of sectarian assassins, a more casual mood now prevailed; people did not scrutinize every car that approached looking for some telltale sign of imminent danger. Soldiers patrolled without helmets, and police officers shed their bulletproof vests. A few streets that ran through the peace line between the Shankill and the Falls, sealed off from each other for a generation, were now opened. Soon civilian searchers were no longer seen at the main department stores, and cars were allowed to park close to the city center. The Europa Hotel, the most bombed hotel in Western Europe, was renovated with a brave new front that bulged out toward the sidewalk, and all its barricades and security checks were lifted for the first time since 1971. In mid-January 1995 all daytime army foot patrols in Belfast ceased. At the end of that month, border patrols were also drastically reduced. The Irish government announced that nine IRA prisoners released on parole for Christmas were free.

The British government continued to move cautiously, however. There were no big gestures. Paramilitary prisoners would stay behind bars for the time being. It was twelve weeks after the IRA cease-fire before Major allowed even a preliminary meeting between his government and Sinn Fein officials. He began speaking about the need for the decommissioning of IRA weapons before Sinn Fein could get into full-fledged talks. Among Nationalists, impatience and unease were growing. There were suspicions that Major was afraid to do anything that might jeopardize the support of the nine Ulster Unionist MPs at Westminster who were helping to keep him in power. Irish officials, in particular, were concerned that the IRA would become restless at the delays and interpret them as a deliberate attempt by the British to undermine its military capacity. To add to the uncertainties, Reynolds, one of the chief architects of the IRA cease-fire, had been replaced as taoiseach by John Bruton, whom republicans viewed as being much less sympathetic to their position. Meanwhile, behind the scenes, civil servants from the two governments were working hard to come up with a political program that would appeal to Nationalists without frightening Unionists and keep the cease-fires on track. The result was the Framework Document, the first political fruit of the peace process; it was revealed by the two governments in February 1995.

It was a complex set of proposals, but they repeated three themes familiar since the 1973 Sunningdale Agreement: the maintenance of the union as long as the majority wished it, the establishment of a devolved assembly in Northern Ireland, and the creation of a "north-south" body with a potential for "dynamic" development. The concept of power sharing was there but not the term; instead, the Framework Document spoke of institutions for local government that respected both traditions; the 1973 Sunningdale provisions for a Council of Ireland became a "north-south body," but its functions remained the same. It was all set within the context of Britain's oft-repeated assertion that it no longer had a "selfish strategic or economic interest in Northern Ireland."

The Framework Document was not what republicans wanted. It did not contain plans for a British withdrawal or even a promise to persuade Unionists of the benefits of a United Ireland. But it was not what Unionists wanted to hear, either. The proposals were an emphatic reminder that Northern Ireland's membership in the United Kingdom was dependent on the consent of the people of Northern Ireland, not on the sovereign claims of a confident imperial power. That kind of union was no longer on offer. Britain, in effect, was telling the Unionists, "Yes, you can stay as long as the majority of you want to, but you are free to leave whenever you like. And in the meantime, you are going to have to accommodate the political aspirations of your Nationalist neighbors."

The sun had long ago set on the British Empire; it was now setting on the union between Great Britain and Northern Ireland.

The Ulster Unionist Party rejected the Framework Document in its entirety, but it had a major advantage over the Sunningdale Agreement and, indeed, every other Northern Ireland initiative that had come before it: The only one to have been born at a time of peace, it was not greeted with strikes, arson, bombs, or bullets. While republicans and Unionists found much to dislike about it, there was no concerted campaign to thwart or destroy it. The only problem was that the document was not itself a settlement, only the outline of what a settlement might look like. It remained to be enacted. It the meantime, much could go wrong, and it did.

During the secret talks between Britain and the Provisional IRA, decommissioning was rarely if ever referred to as a demand needed to be met before the republican movement could be "sanitized" and brought fully into the peace process. Nor was it on the agenda during the months before the Provisionals called their cease-fire, when the Irish government and Hume sought to persuade republicans that armed force was counterproductive. But now Major and his deputy in Northern Ireland, Sir Patrick Mayhew, were raising it with increasing frequency. On March 7, 1995, in Washington, Mayhew announced three steps that the IRA must take before Sinn Fein would be allowed into the conference room: It must agree in principle to disarm; there must be agreement on how to go about it; and there must be a "confidence-building" measure, a token gesture of disarmament to begin the process.

It did not take long for republicans to reply. Martin McGuinness said he wanted to remind the British "just in case reality had escaped them" that "the British army had not defeated the IRA—that the IRA had not surrendered—and that the British government could not even remotely expect Sinn Fein to deliver that surrender to them." Decommissioning, he said, must be "seen for what it is, an excuse to delay the all-party peace talks. . . . All-party peace talks are the inevitable next step in the peace process."[2] But the British argued that unless there was a "token gesture" from the IRA, they could never persuade the Unionists to take part in any peace talks with Sinn Fein present. Decommissioning soon became the major issue of the whole peace process and threatened to destabilize it.

In June 1995, Adams replied to the continued demand from Britain. He told *The Irish Times* that "the surrender of IRA weapons as a precondition to negotiation was never mentioned by the British government before August 31, 1994. . . . In my view, had a surrender of IRA weapons been imposed as a precondition to peace negotiations prior to the cessation, it is possible there would have been no cessation. . . . The British government is not simply interested in a gesture. It is, in reality, demanding the start of a surrender process as a precondition to all-party talks."[3]

The first summer of "peace" was fraught with political and sectarian tension, which erupted in mob violence. A paratrooper convicted of murdering a Catholic teenage girl was freed in early July after serving only four years of a life sentence. Catholic neighborhoods, where tension was high because of the deadlock over disarmament, exploded. At the same time, Orange marchers at Drumcree, near Portadown, County Armagh, were blocked from parading along Garvaghy Road, which skirted a Catholic district. One thousand RUC men confronted ten thousand Orangemen. Loyalists rioted in protest throughout Northern Ireland. Although the violence (at least at an organized level) had ended, the underlying conflict between Catholic and Protestant, Nationalist and Unionist, remained unresolved. By September and the first anniversary of the IRA cease-fire, Sinn Fein was still barred from entering talks, and the peace process was crumbling, thanks to the issue of decommissioning. The IRA repeated its rejection of what it termed the "ludicrous" demand and insisted there would be no surrender of weapons. "There is no possibility of disarmament except as part of a negotiated settlement," it said. Republicans pointed out that decommissioning was never an issue when earlier IRA campaigns had ended. The Official IRA called a cease-fire in May 1972, and its political wing, the Workers' Party, entered the Dail nine years later, without any demands ever being made for the organization to hand over weapons or explosives, of which it was believed to possess three tons—enough to arm about three hundred volunteers. Leading Unionists felt comfortable enough negotiating with Workers' Party representatives, regardless of the fact that the Official IRA was still armed. Indeed, John Taylor, whom the Officials tried to assassinate, later praised them for their commitment to the political process.[4] But such arguments moved neither the Unionists nor the Major government. They quoted RUC sources as claiming that the IRA had murdered a drug dealer in Belfast in April 1995 and was still involved in scouting for potential targets and planning operations.

The Irish government turned to the Clinton administration for help in finding a way around the disarmament dispute. Clinton helped maintain the momentum throughout 1994 and 1995, often doing so at the cost of angering the British. In December 1994, when the British said that Sinn Fein would be barred from an investment conference being held in Belfast, Clinton threatened to withhold his representative, Ron Brown. The British relented. In March, against British protests, he gave Adams permission to raise money in the United States. He shook hands with the Sinn Fein leader (but not in public) later that month during the Saint Patrick's Day festivities in Washington, again defying British protests.[5] May saw Clinton host a Northern Ireland investment conference in Washington. In July, at the height of the turmoil on the streets, the president announced that he would be visiting Northern Ireland beginning on November 30. Neither the British nor Irish governments wanted a stalled peace process and an unseemly row over decommissioning to tarnish the prestige of an American presidential visit.

As the November 30 visit drew closer, the Irish and British strove desperately to get around the obstacle of decommissioning that Major had planted firmly on the path to peace. Eleven hours before Clinton was due to arrive in London on the first leg of his trip, the British agreed to adopt a twin-track approach, as the Irish had been advocating for some months. Former Democratic Senator George Mitchell, Clinton's economic "envoy" to Northern Ireland, was appointed to chair an international committee to report on the decommissioning issue by mid-January 1996. Meanwhile, the two prime ministers stated that their aim was to achieve all-party talks by February. No untidy policy issues would be left lying around when the president arrived. The place would be presentable.

Behind the scenes it was a very different story. Unknown to Clinton, Bruton, and Major, a decision was made at a meeting of the Provisional Army Council in Donegal in October that unless Britain abandoned its demand for the IRA to disarm, it would end the cease-fire. The aim was not to relaunch the armed struggle but to carry out a limited bombing campaign concentrated in Britain. Shortly after this meeting Adams stated that the peace process no longer existed, having been "subverted" by the British government. Sinn Fein leaders chose not to tell the world about the decision of the IRA leadership even though several of their highest-ranking members were at the meeting when the decision was made.

Innocent of these machinations, Bill Clinton and the first lady arrived to celebrate the peace that was about to collapse. Apart from that small matter, the first visit of a U.S. president to Northern Ireland was a spectacular success. Even the weather cooperated for once. It was bright and cold when they arrived in Belfast on the morning of November 30. The president's first stop was on the Shankill Road, where he converted the suspicious Protestants into Clinton enthusiasts with a brief walk and some flesh-pressing. From then on it was one huge welcome after another, with thousands upon thousands showing up along the Falls, where he shook Adams's hand again, this time in public, and in Derry, where he shared a platform with John Hume. It was erected in Guildhall Square, near the city center, not far from where in 1972 the Provisional IRA had exploded its first car bomb. That evening President Clinton lit the Christmas tree in front of Belfast's city hall while some fifty thousand people cheered and applauded. The city was not used to crowds of that size assembling for a happy purpose. Many onlookers contrasted the positive, enthusiastic mood of the Clintons when they spoke of peace with the reluctant, cautious, and sometimes downright suspicious reaction of Major and the Unionists. It was refreshing for a city to find that the president also wanted to celebrate the change, not pick it to pieces with doubts and prevarications. "Hillary and I thank you from the bottom of our hearts for making us so welcome," the president said. "I will remember this day for as long as I live with great gratitude."[6]

Even as the lights went on for Belfast's first Christmas at peace, in a small house in the middle of west Belfast the IRA was holding a meeting with a group of Irish Americans, some of whom had been active in the 1992 Clinton election campaign. They were told that unless the disarmament demand was dropped, the cease-fire would crumble. And it would be sooner rather than later. The Irish Americans left depressed but tried to console themselves with the thought that republicans had been crying crisis now for months, yet the cease-fire still held.[7]

· 2 ·

ON JANUARY 24, 1996, George Mitchell's international body published its recommendations. It advised that the disposal of weapons should not be a precondition for entry into all-party talks but that the two should take place along parallel tracks. Major effectively rejected the report and then added what the IRA saw as a new precondition. Before the all-party talks began, elections would be held in Northern Ireland so that those parties who wanted to take part in them could secure a "democratic mandate." Sinn Fein, with a solid electoral base, saw this as simply another delaying tactic intended to prevent those talks from taking place for as long as possible. Mayhew rejected an appeal from Adams to abandon plans for elections. Meanwhile, there was a series of murders of alleged drug dealers in Belfast. A group calling itself Direct Action Against Drugs claimed responsibility. It was a thinly disguised front for the IRA.

It was now clear that the promise of all-party talks by the end of February would not be met. Sean O'hUiginn, a high-ranking Irish government official who played a key role in the negotiations, commented in early 1996, "I'd be very nervous about saying anything that sounds like a self-fullfilling prophecy. But from last August or so the political graph has been dipping. The question is at what point will it intersect with the killing graph?"[8] It was a prescient remark.

At 5:40 P.M. on February 9, Scotland Yard received a telephone call warning that the Provisional IRA cease-fire was about to end. A short time later an IRA statement followed that read:

> *It is with great reluctance that the leadership of Oglaigh na hEireann announces that the complete cessation of military operations will end at 6 P.M. . . . The cessation presented an historic challenge for everyone, and Oglaigh na hEireann commend the leadership of Nationalist Ireland at home and abroad. They rose to*

> *meet the challenge. The British prime minister did not. Instead of embracing the peace process, the British government acted in bad faith, with Mr. Major and the Unionists leaders squandering this unprecedented opportunity to resolve the conflict. . . . Selfish party political and sectional interests in the London parliament have been placed before the rights of the people of Ireland. . . . The resolution of this conflict in our country demands justice. It demands an inclusive negotiated settlement. That is not possible unless and until the British government lives up to its responsibilities. The blame for the failure thus far of the Irish peace process lies squarely with John Major and his government.*

At one minute after seven that evening a huge bomb exploded in an underground garage in an office building near Canary Wharf (the object of an earlier IRA bombing attempt in 1992) in east London. It killed two men, injured one hundred, and inflicted about $140 million worth of damage. The blast created a crater fourteen feet wide and twenty feet deep. There was dismay, anger, and outrage, but among many Nationalists who were frustrated at Britain's response to the IRA's cease-fire, the bombing did not come as a complete surprise. Nor was it unexpected among the Irish government's advisers and civil servants who had been working for months to defuse the decommissioning crisis. Privately they, too, blamed the Major government for mishandling events since the cease-fire. One Irish official commented that "the British government didn't know why the violence stopped. And they didn't know why it started again." Some among them suspected, as did the IRA, that it was a deliberate policy, not just ineptitude, that led the British to delay and prevaricate, in an effort to debilitate the IRA, the theory being that the longer the organization remained inactive, the more difficult it would be for it to resume its terrorist activities. So by holding back on concessions, the British had nothing to lose and everything to gain. But in public, the British and Irish governments adopted a united front and announced they were breaking off any further meetings with Sinn Fein. However, the Clinton administration said that it would maintain contact with Adams because "it is hard to imagine a process making progress without him." Hume also rejected calls, some from within his own party, to walk away from Adams.

As usual in Northern Ireland, the two communities interpreted the return to violence in diametrically opposed ways. For Nationalists it was final proof of what they were arguing all along, that the demand for decommissioning would destroy the cease-fire; for Unionists it was proof that decommissioning was necessary and Major was correct in refusing to allow Sinn Fein into talks until it took place. But the vast majority of both Catholics and Protestants were vehemently opposed to a renewal of the killing. Six thousand people gathered at a peace rally in Belfast just days after the London bombing. In less than a week, 150,000 people telephoned Belfast's two morning papers demanding the cease-fire be restored.

In his response to the IRA's statement that he was to blame for the failure of the peace process, Major replied that in spite of the cease-fire, the IRA never really abandoned violence but had been preparing for a renewal of operations for some time. The prime minister's assertion was based on accurate intelligence. The IRA's Northern Command set up a special intelligence-gathering unit, the aim of which was to penetrate middle-class areas where high-profile targets such as judges and senior policemen lived. The IRA's return to violence was intended to be spectacular. MI5 warned the government a full month before the Canary Wharf attack that violence would start again. When it came, the RUC's E9 countersurveillance unit was ready. Three days after the bombing, the RUC intercepted an eight-man IRA Active Service Unit as it attempted to pull off a major robbery at a warehouse in south Belfast. Among those arrested was one of the Belfast Brigade's top gunmen. (He had escaped arrest in February 1994 when the police seized the IRA squad planning to assassinate Superintendent Martindale, as noted in chapter 7.)

It was the first of a series of setbacks for the IRA. On February 18 a premature explosion killed an IRA volunteer as he transported a bomb on a London bus. Hundreds were injured in a bomb attack in a shopping center in Manchester in June. But at the end of that month the Irish police raided an IRA bomb factory in County Loais and arrested six leading members of the organization. On July 15 a police raid in London netted eight IRA men and led to the discovery of another bomb-making factory. Another London bombing team was seized on September 23, along with ten tons of home-made explosives, Semtex, and weapons; during the arrest operation, an IRA volunteer was shot dead and five others held. By the fall of 1996, seven months after the ending of the cease-fire, the IRA's strategy of confining its campaign to bombing attacks in Britain was abandoned. The RUC realized that it was only a matter of time before the armed campaign would be resumed in Northern Ireland. The police feared that this would lead to a backlash from the loyalist paramilitaries who so far had maintained their cease-fires.

The IRA resumed attacks in Northern Ireland on October 7 with a double car-bomb attack inside the British army headquarters in Lisburn, near Belfast; by some miracle it killed only one soldier. It was a "spectacular"—proof that the IRA could still carry out headline-grabbing operations and embarrass the security forces. However, whatever satisfaction the IRA felt about this success was short-lived. Within weeks the RUC swooped down on the special intelligence unit they believed responsible for this operation and arrested Bobby Storey, a high-ranking IRA veteran not long out of prison. Police claimed that Storey was the Northern Command's intelligence officer.[9]

The IRA's strategy of going for high-profile targets collapsed, as had its bombing campaign in Britain. Within a period of a few months it lost about thirty of its most seasoned operators in police raids; two were dead. It now attempted to relaunch its campaign in Belfast with attacks on the security forces. However, the IRA's weakness was more apparent than ever, as one bungled effort followed another, and more men were arrested. A senior RUC officer commented that it was a "pathetic, grubby little war."[10] The Belfast IRA was now thoroughly compromised, thanks mainly to RUC intelligence operations, but the "pathetic, grubby little war" struggled on into the new year. Among the units most keen to end the cease-fire were those in south Armagh, where doubts about the peace process were prevalent. An Armagh man, Thomas "Slab" Murphy, was now the chief of staff. It was from south Armagh that the bomb attack on Canary Wharf was launched, like so many others before it. On February 13, 1997, an IRA sniper shot and killed a British soldier as he chatted with a woman at a vehicle checkpoint near the town of Forkhill. The police believed the same sniping unit was involved in a whole series of attacks, using a powerful American-made weapon with a range of up to six thousand feet. Bulletproof clothing was no defense against it. Ten soldiers and a police officer were shot dead between 1992 and 1997, victims of the same or a similar gun, the majority of them in the south Armagh area. In April the sniping tactic was repeated in Derry, where a policewoman was seriously wounded during an attack in the city center. But, as ever, south Armagh was the most dangerous zone, and as long as it was a safe haven for IRA militants, it would remain so.

Over the years the security forces enjoyed few successes there. But finally, on April 13, a surveillance operation involving the SAS, MI5, and the RUC produced results. SAS men burst into an unused farm just as the sniper got ready to begin an operation. He was caught in a mask, gloves, and coveralls, along with five other members of the unit, reading a newspaper and relaxing before going out to kill. Two rifles were recovered as well as an armor-plated car that was used as a sniping platform. For the police it was a major coup. They were convinced they now had south Armagh's "A" team of IRA operators. It was, at any rate, another demoralizing blow to the IRA. For the first time their safe haven had been penetrated.

The IRA leadership would never admit it publicly, but the attempt to resume the armed campaign was proving a disaster. It was just over a year since the campaign resumed. In that time it claimed the lives of two soldiers and two civilians—but at a high cost. Aside from the deaths of two of its volunteers, the IRA saw its bombing teams in Britain broken, a major intelligence-gathering unit of its Northern Command seized, a series of Active Service Units in Belfast intercepted, and a team of top operators in south Armagh under arrest. It strengthened the hand of those who, like Adams, were arguing that the physical force option was no longer viable. Outside events also helped him and his supporters, who were seeking to resume the political process.

In May 1997 the Labour Party won a crushing and historic victory over the Conservatives, who were ousted from power for the first time in eighteen years. Tony Blair became the new prime minister, and Mo Mowlan was made his secretary of state for Northern Ireland. In Northern Ireland, Adams recovered his west Belfast seat, and Martin McGuinness won a second seat for Sinn Fein when he took the Mid-Ulster constituency from Paisley's DUP. Sinn Fein scored its highest percentage of the vote ever. The party's electoral successes stood out in sharp contrast to the IRA's military failures.

Most interpreted the increased votes for Sinn Fein as an expression of the Nationalist desire to see another cease-fire, since bolstering the party, they believed, would strengthen those in the republican movement in favor of such a move. The question now was not *if* but *when* it would happen. Unfortunately, two more lives were lost in the meantime. The North Armagh IRA shot dead two community policemen on patrol in the center of Lurgan on June 16. It was a provocative act. North Armagh was seething with Protestant discontent over the continued crisis at

Drumcree, where every summer Orangemen confronted Catholic residents who wanted to prevent them from marching near their neighborhood. The previous two summers had seen serious violence. It was feared the killing of the two officers would provoke worse. However, the army sealed off the Catholic area and created a secure corridor of troops, armored vehicles, and barricades through which the Orangemen were quickly marched. It infuriated local Catholics, but a new chief constable, Ronnie Flanagan, responded that the alternative would have been a province-wide breakdown of law and order.

The new government quickly put out feelers to the republican leaders about the prospects for another cease-fire. In their response they said that the British would have to set a date for when Sinn Fein could join the talks following any new cease-fire, that those talks must have a deadline, and that constitutional issues would be matters for negotiation.

Blair was eager to restart the peace process as soon as possible and involve Sinn Fein, not because he liked the party but because he knew that without it there could be no meaningful settlement in Northern Ireland. He met Sinn Fein's conditions. His new secretary of state said that if the IRA renewed its cease-fire, Sinn Fein would be included in the talks within six weeks and that the deadline for reaching a settlement would be April 9, 1998—the day before Good Friday and the Easter weekend. Constitutional issues would be on the negotiating table. It was also confirmed that former U.S. Senator George Mitchell would chair the negotiations, giving the U.S. administration a direct role in them—a reassuring factor for the Provisionals. Pressure on the Provisional IRA to call a halt was now irresistible. On July 20 it announced it was ending its campaign of terror. After criticizing the British government and the Unionists for blocking "any possibility of real or inclusive negotiations" during the last cease-fire, the statement went on:

> *The IRA is committed to ending British rule in Ireland. It is the root cause of divisions and conflict in our country. We want a permanent peace and therefore we are prepared to enhance the search for a democratic peace settlement through real and inclusive negotiations. So having assessed the current political situation, the leadership of Oglaigh na hEireann are announcing a complete cessation of military operations from 12 midday on Sunday, 20 July 1997. We have*

ordered the unequivocal restoration of the cease-fire of August 1994. All IRA units have been instructed accordingly.

This time there were no quibbles from the British government about the wording of the announcement. The government was as good as its word, and on September 15, Sinn Fein joined the peace negotiations in Belfast. For the first time since 1921, when Michael Collins went to London to meet with Lloyd George, IRA representatives engaged in direct negotiations with the British government. Seventy-six years earlier, Collins had come away with a measure of freedom for twenty-six of Ireland's thirty-two counties. The question was being raised as to what Adams could get as a result of the talks that he and other Sinn Fein leaders seemed so keen to enter. Among some republicans there was growing disillusionment; even the most positive outcome from their point of view would still fall far short of what the republican movement was seeking. Anthony McIntyre, a former IRA prisoner turned academic, wrote that

to claim . . . that the IRA did not win but had not lost either is demonstrably wrong. The political objective of the Provisional IRA was to secure a British declaration of intent to withdraw. It failed.

The objective of the British state was to force the Provisional IRA to accept—and to respond with a new strategic logic to—the position that it would not leave Ireland until a majority in the North consented to such a move. It succeeded.[11]

Other republican groups such as the INLA and its political wing, the IRSP, were more and more critical of the Sinn Fein strategy, as was Republican Sinn Fein, which had broken with the mainstream organization in 1986. They viewed the IRA and Sinn Fein involvement in the peace process as a sellout and made increasingly bellicose statements that they, at least, would continue what they termed "the fight for Irish freedom." INLA received a shipment of explosives from New Zealand in 1994 and possessed a supply of AK-47s and hand grenades. But as usual it proved more deadly to its own members than to its declared enemies. Another vicious feud weakened the organization in 1996 when it claimed the lives of two of its leaders, Hugh "Cueball" Torney and Gino Gallagher, and four others.[12] But INLA still remained a threat to peace.

Concern was also focused on Republican Sinn Fein and its alleged links to an armed faction calling itself the Continuity IRA. One of the founding members of the Provisionals, Daithi O'Conaill, formed CIRA in 1986 at the same time as Republican Sinn Fein split from the mainstream republican movement. He was its first chief of staff. The organization lay dormant until 1994 and the first Provisional IRA cease-fire. In December that year it planted a small Semtex bomb in Enniskillen and some weeks later another in Newry. The first public statement appeared in its name on January 6, 1996, when it declared that "the Irish Republican Army under the leadership of the Continuity Army Council renews its allegiance to the All-Ireland Republic of Easter 1916 and the First (thirty-two-county) Dail. It is the final custodian of that republic and is the absolute guarantor of continued resistance to British rule in Ireland.

"We wish to clarify our position to the people of Ireland. We are neither Official nor Provisional and rejecting reformism we remain revolutionary as the true Oglaigh na hEireann, Irish Republican Army." The statement pledged "unremitting hostility to the British forces of occupation" and vowed that "action will be taken in the future at an appropriate time to further this objective."

In July 1996, CIRA bombed a hotel in Enniskillen and subsequently carried out a series of bombings and attempted bombings in Belfast and provincial towns near the border. On September 16, 1997, the day after Sinn Fein joined the talks, CIRA exploded a huge bomb in the mainly Protestant town of Markethill, County Armagh, sending a signal to both governments and the Provisionals that there were still militant republicans ready to use terror. Just how many, it was difficult to estimate, but probably CIRA could count on no more than forty or fifty activists. They possessed few weapons—some hand grenades, shotguns, and AK-47s. So it is not surprising that one of CIRA's leaders appealed to the Provisionals not to surrender any weapons to the authorities but to hand them over to "true republicans." It is known that CIRA received a small cache of MAC-10 submachine guns from supporters in New York in 1997.[13] However, intense police surveillance in the Irish republic frustrated many of its operations and limited its capacity to strike.

As the Provisionals were drawn more deeply into the peace process and actual negotiations got under way, a more serious threat emerged. It came from within the Provisional IRA itself. In order for Sinn Fein to take part in the talks, the party was asked to sign up to six principles devised by the chairman of the talks, George Mitchell. These principles committed the talks' participants to forswear the use of violence and to dissociate themselves from any organization that employed violence to achieve its ends. This was a dramatic challenge to the traditional republican claim that as the legitimate "army" of the Irish republic, the IRA possessed the right to wage war. It was a claim that went back to 1919 when the Sinn Fein government in Dublin (outlawed by the British) devolved that right to the IRA and was one of the moral foundation stones on which the republican movement rested. In order for those Sinn Fein talks delegates who were also members of the IRA, including McGuinness, Adams, and Gerry Kelly, to accept the principles, a special army convention would have to be held to give them "special dispensation" to do so. When it took place in October 1997, it was acrimonious. Several leading members walked out in protest, including Mickey McKevitt, the former quartermaster general of the Provisionals' GHQ staff and, for a brief period, a member of the Provisional Army Council. McKevitt was married to Bernadette Sands, a sister of Bobby Sands, the 1981 hunger striker who became a republican icon. He commanded a considerable following in the County Louth area of the border and in south Armagh. It was alleged that as many as twenty other high-ranking Provisionals went with him and that the South Armagh IRA suffered a large number of defections. Sinn Fein, especially in the Louth area, was also shaken with reports of many resignations.

The republican leadership denounced these stories as mostly fictions. *The Irish Times* quoted a veteran republican who compared the dispute to the split of 1969, when the Provisional IRA was born. "It was all claim and counter-claim," he said. "Things were happening on the ground but they were denied. Both sides manipulated the facts. Sometimes it took months, even years, for the whole truth to emerge."

It was clear, however, that Adams and his supporters emerged with the vast majority of republicans still in line, supporting their course. The kind of split that divided the republican movement in 1969 did not take place. Most important, the Belfast organization remained overwhelmingly committed to Adams's leadership.

Still, the security forces could not be complacent. Louth was an important staging area for republicans moving weapons and explosives across the border into Northern Ireland. Whichever faction controlled it possessed the capacity to cause trouble. In addition, McKevitt knew the locations of the organization's major arms dumps. There was much speculation about whether or not the dissidents had access to supplies of Semtex and weapons or would dare to seize them from their former colleagues. (Such a move would certainly have provoked a bloody feud.) Equally disturbing for the peace process was the revelation that one of the heads of the IRA's bomb-making department joined the dissidents.[14] As 1997 came to a close, just as people's hopes brightened, the prospect of a new campaign of terror cast a shadow over the future.

The dissident republicans went public and formed the 32-County Sovereignty Committee, with Bernadette Sands-McKevitt as its vice president. At its first press conference in Dublin on December 7, the committee spelled out its aims. Its primary goal was to bring about "total British disengagement from Ireland and to oppose any internal settlement in the 6 Occupied Counties or any settlement which provides for continued British Rule in any form." The committee said it would oppose "all groups who call for such internal settlements." That now included Sinn Fein, which according to the committee's view was part of a process that guaranteed a "unionist veto" and prohibited "an end of partition." The new group reaffirmed "the right of the Irish people to armed struggle in pursuit of national sovereignty." At the same time it denied that it was anything other than a pressure group or possessed an armed wing. Sinn Fein acted rapidly against any party members who were also involved with the 32-County Sovereignty Committee and expelled them.

The peace process was threatened on other fronts. Much to the disgust of a few militant loyalists, the cease-fires of the UDA and UVF had remained intact even after the IRA resumed its bombing campaign in February 1996. They were further angered as the authorities rerouted some Orange parades away from Catholic areas or blocked others, seeing this as the appeasement of republicans. In July 1996, under the leadership of a local gunman, Billy Wright, nicknamed "King Rat," a section of the UVF in north Armagh split away from the organization. North Armagh loyalists were among the most violent and sectarian killers in Ulster; in the mid-1970s the area where they operated became known as the Murder Triangle. As the police and army blocked Orange marchers at Drumcree on July 6, 1996, loyalist gunmen murdered a Catholic taxi driver. The former UVF men soon began using the name Loyalist Volunteer Force. Like the dissident republicans, they viewed their leadership's commitment to the peace process as a sellout. The LVF victims included a teenage Catholic girl, murdered as she slept in her Protestant boyfriend's home, and a teenage boy, who was tortured before being shot and dumped in a slurry pit. The group's support was mainly confined to rural areas. The Belfast UVF and UDA suffered only a handful of defections.

Not long after forming the LVF, Wright was jailed on charges of intimidating a witness. On December 27, 1997, two INLA prisoners, using guns smuggled into the Maze prison, shot Wright dead as he was being moved from his cell block to the visiting area. It was the most sensational assassination the organization had carried out since its booby-trap bombing of Conservative Party chairman Airey Neave in March 1979.

Wright's murder was revenged in the traditional loyalist fashion—through indiscriminate attacks on Catholics. Within days, two were murdered and eight seriously wounded as LVF gunmen struck in Tyrone and north Belfast. There were concerns that the Belfast UDA was behind some of the incidents, which could mean that the loyalist cease-fire was about to unravel. By the end of January 1998, twelve people were dead mainly as a result of LVF violence. Ominously, imprisoned UDA men stated that they were withdrawing their support for the peace process, claiming it was a "one-way street" of concessions to republicans. Once more Ulster's hopes for peace seemed doomed to disappointment.

Pessimism deepened when the IRA retaliated and killed a UDA member in February 1998. It also took responsibility for the murder of an alleged drug dealer. Sinn Fein was temporarily suspended from the talks.[15] It returned after two weeks, and the peace talks struggled on. With only two months to go before the April 9 deadline for a settlement, few believed that it could be achieved. Violence from dissident republicans and angry loyalists was not the only difficulty. Throughout the negotiations, the Ulster Unionist Party delegates refused to speak with Sinn Fein, even after an appeal from President Clinton. But David Trimble, the party leader, pledged that Unionists would not meet with republicans until the IRA disarmed.

Both dissident republicans and disaffected loyalists hoped that their attacks would bring the talks crashing down. As Easter approached, they tried to apply more pressure on the beleaguered negotiations. During the last week in March, republicans fired mortars at an RUC base in south

Armagh and attempted to set off a huge bomb consisting of thirteen hundred pounds of explosives. But it was intercepted near Dundalk in a garage. Two men linked to the Sands-McKevitt committee were arrested. The bomb was a sophisticated device with Semtex stuffed into booster tubes to enhance its power; it resembled those the Provisional IRA once manufactured that caused such devastation in London. The dissident republicans' attempts to disrupt continued throughout March and April. A week before the settlement deadline, the Irish police seized another large bomb at a ferry dock near Dublin as it was on its way to England. LVF gunmen, meanwhile, murdered two young friends, one Catholic and one Protestant, as they chatted in a pub in Poyntzpass, County Down.

The talks became a race against the gunmen as the politicians strove for a settlement before some awful act of violence could set off a chain reaction of killings and draw in the Provisionals and the major loyalist paramilitary organizations.

The eight parties involved were sequestered near the site of the old Northern Ireland parliament at Stormont, just outside Belfast.[16] All the skills that Chairman George Mitchell honed as majority leader of the U.S. Senate were tested as he sought to find common ground between Unionist and Nationalist, loyalist and republican. Sinn Fein and the UUP proved the most implacable opponents. Since the UUP refused face-to-face meetings with the republicans, Mitchell was the go-between. Sinn Fein was pushing for maximum change, the Unionists for minimum. The fiercest battles took place around the number and scope of any cross-border bodies, the powers of the new assembly, the fate of paramilitary prisoners, and the future of the RUC. During the first week in April, Mitchell worked feverishly on a document that outlined what the agreement would look like. On April 7, two days before the talks' deadline, he delivered it. The outline's most important proposals were for between five and eight cross-border bodies to handle such matters as tourism, agriculture, and railway links, set up by legislation in the British and Irish parliaments, a north-south council of ministers to select membership of those bodies, a commission to look at how the RUC might be made more amenable to Catholics, and a commitment from the British to speed up the release of prisoners.

Within twelve hours Unionist leader David Trimble rejected it as a "Sinn Fein wish list" and a "charter for a United Ireland." His deputy,

John Taylor, proclaimed that he "wouldn't touch it with a forty-foot pole." The Unionists stormed out of the negotiations and demanded that the sixty-five-page document be rewritten. Trimble wrote to British Prime Minister Tony Blair that "it is now 25 years from the failed Sunningdale Agreement and it now appears that the Irish government has learned nothing from the reasons for its failure."[17]

The deal seemed about to collapse. Clinton rang Bertie Ahern, the Irish taoiseach, from Air Force One, offering to "do anything we can" to help. British Prime Minister Blair flew into Belfast and held talks with Trimble. An air of crisis prevailed as television crews and reporters from all over the world gathered around Stormont. It began to seem foolishly optimistic for anyone to have dared to declare that a problem which some traced back to 1169 could be resolved by a specific date, that is, April 9, 1998. Yet Blair insisted he was sticking to his deadline. The Unionists saw the cross-border bodies established under government decree as too independent; they wanted them demoted and under the assembly's control. They wanted the proposed 108-seat assembly to be restricted in its powers, more like a county council than a real government. Ironically, the Ulster Unionists, who for many years lamented the loss of their parliament at Stormont, were now pressing for weak, not strong, devolved government. They were worried that under the new dispensation, a strong assembly, with a large number of Nationalist deputies and powerful links to the Irish republic, would slip out of their control. Most problematic of all, they were demanding that the paramilitaries disarm before their political representatives be allowed into any new government. Sinn Fein warned, meanwhile, that any such concessions would not be acceptable to republicans and nationalists.

April 9 dawned, and Blair was still arguing with Trimble, at one point blocking the doorway to prevent him from walking out again. Would the Unionists, who rejected so many initiatives to settle the Irish conflict, play the wreckers' role yet again? Irish officials involved in the negotiations were less pessimistic. The walkout threat to them seemed more of a negotiating stunt than a real rejection. After all, where would Trimble go? Paisley already occupied Ulster's political wilderness.

At 11 P.M. (U.S. Eastern Standard time), Prime Minister Blair called President Clinton in Washington to ask for his help in persuading the Unionists and republicans to accept a compromise on their core issues, including weaker cross-border bodies and no immediate disarmament. Clinton manned the telephones into the early hours of Friday morning, cajoling Trimble and Adams to reach an agreement. Trimble was assured that disarmament would not be ignored, and Adams that the north-south arrangements would be meaningful, that police reforms would be sought, and the prisoners not forgotten. On Good Friday, April 10, at 4:30 P.M., after a series of last-minute doubts, Trimble said to his still uneasy Unionist Party colleagues, "I'm going for it. Who's with me?"

One of those closest to him, Jeffrey Donaldson, walked out, angry that disarmament of the paramilitary groups was being shunted aside. But what seemed impossible only a few days before occurred: Agreement was reached.

Clinton's intervention was judged crucial. Commented George Mitchell, "I was there from the first day to the last. There would not have been a peace agreement in Northern Ireland without the efforts of Bill Clinton."[18]

The governments moved swiftly to shore up the agreement. At the end of May, referenda were held simultaneously in Northern Ireland and the Irish republic on the Good Friday Agreement. As part of the agreement the Irish government was asking its citizens to dilute the state's claims to jurisdiction over Northern Ireland, contained in articles two and three of the Irish constitution. They were to be changed to express an aspiration for unity, based on consent. Rewriting the constitution was aimed at placating Unionists who for years had cited the articles as an obstacle to any agreement between the two states. Militant republicans attacked the proposed changes as an abandonment of the last vestiges of Ireland's claims to sovereign status on a thirty-two-county basis. In the north, Paisley ran a "no" campaign against the agreement. He argued that it was an IRA ruse to get its prisoners out of jail. Paisley's claims gained emotional credence when a group of IRA bombers serving long sentences for a string of murders in Britain were released on bail and went to a Sinn Fein pro-agreement conference where they received a thunderous welcome. Many ordinary Protestants were disgusted, as they were a few days later when a UDA killer, also on parole, was accorded a similar reception at a loyalist conference in Belfast. Undoubtedly the spectacle reduced the "yes" vote in the north, especially among Protestants. But the Good Friday Agreement still received an enormous endorsement: 94.4 percent voted in favor of it in the Republic, and 71.1 percent in Northern Ireland. The accord laid foundations for a settlement; the referenda strengthened them. Anyone who set out to oppose the Good Friday Agreement, republican or loyalist, could now be accused of defying the will of the Irish people, democratically expressed, north and south, in the referenda.

However, amid the optimism the overwhelming "yes" vote created, there was a cause for concern. While northern Nationalists overwhelmingly supported the agreement, about 95 percent voting in favor, only 55 percent of Unionists agreed with them. Paisley and the others in the "no" campaign claimed a moral victory. The uncertain response to the agreement among Protestants invigorated the rejectionists' campaign for places in the new 108-seat assembly, for which elections were held at the end of June. Once more the pro-agreement parties won a majority, with Sinn Fein securing eighteen seats and 17.65 percent of the vote, its biggest ever. It was now just six seats behind its nationalist rival, the SDLP.

Once more there was a marked difference between the two communities in how they responded to the new arrangements. Within the Nationalist community there was in effect no serious electoral opposition to the agreement. But within the Protestant community, Paisley and other dissident Unionists who ran against it translated the 45 percent "no" vote they achieved in the referendum into twenty-five seats in the assembly. While Trimble's mainstream UUP took twenty-eight seats, it left the pro-agreement Unionists with only a narrow majority. However, the Progressive Unionist Party, which was pro-agreement and could be expected to support Trimble, took two seats. But in the months of negotiations that lay ahead for the setting up of the assembly executive and the cross-border bodies, the UUP leader was forced to move slowly to avoid desertions to the anti-agreement camp. After the election, Trimble was elected to be first minister in the new government, with SDLP member Seamus Mallon as his deputy, when it took office in February 1999. Some expressed surprise that Hume, the man who more than any other was responsible for creating the peace process that led to the agreement, did not become deputy leader of the new assembly. But for Hume the Northern Ireland political arena was too narrow. Its still-divisive sectarian squabbling held little interest for him, as did the more august corridors of Westminster. It was thought that he would not defend his seat there in the next British general election. The man who in 1959 as a university debater advocated Ireland's membership in the Common Market, as the European Union was then known, was happiest in the Brussels parliament, dealing with issues that were on a scale more commensurate with his vision.

· 3 ·

THROUGHOUT MAY and June 1998 it was apparent that Ulster was entering a new stage of its history when a former RUC chief constable, Jack Hermon, and a Sinn Fein president and IRA leader, Gerry Adams, were seen canvassing support for the same agreement. In spite of many difficulties and dangers, a remarkable consensus was being built, one that would have been unimaginable even a few years earlier.

In May, Sinn Fein announced that it would allow its members to sit in the new Northern Ireland assembly—the first time in the party's history that it agreed to take part in the government of a state it previously tried to violently overthrow. Sinn Fein's goal was still a united Ireland. But the party now believed that it could be better achieved by working within the new institutions of government, especially the cross-border bodies, than attempting to destroy them from the outside through violence.

On the loyalist side, the referendum and election campaigns revealed an equally startling change. During the entire period, Paisley, once the voice of loyalism, did not appear on the Shankill Road for fear, it was said, of being heckled. The Shankill, the heartland of Ulster loyalism, was where in 1966 Paisley's rhetoric inspired UVF men like Gusty Spence to take up the bomb and the gun. When the referendum result in favor of the agreement was announced in Belfast's King's Hall, a group of UVF men and their political spokesmen chanted like fans at a soccer match: "Cheerio, cheerio, cheerio," as a flushed and angry Paisley strode from the scene of the count. His son, Ian, Jr., who was following his father's political path, accompanied him. "Where are you going to lead us now?" one of the UVF men asked, running after him. "We're not going to prison for you anymore," another shouted.

"Try to smile," said Paisley's son.

It was wasted advice. Paisley stalked from the hall, scowling.

"The people have spoken. The modern world awaits," commented Davy Ervine, a spokesman for the UVF, which thirty-two years earlier had begun the killing.

· 4 ·

THE TROUBLES were over, but the killing continued. Some of the heirs to Ireland's violent traditions refused to give up their inheritance.

As the Irish people were getting ready to vote in the referenda, a group calling itself the "Real" IRA emerged. On May 8, 1998, it announced its existence, claiming to represent "true" republicans. It stated that Sinn Fein had no right to enter the new assembly, which was "a complete betrayal of the claim of Irish self-determination for which volunteers gave their lives. . . . The cease-fire as called by the old leadership is over and our war machine will once again be directed against the British." The "Real" IRA was made up of about thirty or more former Provisionals who had left the organization late in 1997. They were associated politically with the 32-County Sovereignty Committee. Their leader was former Provisional IRA Army Council member and quartermaster general Micky McKevitt. One of its members was shot dead during a bungled raid on a security van a few miles outside Dublin at the beginning of May. During the summer of 1998, the group bombed Banbridge, County Down, and tried and failed to launch several bombing attacks in Britain.

On Saturday afternoon, August 15, 1998, the market town of Omagh, County Tyrone, was swarming with shoppers. Several days of mist and rain had given way to sunshine, drawing more people to the town's main shopping area around Market Street. Among the shoppers were many women and children, getting ready for the new school year only a couple of weeks away.

The population of Omagh was mainly Catholic, but for many years, long before the Troubles, the town had been the home of a British army garrison. Over the years Omagh experienced its share of political and sectarian killings, but it was never regarded as an especially dangerous place. Indeed, it was quieter and more integrated than most towns and villages in Tyrone. With the peace process firmly in place and the cease-fires in force, there was even less reason for those milling about in the streets that August afternoon to worry about violence.

Shortly before three P.M. newspapers received a warning that there was a car bomb parked between three hundred and four hundred yards from the courthouse, not far from the town center. The RUC was informed and began moving the crowds away from the suspect area toward the already bustling Market Street, where a fatal Vauxhall Cavalier was parked. For whatever reason—stupidity, confusion, or sheer ruthlessness—the person who called in the warning had misled people. The bomb was not close to the courthouse but ticking away in the Cavalier in the middle of the crowd of shoppers, now swollen by those fleeing into what they thought was the safe zone. At 3:10 P.M. the five-hundred-pound device exploded, killing twenty-eight people, including fourteen women. Seven children died. Three generations of one family were wiped out: Mary Grimes, sixty-five; her daughter, Avril Monaghan, thirty; and her granddaughter, Maura, eighteen months. Mrs. Monaghan was pregnant with twins.

Another victim died two months later, bringing the total to twenty-nine and making the Omagh bombing the single worst atrocity in the history of the Ulster conflict.

The "Real" IRA claimed responsibility and apologized to the victims' loved ones. It said that it did not intend to kill civilians but that its warning had not been acted upon properly. As ex-Provisionals, this excuse came easily to them. However, the resignation with which such excuses were once accepted was no longer in evidence. By 1998 hope had replaced it.

Shock quickly turned to anger and disgust. Protesters picketed the home of Bernadette Sands-McKevitt and her husband, Micky McKevitt—the two most public figures associated with the new organization. It became obvious that what was left of the tradition of violent republicanism was completely discredited. Sinn Fein, past master in the art of evasive language thanks to decades of IRA "mistakes," now joined the chorus of unequivocal condemnations. The time for waffling about violence was over. The INLA, too, issued a statement saying that "there was now no basis for the continuation of armed struggle by republicans." For the first time in its history, it called a cease-fire. Not long afterward, the "Real" IRA announced that it also was calling a cease-fire. Violent republicanism was drowning in the blood of ordinary Catholics and Protestants, the very people for whom it claimed to be waging its war.

A similar fate befell extreme loyalism. In July 1998, during the annual Drumcree crisis, the Orange marchers tried yet again to force their way past the Catholics on Garvaghy Road. But this time the police and army blocked their path. As the standoff continued, Protestant gasoline bombers set fire to the home of a Catholic woman who lived in a loyalist district with three of her sons. The three young boys, who were, ironically enough, being raised Protestants, were burned to death. The Drumcree protest effectively collapsed.[19] Within weeks the Loyalist Volunteer Force, the last of the Protestant paramilitary groups still defying the peace process, said it was ending its campaign.

On September 1, 1998, two weeks after the Omagh massacre, Gerry Adams made a momentous statement in which he said that "violence must be a thing of the past—over, done with." Though "must" implied a moral imperative, not a statement of fact, it was the closest the republican movement had come to saying that the armed campaign was ended forever. It was sufficiently close to allow Trimble to do what he said he would not do until the IRA disarmed: meet with Adams. The two held face-to-face negotiations on September 10. This was the first meeting between a leader of the republican movement and a leader of Ulster Unionism since 1922, when Michael Collins held talks with James Craig, the prime minister of the new state of Northern Ireland, in an effort to halt the sectarian violence then sweeping Belfast. In 1922 the talks failed. The killings continued. And when they stopped, the two communities were hunkered down behind the barricades from which they had viewed each other with hatred and suspicion over the long, dark decades.

In 1998 the problems the two leaders discussed concerned that distrust, fear, and insecurity, immeasurably deepened now thanks to the years of killing. Trimble's demand for paramilitary disarmament was still the chief obstacle to accommodation between the two communities. The refusal to concede to the demand, principally by the IRA, was blocking progress on the setting up of the power-sharing executive, which was supposed to take place in "shadow" form by the end of October, with departments and their ministers nominated, and decisions reached on the number and scope of the cross-border bodies. Failure to resolve these matters would delay the time when the assembly formally assumed power as the new government of Northern Ireland, which was supposed to occur in February 1999.

Agreement between Trimble and his deputy, Mallon, was not reached until December 18, following another round of long and arduous negotiations. The first minister announced that there would be ten ministerial departments in the new power-sharing executive and six cross-border bodies to deal with matters such as inland waterways, trade and business development, and special European Union projects. Most significant of all, perhaps, was the breakdown in the distribution of the ministerial departments, which were apportioned to different parties according to the number of seats they held in the assembly. Of the ten departments, three would go the Ulster Unionist Party, two to the Democratic Unionist Party, three to the SDLP, and two to Sinn Fein. That is, there would be five Unionist-controlled departments and five controlled by nationalists.

For the first time in Northern Ireland's history, Nationalists, though still a minority, had achieved political parity with Unionists.

Another "first" occurred the same day. The LVF under police escort brought a small cache of weapons to a workshop in east Belfast used by the International Body on Decommissioning. It consisted of nine guns, 350 rounds of ammunition, two dozen shotgun shells, six detonators, and two pipe bombs. Shortly after 10 A.M., before a small group of reporters, disarmament made a modest beginning as two guns were chopped to pieces in a metal slicing machine, their fragments dumped in a garbage can. The LVF became the first paramilitary group in Ireland's long history of illegal militias and secret brotherhoods to voluntarily disarm.

The bigger paramilitary organizations like the Provisional IRA and UVF shrugged it off as a publicity stunt, knowing full well that if the settlement was to survive, they would eventually have to do the same.

· NINE ·

IN CONCLUSION

TIME PAST AND TIME PRESENT

HISTORY IS often made in unlikely places. A drab building, a dreary market town, a street corner, a field, an alleyway, a dingy pub. In Northern Ireland the scale is small, the location precise. Saint Comgall's, Belfast, is one such spot, a nondescript building that has served as a primary school to the Falls community since the 1920s. Centuries before that, local legend has it, a Fairy Thorn grew on the spot. It was there that the Troubles assumed the form they were to keep for thirty violent years. In the early hours of August 15, 1969, a small group of IRA men fired on Protestant mobs threatening their neighborhood, drove them off, and in doing so for all intents and purposes created the Provisionals. Almost thirty years later, Saint Comgall's was a polling station for the referendum on the Good Friday Agreement, the aim of which was to take the gun out of Irish politics forever.

A few streets away, Billy McKee, ex-leader of the Belfast Provisionals and one of the small band who in August 1969 had occupied the school, sat in his parlor reflecting on the past and present. "You can see it all like a picture," said the spry seventy-six-year-old of the events of August 1969, "the flames everywhere." Except for a few years in Dublin and various spells in jail for IRA activities, McKee has lived in this neighborhood all his life. But the old Falls is gone—the maze of narrow streets of tiny red-brick homes with black slate roofs has been completely remodeled. The neighborhood is greener now; the homes have gardens. "It's strange to see the trees," he mused. "There's trees in every garden." Outside, a British patrol edged along the hedgerow in what was once a sniper's alley but is now a wide street with no gunmen lurking at the windows of its pleasant houses.

He spent time in jail with Gerry Adams's father and also with Gerry Adams but has no kind words for the son. "He was never a republican of our type," according to McKee. He greets with anger and disbelief the prospect of Sinn Fein entering a Northern Ireland government. "I don't know how anyone who calls himself a republican can build it up. . . . Back to Stormont is back to the status quo.

"I still follow the old line," he said. But he has no illusions that there is much support for his line. "There's despondency among good republicans," he admitted. "They're actually broken."

On the day Ireland said yes to the agreement, up and down the Falls Road black flags on lampposts flapped in the mild May breeze. They commemorated the seventeenth anniversary of the hunger strike that began the transformation of the republican movement into a political party ready to take its place in the new government as part of the settlement reached on Good Friday 1998.

In the wake of the IRA cease-fire, a settlement became possible. A majority of Unionists recognized that their goal of an "Ulster" that incorporated and protected only a Protestant sense of identity was no longer viable. The new Northern Ireland that, it is hoped, will emerge from the Good Friday Agreement has to express the messy reality of two conflicting aspirations, Nationalist and Unionist, which for better or worse constitute the nature of the state. "To see what is in front of one's nose requires a constant struggle," George Orwell wrote in 1946.[1]

In the 1960s it was believed that the clashing aspirations of Nationalists and Unionists, could be resolved through raising Catholics up to the same economic level as Protestants and removing at the same time the various obstacles to their full integration within the state. This encountered a simple problem: It was impossible to integrate Catholics into Northern Ireland without radically changing the nature of the state. From the days of Spence's UVF to Paisley's "no" campaign against the 1998 agreement, some Protestants resisted that prospect, viewing it as a threat to Northern Ireland's existence.

Johnny White had been one of those, and in August 1969, as a nineteen-year-old vigilante, he was in the Protestant mob throwing gasoline bombs at Catholic homes only a few streets away from where Billy McKee and his men were crouching, guns in hand. In the summer of 1998, White's face adorned election posters that hung from walls and lampposts along the Shankill Road and the streets of north Belfast, a reminder of his failed attempt to win a seat in the new Stormont assembly as a member of the UDA-linked Ulster Democratic Party. As leader of the UDA's most dangerous assassination squad in 1973, he prowled those same streets looking for Catholics to murder. Now the bespectacled face of candidate White beamed a reassuring smile on all who passed. He was not long back from a cruise that took him, among other places, to Rome, where he visited the Vatican. Michelangelo's Sistine Chapel ceiling deeply impressed him.

On a trip up the Shankill he paused at a new mural depicting the history of the UDA. Had he won a seat in the new assembly, his portrait would have been part of the mural. Near election time, however, the local BBC television station did a profile of him and described his role in the murder of SDLP councilor Paddy Wilson and Wilson's companion, Irene Andrews, stabbed to death on the outskirts of north Belfast. "They showed the funerals," White said. "It was very emotive." He shrugged off the disappointment of his defeat and inspected the unfinished mural from various angles. "It isn't just the way we wanted it," he said.

Ultimately, Protestant resistance failed, as did the IRA's armed campaign. And it failed mainly because Northern Ireland was not "Ulster." Ulster was a Unionist vision, the secure homeland that the Protestant planters sought to establish. Northern Ireland was the complex reality, a "Little Ulster," six counties carved out of nine, securing them a majority but one that was brittle and subject to change. Census figures from 1991 showed that Catholics were an increasingly large minority, around 43 percent of the population. Over the years, that change was most noticeable west of the River Bann in the counties of Derry, Tyrone, and Fermanagh, where Catholics were an overall majority. Were Unionists to attempt through a new partition to carve out a "safer," more homogeneous, homeland today, they would be constrained to draw the border down the east bank of the Bann, with a salient around the Protestant enclave of Coleraine. But even within that new, even littler "Ulster," there would be areas where Catholics were in a large majority, such as south Armagh and south Down.

Meanwhile, in Belfast, once a "jewel" of the British Empire, Catholics have been growing in numbers since the 1960s, as evidenced by the abandoned Protestant churches and Orange halls engulfed in the demographic shift. Some have fallen to ruin. One Orange hall in west Belfast has become a well-appointed republican drinking club, and a Protestant church in the same area is now a cultural center where the Irish language is taught and Irish events held. The population of the Shankill Road, the working-class heart of loyalist Belfast, fell from 76,000 in the late 1960s to 27,000 in the early 1990s. In north Belfast, in the decade between 1982 and 1992, the Protestant population dropped from 112,000 to 56,000.[2] In the prosperous Malone Road district of south Belfast, once a bastion of middle- and upper-middle-class Protestants, there is one Catholic church. It was originally erected for the servants who worked in the surrounding mansions owned by wealthy businessmen. Now it has undergone a major expansion in order to accommodate the drastic rise in the number of its parishioners. They are no longer servants. They now own the mansions.

In 1997, after more than one hundred years, Unionists' political domination of the city was broken when the first Catholic lord mayor of Belfast, SDLP member Alban Maginness, took office. The Ulster homeland proved an unrealizable dream, as did the Provisional IRA's thirty-two-county socialist republic.

Almost as dramatic were the political changes within Belfast's expanding Catholic community. By the mid-1990s, Sinn Fein was the biggest nationalist party in the city, with thirteen council seats, almost twice as many as the SDLP and the same number as the Ulster Unionist Party. It is only a matter of time before there is a Sinn Fein lord mayor of Belfast.

The changing demographics and the rise of a new Catholic middle class has attenuated the long-prevailing sense of grievance in the Catholic community. The explosion of violence in August 1969 was mainly a working-class phenomenon, but it was originally set off because of frustration as upwardly mobile, well-educated Catholics ran into the old barriers of discrimination. With the rise of the Provisional IRA, who sought not the reform of the Northern Ireland state but its destruction, civil rights concerns soon became secondary to the violent pursuit of a united socialist Ireland, the Holy Grail of republicanism.

Direct rule brought about the dismantling of the Unionist structures from 1972 onward, and the barriers to social and economic progress for middle-class Catholics gradually came down. However, working-class Catholics still suffered disproportionately from unemployment and other forms of disadvantage. And they bore the brunt of the security forces' response to republican violence launched mainly from working-class Catholic districts. Their sense of grievance remained and spurred the rise of Sinn Fein as a political power. But within the working-class Catholic community, changes were also apparent.

The kind of poverty and bad housing typical of the 1960s was all but eradicated in the 1980s and 1990s. While unemployment remained high, a black economy flourished (usually controlled by the republican paramilitary groups), with people collecting welfare and working at part-time jobs. Even the poorest housing developments of west Belfast in the mid-1990s show a remarkable transformation from the way things were in the 1960s: streets of well-kept houses with neat gardens, cars parked at the gate, and satellite dishes on nearly every home have replaced the Victorian slums. Large shopping malls flourish, their parking lots nearly always full. What sense of grievance remained became more focused on specific issues, such as the police and the need to reform it to make it more acceptable to Nationalists. Demands for reform of those aspects of Northern Ireland that most offended Catholics, including the handful of Orange marches that their organizers insist on forcing through Nationalist areas, have gradually replaced the old, generalized hostility against the state. As the millennium approaches and Catholics get ready to take their share of responsibility for running Northern Ireland's government, a new self-confidence characterizes their community, replacing the deep sense of alienation that it felt for almost a century.

How much "credit" the Provisional IRA can claim for this transformation is a matter of debate. Undoubtedly, the fall of Stormont in 1972 was due at least in part to the IRA. But ultimately it was not the IRA that determined the nature of the changes which overtook Northern Ireland. More than anything it was the failure of Unionism to create a moderate center able to accommodate Catholic demands that forced the British to rethink and then restructure the 1920 settlement. That failure dated back to the mid-1960s and the Unionist government's inability to advance the reforms Prime Minister Terence O'Neill sought. At the same time, the progress of Paisleyism helped open and then exploit the first crack in the Unionist monolith. The rise of the Provisionals made it harder for any moderate center to develop later. But the chief obstacle to its development always lay within Unionism itself. Even after the peace process was in place, the IRA's campaign ended, and Sinn Fein was ready to take part in the new institutions of government, Unionist leaders were still wavering on the Good Friday Agreement, uncertain about their ability to deliver a majority of their party in favor of the new reforms.

The rise of confidence within the Nationalist community has been accompanied by a corresponding decline in the morale of Unionists. In Protestant working-class communities throughout the 1990s there were echoes of the kind of complaints that once were typical of poor Catholics. They expressed a sense of alienation from the state made still more bitter because, unlike Catholics, they once identified with it and saw it as "theirs." It was partly explained by the rise of unemployment in Protestant areas where before jobs were once virtually guaranteed. Working-class alienation from the predominantly middle-class Ulster Unionist Party took the form of growing support for "fringe" loyalist parties like the UVF-linked Progressive Unionist Party. A deep sense of betrayal characterized the feeling many loyalists harbored toward the Protestant middle class who, they believed, reaped most of the benefits of the state while condemning and dissociating themselves from the Protestant paramilitaries who "defended" it. Middle-class Protestants, meanwhile, regarded loyalist paramilitaries as criminals. There was no equivalent sympathy for them as is found for IRA prisoners in virtually all sections of the Catholic community. "Respectable" Protestants of all classes were angry at the sight of convicted gunmen and bombers being released in a steady stream from the Maze prison until by the end of 1998 it was almost empty. To them the Good Friday Agreement was simply awarding the wicked. By the 1990s, increasing numbers of the children of the Protestant middle classes, rather than finishing their education at Queens University or the University of Ulster, were choosing instead to go to universities in England and Scotland. Many would settle there.

Protestants were clearly more uncomfortable with the new Northern Ireland than their Catholic counterparts. However, in late 1998, when it was announced that the Nobel Peace Prize was to be awarded to John Hume and David Trimble, it was thought that this international recognition of the role Protestants played in the peace process might help them adjust more easily to some of its consequences. In fact, it highlighted their continued defensiveness and suspicion. Many of them scoffed at the award as an attempt by the outside world to "bribe" them through flattering Trimble, claiming (like many Nationalists) that it was given for purely political reasons in order to shore up his commitment to implementing the accords; a few, even in his own party, could hardly disguise their hostility to the honor. Their reactions made obvious the isolated nature of Unionism as an ideology, and the self-referential narrowness of its vision.[3]

The honoring of Hume, in contrast, was welcomed in the Nationalist community and beyond almost without reservation. There was no problem in recognizing Hume's role in the peace process (after all, without him it would not have happened); nor was the world's attention viewed suspiciously as containing some kind of threat or bribe. Quite the opposite was the case: Ulster's Nationalist community has always welcomed, indeed sought, outside attention, perhaps because they were convinced that the world could not but see things their way.

Until fairly recently it appeared extremely unlikely that it ever would be possible to write a "conclusion" to the story of the Ulster Troubles. Few dared predict that a conflict involving such irreconcilable demands could be brought to an end. Indeed, some doubt that it is as yet possible. Since there is a dispute about when the Troubles actually began, it is fitting that there should be controversy over if and when they came to an end.

The conflict known as the Troubles was never a continuous, unchanging struggle, however. As is argued in these pages, the "classic" period of the Troubles ended more than twenty years ago, in 1977. Loyalist paramilitary organizations drastically reduced their level of activity, as did the Provisional IRA. But organized violence remained in the form of terrorism linked to a developing political organization that attempted to articulate the republican movement's aims but ended up spending most of the time justifying its methods. By the early 1990s it was clear to some of those involved in that campaign that it would not achieve its aims, thanks mainly to the successes of the security forces and the measures taken by the RUC against terrorism. Within the republican movement there was a growing feeling that violence was counterproductive and was limiting the capacity of Sinn Fein (having tasted electoral success) to make further political progress. It was the ending of the armed campaign that allowed the moderate political center to develop into a public sphere where compromise would eventually replace the clash of contending absolutes, the dogmas of Unionism and republicanism.

For too long those dogmas proved deadly, as the burned-out shell of a house where three young brothers died and the devastated shopping street of a quiet market town where twenty-nine men, women, and children were slaughtered mutely testify. But hope, too, is found in unlikely places.

The IRA Family Tree

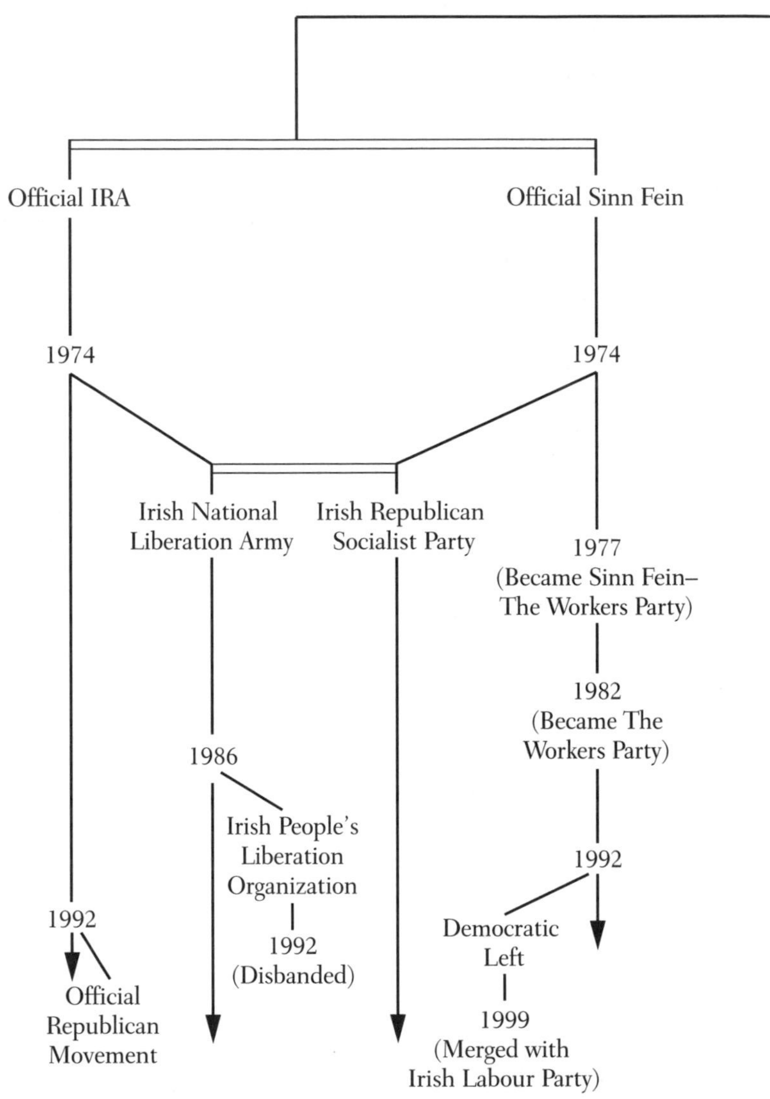

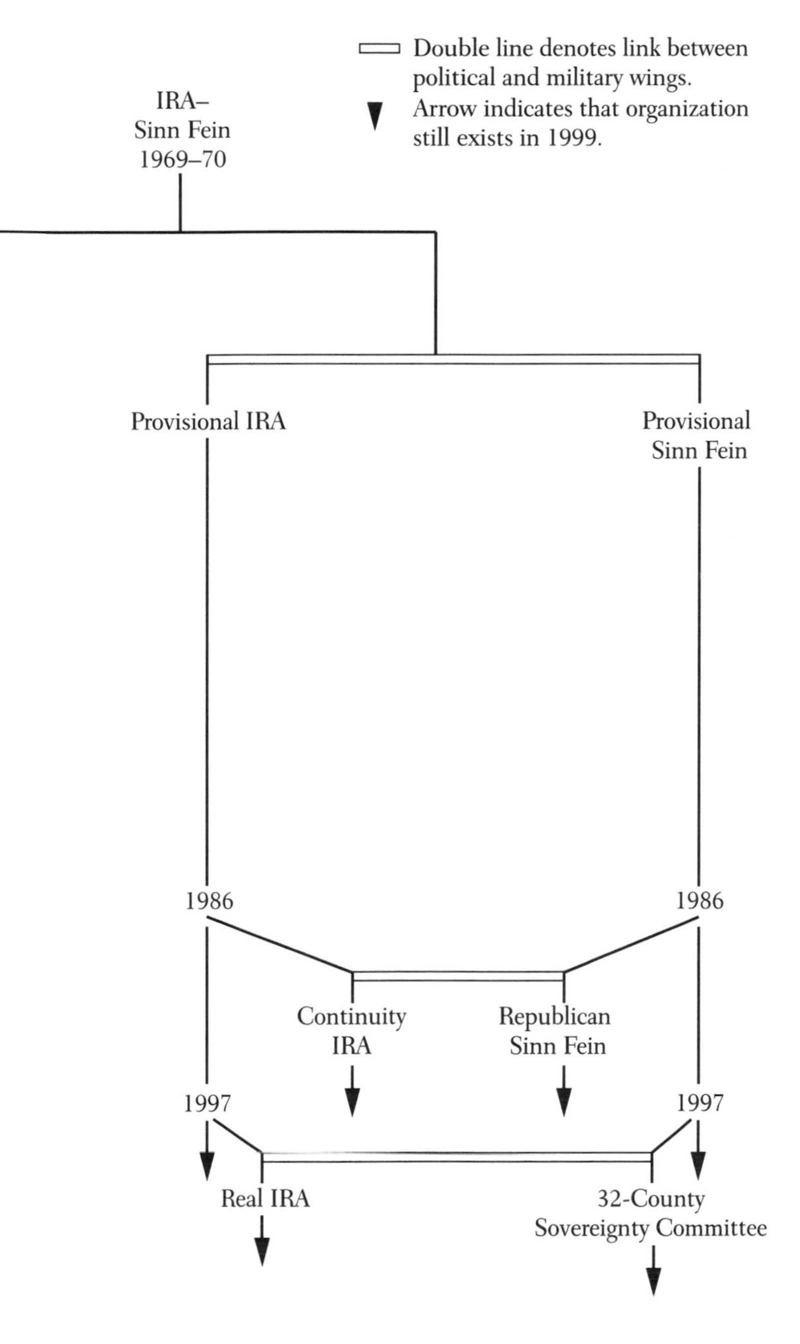
Double line denotes link between political and military wings.
Arrow indicates that organization still exists in 1999.
IRA–
Sinn Fein
1969–70
Provisional IRA
Provisional
Sinn Fein
1986
1986
Continuity
IRA
Republican
Sinn Fein
1997
1997
Real IRA
32-County
Sovereignty Committee

NOTES

CHAPTER 1
RETURN OF THE GUNMAN: 1966–1969

1. The Ulster Volunteer Force took its name from a militia established in 1912 to oppose Home Rule for Ireland. The original UVF was one hundred thousand strong. Incorporated into the British army en masse during World War I, it lost over five thousand men in the first hour of the Battle of the Somme on July 6, 1916.

2. David McKittrick and Jack Holland, *The Assassins: A History of the Ulster Defense Association.* Unpublished.

3. A. T. Q. Steward, *The Narrow Ground: Aspects of Ulster, 1609–1969* Belfast: Blackstaff Press, 1997.

4. Ibid.

5. Thomas Hennessy, *History of Northern Ireland, 1920–1996.* New York: St. Martin's Press, 1997.

6. Ibid. In 1958, of the twenty full-time clerical staff working for Newry Urban District Council, all were Catholics. Of the seventy outdoor full-time workers, all were Catholics. Of the 765 houses belonging to the council, only twenty-two were occupied by Protestants although Protestants represented one-fifth of the population.

7. Daniel O'Connell used the tactics of protest march and passive resistance in the mid-nineteenth century in his successful campaign to end the anti-Catholic penal laws. O'Connell was greatly admired by the black antislavery campaigner Frederick Douglass, who visited Ireland. When NICRA took up the same tactic from the black civil-rights marchers, it had come full circle.

8. *The Irish Times,* June 20, 1998.

9. Eamonn McCann, *War in an Irish Town.* London: Pluto Press, 1980.

10. Gerry Adams, *Before the Dawn.* New York: William Morrow, 1996.

11. Alexis de Tocqueville, *The Old Regime and the French Revolution.* New York: Knopf.

12. Michael Farrell, *Northern Ireland: The Orange State.* London: Pluto Press, 1980.

13. Bernadette Devlin, *The Price of My Soul*. London: Andre Deutsch, 1969.

14. *Disturbances in Northern Ireland (1969),* The Lord Cameron Report. A subsequent inquiry found the RUC guilty of "misconduct which involved assault and battery."

15. McKittrick and Holland, *The Assassins.*

16. Ibid.

17. Patrick Bishop and Eamonn Mallie, *The Provisional IRA*. London: Corgi Books, 1988.

18. Interview with Billy McKee, 1998.

19. Sean MacStiofain, *Memoirs of a Revolutionary*. Edinburgh: Gordon Cremonesi, 1975.

20. Gerry Adams, *Before the Dawn.*

21. MacStiofain, *Memoirs.*

22. Adams, *Before the Dawn.*

23. MacStiofain, *Memoirs.*

24. Henry Patterson, *The Politics of Illusion: A Political History of the IRA*. London: Serif, 1997. In fact, O'Donnell was exaggerating the amount of sectarianism within the Belfast IRA. In late 1932 striking railway workers in Belfast, most of them Protestant, successfully enlisted the IRA's aid in trying to stop scabs from taking supplies by road into the city. During an attack on scabs, the IRA shot dead a RUC officer, the police force's first fatality. The Belfast IRA at one time even succeeded in recruiting a unit of Shankill Road Protestants.

25. Interview with Billy McKee, July 1998.

26. Bishop and Mallie, *The Provisional IRA.*

27. Hugh McCabe, a Catholic, was home on leave at the time of his death. He joined the British army in 1966 after refusing a job as a bartender at the International Hotel in Belfast. The position was filled instead by Peter Ward, whom the UVF murdered a few months later. An American television crew caught McCabe's death on camera.

28. During the disturbances of July and August, gunfire wounded 154 people and killed ten, eight of them in Belfast. In the city, 1,820 families were forced from their homes, 1,505 of them Catholic. Most of the damage and casualties occurred between August 12 and 15. Protestants especially targeted Catholic-owned or -managed pubs. Thirty were destroyed and forty-six damaged.

29. *Daughters of the Troubles: Belfast Stories,* a documentary produced by Marcia Rock and cowritten by Jack Holland and Marcia Rock.

CHAPTER 2
OUT OF THE ASHES: 1969–1972

1. McKittrick and Holland, *The Assassins: A History of the UDA,* unpublished.

2. Interview with Billy McKee, 1998.

3. Gerry Adams, *Before the Dawn.* New York: William Morrow, 1996.

4. Quoted in Paul Bew, Peter Gibson, and Henry Patterson, *Northern Ireland, 1921–1996: Political Force and Social Classes.* London: Serif, 1996.

5. On a visit to London in 1965, the author astonished his hosts—university students—by informing them that Northern Ireland was still part of the United Kingdom. They had assumed Britain had left Ireland in 1922.

6. Bew, Gibson, and Patterson.

7. Bew and Gillespie, *Northern Ireland: A Chronology of the Troubles, 1968–1993.* London: Serif, 1996.

8. A. T. Q. Steward, *The Narrow Ground: Aspects of Ulster, 1609–1969.* Belfast: Blackstaff Press, 1997. The Hunt report, the latest in a long line of inquiries into Belfast's street disorders, repeated familiar themes about the inefficiency and partiality of the police. In 1864 a report had observed that "as regards the local police, the absolute necessity for change is universally acknowledged." The Royal Irish Constabulary and the Royal Ulster Constabulary were each in turn "criticized for allowing riots to develop, and failing to contain them when they did develop. If they were unarmed, it was recommended that they should be armed; if they used their arms, it was recommended that they should be disarmed. When Lord Hunt recommended in 1969 that the RUC be instantly disarmed, he was, whether he knew it or not, following a well-established precedent."

9. For a time McKeague was associated with Paisley's UPV, the UVF, and an obscure organization, Tara, which was run by Billy McGrath, also a homosexual and pedophile.

10. Henry Patterson, *The Politics of Illusion: A Political History of the IRA.* London: Serif, 1997.

11. Ibid.

12. Sean MacStiofain, *Memoirs of a Revolutionary.* Edinburgh: Gordon Cremonesi, 1973.

13. Interview with Billy McKee, 1998.

14. Interview with Billy McKee, 1998. Adams has stated that he did support certain aspects of the Goulding strategy, such as the building of a nationalist liberation front.

15. In contrast, the Provisionals used pins to affix their lilies and for a while were called "Pinheads." But this nickname did not last.

16. Interview with George Harrison, 1998.

17. Jack Holland, *The American Connection: U.S. Guns, Money and Influence in Northern Ireland.* New York: Viking, 1987.

18. A second Provisional IRA team was also trawling through the United States with the approval of a member of the Irish government, which had made over £105,000 available to the Catholic "defense committees" for the "relief of distress in Northern Ireland." The 1969 crisis had caught Dublin unaware, and in a desperate effort to do something, its agents linked up with a few leading Provisionals who were involved in Belfast's Catholic defense groups. Subsequently, controversy erupted in which the Official IRA alleged that the Irish government was responsible for creating the Provisional IRA, with the intention of splitting the republican movement and weakening its socialist program in the south. The Provisionals dismissed this conspiracy theory and countered that their organization would have come about anyway, thanks not to the Irish government but to the circumstances. Later, several high-ranking ministers in Dublin would stand trial for arms smuggling, including Charles Haughey, who later became taoiseach (prime minister). They were acquitted after a sensational trial in 1970.

19. Adams, *Before the Dawn.* Disapproval of local women who went out with soldiers gradually grew. From 1971 onward, shaving the offender's hair and then tarring and feathering her became the punishment for women who violated this communal rule.

20. The residents accused the soldiers of stealing and abusive behavior, which later led to several court cases.

21. McKittrick and Holland, *The Assassins.* Members of the UDA later claimed to have started the whole episode. They said that a few of their members went to the fringes of the Falls district on July 1 and opened fire on troops in order to provoke the army who blamed republicans into raiding for weapons. The UDA used a similar tactic on several occasions in 1972 and 1973, intending to spark clashes between Catholics and soldiers.

22. Colonel Michael Dewar, *The British Army in Northern Ireland.* London: Arms and Armour Press, 1997.

23. South Armagh had been the scene of the first fatality experienced by the Ulster Special Constabulary, which preceded the RUC, when, in January 1921, the IRA shot and killed a special constable in the village of Crossmaglen. In 1985, Donaldson's brother, Alexander, who was also in the RUC, died along with eight other constables in a mortar bomb attack on the police station in Newry, County Down.

24. Sunday Times Insight Team, *Ulster,* London: Penguin Books, 1972.

25. Patricia McCluskey, quoted in Thomas Hennessey, *History of Northern Ireland: 1920–1996*. New York: St. Martin's Press, 1997.

26. Ibid.

27. Ibid.

28. *Fortnight,* February 5, 1971, quoted in Hennessy, *History.*

29. Interview with Billy McKee, 1998.

30. In late June 1970, an IRA sniper shot and seriously wounded a soldier in north Belfast during the riots between Protestants and Catholics. There were many other instances when troops were fired on.

31. MacStiofain, *Memoirs.*

32. Patrick Bishop and Eamonn Mallie, *The Provisional IRA*. London: Corgi Books, 1988. Billy Reid died three months later in a gun battle with soldiers. A popular ballad still celebrates his life and death.

33. Interview with Billy McKee, 1998.

34. These figures are taken from the European Commission of Human Rights report, *Ireland Against the United Kingdom of Great Britain and Northern Ireland: Application No. 5310/71.*

35. Jack Holland and Susan Phoenix, *Phoenix: Policing the Shadows: The Secret War Against Terrorism in Northern Ireland.* London: Hodder and Stoughton, 1996.

36. Jack Holland, *Too Long a Sacrifice: Life and Death in Northern Ireland Since 1969.* New York: Dodd Mead, 1981.

37. *Report of the Committee of Privy Counselors appointed to consider authorized procedures for the interrogation of prisoners suspected of terrorism.* Chairman Lord Parker of Waddington.

38. MacStiofain, *Memoirs.*

39. Adams, *Before the Dawn.*

40. Ibid.

41. Holland and Phoenix, *Phoenix.*

42. *Report of the Committee.* Lord Gardiner also revealed that the techniques derived from KGB interrogation practices.

43. Holland, *Too Long a Sacrifice.* Seven years later the European Human Rights Court at Strasbourg, after a lengthy and exhaustive investigation, found Britain guilty of violating the European Human Rights Convention, to which it was a signatory. The European Human Rights Commission's inquiry was initiated by the Irish government. It uncovered the fact that contrary to what the British asserted—that the use of the five techniques was "informal" and never authorized in any written document—there were written instructions concerning their application in the hands of British army intelligence officers. An Irish psychiatrist, who appeared as an expert witness for the Irish government, produced the document during secret hearings into the allegations held by the

commission. He had acquired it during a conference on the uses of sensory deprivation at a security services intelligence center in England in 1969. Most embarrassing, it showed that there were, in fact, six techniques, the sixth being the use of beatings to force prisoners to their feet again when they collapsed at the wall. The document was subsequently suppressed.

44. The only Protestant arrested was a member of the Official IRA, Ronnie Bunting. His was an unusual political evolution. The son of a leading Paisleyite, Bunting joined the civil rights movement as a student and then became active in the Officials, eventually ending up as a leader of the Irish National Liberation Army.

45. In their accounts of the IRA, MacStiofain and Adams ignore this attack, as they do the murders of the three Scottish soldiers. Likewise, "Freedom Struggle," the Provisionals booklet that recounts the story of the organization's first four years, completely omits this and other sectarian attacks, in claiming that in over one thousand IRA operations between the beginning of 1971 and March 1972, civilian casualties "were about nil."

46. McKittrick and Holland, *Assassins.*

47. Ibid.

CHAPTER 3
THE BLOOD-DIMMED TIDE: 1972–1977

1. *Bloody Sunday and the Report of the Widgery Tribunal: The Irish Government's Assessment of the New Material.* Dublin, 1998.

2 Ibid. This has led some experts to surmise that a dumdum bullet was used.

3. The wounds of all three, experts claim, showed the bullets that hit them were fired from above at a trajectory of 45 degrees. Evidence to this effect comes from Dr. Raymond McClean, who was at the march on January 30, attended to some of the victims, and later was at the postmortems, and from the examination of the photographs, statements, and inquest reports carried out twenty-five years later by Robert Breglio. Breglio was a detective in the New York Police Department's ballistics squad for a quarter of a century. In a report he concluded that "the angles of trajectory of bullet wounds of three deceased named William Nash, John Young and Michael McDaid originated from an area in the vicinity of Derry Walls."

4. *Bloody Sunday.*

5. Paul Bew and Gordon Gillespie, *Northern Ireland: A Chronology of the Troubles, 1968–1993.* London: Serif, 1996.

6. *Bloody Sunday.*

7. Ibid.

8. European Commission of Human Rights report, *Ireland Against the United Kingdom of Great Britain and Northern Ireland: Application No. 5310/71.*

9. Colm Keena, *A Biography of Gerry Adams.* Cork: Mercier Press, 1990.

10. Ibid.

11. Quoted in Bew and Gillespie, *Northern Ireland.*

12. Interview with Billy McKee, 1998.

13. Prime Minister Edward Heath later revealed in his account of those years that he had the Royal Navy and the RAF on standby near Derry in case his troops should encounter severe resistance when they moved in the Bogside and Creggan areas.

14. Interview with John White, 1998.

15. W. D. Flackes and Sydney Elliott, *Northern Ireland: A Political Directory, 1968–1993.* Belfast: Blackstaff Press, 1994.

16. David McKittrick and Jack Holland, *The Assassins: A History of the Ulster Defense Association*. Unpublished.

17. Interview with John White, 1998.

18. Interview with Jackie Hutchinson, 1977. Hutchinson, who was an active member of the Shankill Road murder squad, said that before McCartney was killed there was talk of raping her so as not to let her "go to waste." But this was rejected in favor of a song. In July 1977 the UDA "executed" Hutchinson as an informer.

19. There were several other torture killings in Belfast in 1972 for which the UDA was to blame. On August 14, forty-eight-year-old Thomas Madden's body was found in a shop doorway in north Belfast with over 150 stab wounds. James McCartan was abducted from an east Belfast hotel on October 3, and his badly beaten body was found the next day; he had been hung by the heels, stripped, and beaten with bats. Two months later the UDA team in south Belfast tortured and killed Patrick Benstead. He had been burned on his feet and fingers, and a cross and the number 4 branded on his back with a hot poker. His eyes were gouged out. His body was dumped in east Belfast to make the police think it was the responsibility of Herron's gang, much to his annoyance.

20. The Provisional IRA denied responsibility for the Claudy bombings, as they did the deaths of the three Scots soldiers in March 1971. However, shortly before the bombs exploded, at 10:15 A.M. on the morning of July 31, three youths were seen desperately trying to find a telephone that worked in the nearby village of Dungiven, in order to call the Claudy RUC station with a warning about the bombs. Unfortunately, they could not find a working telephone, thanks to the fact that a few days earlier the IRA from Derry had knocked out the local telephone installation. The men involved in the operation were from Claudy. One was a priest. Another one of those involved was working as a barman in New York City as of 1998.

21. Report of the European Commission.

22. McKittrick and Holland, *The Assassins.*

23. Interview with John White, 1998.

24. Interview with UDA activist, 1977.

25. Interview with John White, 1998. White said that Wilson and Andrews were murdered in reprisal for the Official IRA's killing on June 21 of a mentally retarded Protestant teenager, David Walker, whom the Officials mistakenly believed was involved in sectarian murders. He also said that the reason Wilson and Andrews were stabbed so many times was that the knife used, a common commando-style knife available in any sports shop, had a short blade, and he wanted to make sure the couple was dead. But he admitted that the UDA also wanted to provoke another Jack the Ripper scare such as had gripped Catholic areas in the summer of 1972. "Murder is murder no matter what way you do it," he added.

26. The detective who investigated the Herron assassination said it was one of the most puzzling he had ever encountered. Among the possibilities that the RUC considered was that an undercover army unit had killed him; then, an RUC detective with whom Herron was known to have had a link was questioned, to no avail. Almost certainly, Herron was murdered by fellow UDA men who suspected he was stealing money from the UDA prisoners' funds.

27. Quoted in Bew and Gillespie, *Northern Ireland.*

28. Michael Farrell, *Northern Ireland: The Orange State*. London: Pluto Press, 1980.

29. Ibid.

30. *Belfast Newsletter,* May 17, 1974, quoted in Farrell, *Northern Ireland.*

31. J. Bowyer Bell, *In Dubious Battle: The Dublin and Monaghan Bombings, 1972–1974.* Dublin: Poolbeg Press, 1997.

32. Ibid.

33. Interview with Anne Massey's family, 1994.

34. In 1977, the UDA claimed that one of its units from Mid-Ulster had carried out the Monaghan bomb attack, which they said was supposed to take place before the Dublin bombings. The aim was to hire Irish security forces away from the capital and allow the twelve UVF men delivering the bombs a free run. But the Monaghan bomb had a faulty timer and exploded after those in Dublin. McKittrick and Holland, *The Assassins.* While no one was ever charged in connection with the Dublin and Monaghan bombings, most of the names of the twenty-six or so men allegedly involved have been made public. They include several who have since been killed: Billy Hanna, Horace Boyle, and William "Frenchie" Marchant. Hanna was killed during an internal UVF dispute on July 27, 1975. Four days later Boyle died when a bomb he was planting exploded prematurely. The Provisional IRA shot Robert McConnell,

who was in the UDR, at his home on April 5, 1976. Marchant was standing outside the Shankill Road offices of the Progressive Unionist Party, the UVF's political wing, when the Provisionals shot him dead on April 28, 1987. The UVF did not claim responsibility for the bombings, perhaps because shortly before the attacks the Northern Ireland secretary of state, Merlyn Rees, had lifted the ban on the organization to encourage it to go into politics. Claims that undercover British agents were involved were denied by the organization in 1994.

35. Quoted in Bew and Gillespie, *Northern Ireland.*

36. Ibid.

37. European Commission of Human Rights report.

38. Interview with Billy McKee, 1998.

39. The unit was arrested when attempting to return to Ireland. Among those apprehended were Dolours Price and her sister, Marion. Dolours had been a student civil rights protester on the Burntollet march in early 1969. Along with them was Gerard Kelly from Ballymurphy. He would later become a leading member of the Provisional Army Council.

40. Seven people were later arrested and charged in connection with these murders. Four of them, Paul Hill, Gerard Conlon, Patrick Armstrong, and Carole Richardson, who became known as "The Guildford Four," were convicted of the Guildford bombing itself. All later had their convictions overturned, but only after serving long sentences. The experience of Paul Conlon, whose father, Giuseppe, died while still imprisoned because of the bombings, became the basis of the successful movie *In the Name of the Father*.

41. Chris Mullin, *Error of Judgment: The Truth About the Birmingham Bombs.* Dublin: Poolbeg Press, 1989. One of the IRA men involved later claimed to journalist Chris Mullin that they had given thirty minutes warning. Even if true, as Mullin points out, the warning was so vague as to be misleading.

42. Four of the six signed confessions. There was forensic evidence against two—traces of an explosive substance were found on their hands. But in October 1985 an investigative television program, *World in Action,* showed that the original forensic tests were not reliable enough to sustain convictions. After several appeals, all were released in January 1990.

43. Mullin, *Error of Judgment.*

44. Quoted in Bew and Gillespie, *Northern Ireland.*

45. McKittrick and Holland, *The Assassins.*

46. In 1993, during secret talks between the British and the Provisionals, a British government representative would admit that in 1975 the Labour government had set out to "con" the IRA and had succeeded. See chapter 7.

47. By 1977, eighteen hundred people had died as a result of the conflict, which is more than half of the total number killed between 1969 and 1994.

CHAPTER 4
THE POLITICS OF DESPAIR: 1977–1981

1. By 1976 unemployment in the majority nationalist counties Derry, Tyrone, and Fermanagh had risen to 21.3 percent—more than double what it had been five years earlier. In Belfast during the same period it had risen to 8.3 percent from 4.6 percent.

2. Chairman Lord Gardiner, *The Report to Consider in the Context of Civil Liberties and Human Rights, Measures to Deal with Terrorism in Northern Ireland.*

3. Ibid.

4. The gang carried out a series of mass murders, beginning in October 1975, when they murdered four Catholics in a bottling plant. Included among the dead were two sisters. In February 1976 the gang murdered two Protestants, mistaking them for Catholics, in a gun attack on a truckload of workmen. In June the same year they shot up a downtown bar, killing five customers, three of whom were Protestants; one of them was a UVF man. Murphy and his men also killed at least three UDA men, one of whom, Noel Shaw, he tied to a chair and "executed" on a stage in a loyalist drinking club in front of a crowd of drinkers.

5. Martin Dillon, *The Shankill Butchers: A Case Study of Mass Murder.* London: Hutchinson, 1989.

6. Interview with John White, 1998. In jail White struck up friendships with members of the Official IRA, who impressed him with their socialist analysis of the Northern Ireland situation and helped convince him of the futility of sectarian violence. When released seventeen years later, he became active in the peace process.

7. Peter Taylor, *Beating the Terrorists? Interrogation in Omagh, Gough and Castlereagh.* London: Penguin, 1980.

8. Drumm's wife, Maire, had been the firebrand vice president of Sinn Fein. She once threatened in a speech to dismantle Belfast brick by brick. On October 28, 1976, a joint UDA-UVF hit squad murdered her in the Mater Hospital, Belfast, where she was a patient.

9. Interview with Billy McKee, 1998. Soon afterward, McKee was sent to New York to look into fund-raising problems. A former IRA man and ex-paratrooper, Pete "the Para" McMullen, who had been extorting money from Irish-American bar owners in the city, supposedly on the IRA's behalf, assumed he was the target of McKee's inquiry and fled to San Francisco. There, he handed himself over to the police and became the subject of a long-running extradition battle with the British government, which he eventually lost.

10. Taylor, *Beating the Terrorists?*

11. Ibid.

12. David McKittrick, *Endgame: The Search for Peace in Northern Ireland.* Belfast: Blackstaff Press, 1995. This pattern persisted over the decades. In one small Protestant border community of west Tyrone, Victoria Bridge, the IRA murdered fourteen men between 1983 and 1991.

13. Chris Ryder, *The RUC, 1922–1997: A Force Under Fire.* London: Mandarin Paperback, 1997.

14. Interview with Andy Tyrie, 1979. Only eight Catholics were killed during 1978, the lowest number since 1970. Of those eight only one, twenty-nine-year-old Thomas Trainor, was a member of a republican group. Trainor was commanding officer of the INLA in Armagh when he and a friend were shot to death by the UVF on March 8.

15. The other sections were E1, administration; E2, training; E7, TCG work; and E9, specialized surveillance, which was established in 1988. (See chapter 8.)

16. Jack Holland and Susan Phoenix, *Phoenix: Policing the Shadows: The Secret War Against Terrorism in Northern Ireland.* London: Hodder and Stoughton, 1996.

17. Mark Urban, *Big Boys' Rules: The SAS and the Secret War Against the IRA.* London: Faber and Faber, 1992.

18. On December 12, 1977, an SAS unit in Derry shot dead an eighteen-year-old member of INLA, Colm McNutt, as he tried to hijack a car. McNutt was unarmed at the time. On February 26, 1978, the SAS struck again, killing Provisional IRA member Paul Duffy, age twenty-three, at an IRA arms dump in an unoccupied farmhouse in County Tyrone. Denis Heaney was shot dead in Derry on June 10 by SAS men who said he had tried to hijack their car. Witnesses claim he was shot without warning as he walked along the street. Another Derry member of the Provisional IRA, fifty-year-old Patrick Duffy, was shot dead on November 24 in a house that was being used as an arms dump. SAS soldiers said he had taken a gun from a wardrobe when they opened fire. This was disputed by the dead man's widow. And between July and September, the SAS killed two innocent civilians, John Boyle and James Taylor. Boyle, sixteen, was shot dead at an IRA arms dump, which he had discovered earlier and which had been reported to the police. Two SAS men were charged with his murder and acquitted. Taylor was out wildfowling when he became caught up in an undercover operation and was shot.

19. Holland and Phoenix, *Phoenix.*

20. Ignorance about groups like the UDA was common among Irish Americans, partly as a result of the fact that the U.S. media virtually ignored loyalist terrorism. But it was also because it served the interests of republican propaganda not to play it up except when Sinn Fein could present Protestant paramilitaries as British controlled. They were able to do that only because of widespread ignorance as to the nature of the UDA and UVF.

21. The Irish government compiled a document showing links between the caucus and the Provisional IRA. However, by 1979 the INC and the Provisionals had parted company following an acrimonious dispute.

22. Jack Holland, *The American Connection: U.S. Guns, Money, and Influence in Northern Ireland.* New York: Viking, 1987.

23. Ibid.

24. Ibid.

25. In 1979, however, Biaggi succeeded in getting Congress to block the sale of weapons from a U.S. company to the RUC, citing a law that prohibits U.S. companies from selling guns to any group that has violated civil rights. The vote banning the sale could not have been taken on a more provocative date: July 12.

26. Connors was later murdered by the Mafia in a gangland dispute.

27. Holland, *The American Connection.*

28. By that time all but one of the original six M-60s from Harrison had been captured, after claiming the lives of twelve soldiers and RUC men. An M-60 was recovered on May 2, 1980, after a gun battle in which an SAS officer, Herbert Westmacott, was killed. One of those arrested at the scene was Joe Doherty, who later escaped prison and fled to the United States where he became the subject of a celebrated extradition battle. Among his most prominent defenders was George Harrison.

29. Harrison believed that McLogan, who was found dead with a bullet wound in the head, had been murdered on the orders of the IRA leadership because of his opposition to the course of reform being undertaken at the time. An inquiry was promised but never undertaken.

30. Interviews with George Harrison, 1985, 1998. In a later account, *The IRA and Sinn Fein* by Peter Taylor (London: Bloomsbury, 1997), it was claimed that the IRA told Harrison he was being replaced. According to Harrison the claim is untrue. In fact, he says he came under increasing pressure from the leadership to supply more weapons in 1980 and 1981.

31. Interview with George Harrison, 1985.

32. All five men were eventually acquitted in 1982 after a trial notable for the ingenuity of its defense. The defense convinced the Brooklyn jury that De Meo had been working all along with the CIA. Since the CIA is authorized to export weapons without a license, none of the five IRA supporters was breaking the law because they were under CIA supervision. Official sources dismissed the allegations about De Meo as absurd. However, there was proof that at some point De Meo worked for government agents. In 1969, gunrunning charges were dropped against him to protect a source. Wisely, the defense did not ask Harrison, a convinced leftist, to take the stand.

33. Tim Pat Coogan, *The Troubles: Ireland's Ordeal, 1966–1995, and the Search for Peace.* London: Hutchinson, 1995.

34. Gerry Adams, *Before the Dawn.*

35. Jack Holland and Henry McDonald, *INLA: Deadly Divisions.* Dublin: Poolbeg, 1994. INLA had enjoyed something of a resurgence in the late 1970s even though its founder, Seamus Costello, had been assassinated in 1977 by the Official IRA. It had linked up with Al Fatah shortly afterward and began receiving regular arms and explosive supplies from them. It had originally targeted Sir Robert Haydon, the British ambassador to Ireland, who had replaced Sir Christopher Ewart-Biggs, assassinated by the Provisionals in July 1976. On Remembrance Day, November 1978, a remote-controlled bomb planted under his prayer stool in Christchurch Cathedral in Dublin failed to explode, thanks to the fact that the ancient cathedral walls were too stout for the radio signal to penetrate. They then launched an elaborate plot to murder Roy Mason, sending a sniper team to his Barnsley constituency to stalk him. But this plot was aborted when it became clear that Labour was going to lose the election.

36. Colonel Michael Dewar, *The British Army in Northern Ireland.* London: Arms and Armour Press, 1996.

37. Ryder, *The RUC.*

38. Thatcher did, however, appoint a security coordinator to liaise between the army and the RUC. He was Sir Maurice Oldfield, former head of MI5—made famous in the James Bond thrillers as "Uncle." Oldfield, a homosexual, was forced to leave his post within six months after a compromising incident in a pub. He died shortly afterward of stomach cancer.

39. Adams, *Before the Dawn.*

40. Holland and McDonald, *INLA.*

41. The attack on McAliskey was different from the other three incidents, not only in that the assailants failed and were caught. McAliskey described later how they had burst into her home screaming and shouting, a demeanor far different from the calm, self-possessed assassins whom Suzanne Bunting had confronted in her bedroom a few months earlier. The fact also that the murderers of Daly and Bunting carried out their killings in the very heart of west Belfast, which they entered and left without leaving a trace—not even a getaway car linked to either incident was ever recovered—has suggested to some the involvement of the security forces. But the most likely culprit remains the UDA, which later did claim responsibility for the murders. They might well have acted on information from sympathetic UDR or RUC men. In July 1994 the Provisional IRA murdered Ray Smallwoods, who had been one of the three UDA men charged and convicted of the attempted murder of Mr. and Mrs. McAliskey.

42. The titles of some of the poems, ballads, and meditations will give an idea of their nature: "The Lark and the Freedom Fighter," "Weeping Winds," "The Windows of My Mind," "The Rhythm of Time," "Flowers, My Friend, Flowers," "The Rose of Rathfarham," and "Stars of Freedom."

43. Adams, *Before the Dawn.*

44. Ibid.

45. The ten who died were Bobby Sands (May 5), Francis Hughes (May 12), Ray McCreesh and Patsy O'Hara (May 21), Joe McDonnell (July 8), Martin Hurson (July 13), Kevin Lynch (August 1), Kieran Doherty (August 2), Thomas McElwee (August 8), and Michael Devine (August 20). Doherty endured the longest, going seventy-three days without food. Hurson died after only forty-six days. O'Hara, Lynch, and Devine were members of the INLA, the others of the Provisional IRA.

CHAPTER 5
BULLETS AND BALLOTS: 1981–1985

1. John Hume, *A New Ireland: Politics, Peace, and Reconciliation.* Boulder, Colo.: Roberts Rinehart, 1996.

2. Gerard Murray, *John Hume and the SDLP.* Dublin: Irish Academic Press, 1998.

3. Hume, *A New Ireland.*

4. Murray, *John Hume.*

5. Ronnie Munck, *The Irish Economy: Results and Prospects.* London: Pluto Press, 1993.

6. Murray, *John Hume.*

7. Jack Holland and Susan Phoenix, *Phoenix: Policing the Shadows: The Secret War Against Terrorism in Northern Ireland.* London: Hodder and Stoughton, 1996.

8. At a trial in 1985 involving Steenson, one of the police officers admitted that although he had been in the next street, he had been "taking a rest" when the gunmen murdered Stockman.

9. McCreery later fled to London, where his name was mentioned in a murder trial in 1993. He was believed to have been involved in providing ex-paramilitaries for London underworld figures who hired them as hitmen. By then he had disappeared. Craig's name was linked to a series of murders of loyalist figures by the Provisionals and the INLA. In October 1988 the UDA shot him dead in a pub in east Belfast.

10. During the course of the Ulster conflict, republicans murdered eight members of the judiciary, three judges, four magistrates, and an official who worked in the office of the director of public prosecutions.

11. Fitzsimmons and Murphy were acquitted and released to continue their violent careers. McCann was also returned to active service with the Provisionals. In March 1988 the Special Air Service killed him and two other IRA volunteers in Gibraltar (see chapter 6). Murphy was later convicted in connection with the deaths of two soldiers caught by an enraged Catholic mob at the

funeral of an IRA man killed during a loyalist attack on the funeral of those killed in Gibraltar.

12. His brother, Dessie, had been involved in a series of INLA murders in the Armagh area, including that of a UDR officer, killed with a UCBT in March 1979, and a female prison officer, shot dead as she left the Armagh women's prison in April 1979. He would later join the Provisional IRA and become the commanding officer of IRA operations in continental Europe. The SAS shot him dead along with another IRA man at an arms dump near Loughgall, County Armagh, in October 1990. Because of his expertise with UCBTs, Grew was one of the few INLA members ever questioned about the assassination of Airey Neave, in which he was not involved.

13. The judge at one of the trials, Lord Chief Justice Maurice Gibson, congratulated the accused officer for his marksmanship and for dispatching the terrorists to "the final court of justice." These remarks did not endear him to the Provisional IRA. An IRA bomb killed him and his wife in April 1987.

14. John Stalker, *The Stalker Affair.* London: Harrap, 1988.

15. Ibid.

16. When it is borne in mind that the RUC was subjected to a prolonged and organized campaign of violence that targeted its members both on and off duty, claiming the lives of 199 full-time constables and 101 reservists, its record in this regard stands up well when compared to that of other forces. For example, according to figures published in *The New York Times* (April 9, 1997), the New York City police killed more than one hundred civilians between 1992 and 1997.

17. In his career McGlinchey antagonized many fellow republicans. Two months after Dale's murder he murdered two south Armagh republicans, Eamon McMahon and Patrick Mackin, accusing them of cheating him of money from a robbery. His wife, Mary McGlinchey, was also involved, luring them to their deaths. McMahon came from a powerful south Armagh republican family. In February 1987 in revenge they murdered Mrs. McGlinchey at home as she bathed her two sons. By this time McGlinchey himself was behind bars. In February 1994, eleven months after he was released, he was gunned down on a street in Drogheda, County Louth, in front of his son, Dominic, who seven years earlier had witnessed his mother's murder. It is believed "Mad Dog" was murdered by the same killers who had claimed his wife.

18. Derek Dunne, *Out of the Maze: The True Story of the Biggest Jail Escape Since the War.* Dublin: Gill and MacMillan, 1988.

19. Previously, the biggest escape occurred on May 5, 1976, when nine INLA members dug a tunnel from Long Kesh. Two, including Gerard Steenson, were recaptured shortly afterward, but the others got safely south of the border in spite of an SAS attempt to stop them.

20. As of August 1992, five of the nineteen had been recaptured, three were

dead at the hands of the SAS, and eleven were still at large. Four of the eleven were in the United States: Kevin Barry McArt, Pol Brennan, Jimmy Smyth, and Terence Kirby—and later fought extradition battles to avoid returning to Northern Ireland.

21. Patrick Bishop and Eamonn Mallie, *The Provisional IRA.* London: Corgi Books, 1988.

22. Holland and Phoenix, *Phoenix: Policing the Shadows.*

23. Ibid.

24. W. D. Flackes and Sydney Elliott, *Northern Ireland: A Political Directory 1968–1993.* Belfast: Blackstaff Press, 1994.

25. Colm Keena, *A Biography of Gerry Adams.* Cork: Mercier Press, 1990.

26. Adams claimed that British intelligence was involved in the assassination attempt, as evidenced by the presence of undercover RUC operatives. However, given his prominence, their presence is hardly surprising. Had there been no RUC men present, Sinn Fein no doubt would have pointed to that as proof of collusion between loyalists and the security forces.

27. The first "supergrass" occurred in 1974 when UDA hitman Albert "Ginger" Baker gave evidence that led to the arrests of many leading UDA men in east Belfast.

28. Steenson was by now known as "Dr. Death." When he emerged from prison, the INLA split, and during the subsequent feud he was shot dead on March 14, 1987.

29. Margaret Thatcher, *The Downing Street Years.* New York: HarperCollins, 1993.

30. Murray, *John Hume.*

31. *The New Ireland Forum Report.*

32. Paul Bew and Gordon Gillespie, *Northern Ireland: A Chronology of the Troubles, 1968–1993.* London: Serif, 1996.

33. *The Sunday Times,* Sept. 20, 1998.

34. His administration pressed cases against IRA fugitives Peter McMullan, Dessie Mackin, William Quinn, and Joe Doherty. The courts found that all but Quinn were protected by the law's political offense provision and could not be extradited. It was a politically embarrassing setback since it recognized that the IRA's violence was politically motivated, not criminal as Reagan and Thatcher's propaganda claimed. Undeterred by the court's decisions, Reagan pressed ahead. In July 1985 he got the Senate to pass a redrafted version of the extradition treaty between the United States and Britain, diluting the political offense clause. All but Mackin ended up back in British jails.

35. Jack Holland, *The American Connection: U.S. Guns, Money and Influence in Northern Ireland.* New York: Viking, 1987.

36. John Hume, *A New Ireland.*

37. Robert Fisk, *The Point of No Return: The Strike Which Broke the British in Ulster.* London: Andre Deutsch, 1975.

38. Bew and Gillespie, *Northern Ireland.*

CHAPTER 6
QADDAFI'S GIFT: 1985–1990

1. Jack Holland and Henry McDonald, *INLA: Deadly Divisions.* Dublin: Poolbeg, 1994.

2. In June 1992 the Libyans offered to reveal details to the British government of arms shipped to Ireland. But it was not until late 1995 that they actually handed over such information. The U.N. acted as an intermediary when a breakdown of the arms supplies was made available in a series of exchanges between October 31 and November 20. (*Irish Echo,* December 20–26, 1995.) Although Britain found some gaps in the information, it acknowledged that it was comprehensive. Libya agreed to the arrangement as part of its efforts to have U.N. sanctions against it lifted.

3. Interview with republican activist, 1998.

4. Interview with republican activist, 1995.

5. Portacabins, huts made of lightweight material, were used to house Special Branch, MI5, SAS, and army intelligence officers assigned to the Tasking Coordination Groups. Whether the IRA realized this, and targeted McAvoy as a result, is not known.

6. The local Provisionals later justified this callous murder to a journalist. According to Kevin Toolis (*Rebel Hearts: Journeys within the IRA's Soul.* New York: Picador, 1995), "The Henry brothers are collaborating in the oppression of the nationalist people by taking part in that work, just as the British crown is forcing those workers to prostitute themselves because of the huge money involved. They are corrupting the people. They have been warned countless times to stop."

7. Brendan O'Brien, *The Long War: The IRA and Sinn Fein, 1985 to Today.* Dublin: O'Brien Press, 1993.

8. Jack Holland and Susan Phoenix, *Phoenix: Policing the Shadows: The Secret War Against Terrorism in Northern Ireland.*

9. *Just News, Bulletin of the Committee on the Administration of Justice,* June 1995.

10. At an inquest into the shootings in 1993, a coroner described the crime-scene photographs as "quite horrifying."

11. The feud started over a dispute as to whether or not the INLA should disband. Steenson and his men believed it was so badly corrupted that it had to be replaced. The leaders of the opposite faction, including its chief of staff,

John O'Reilly, were invited to meet with Steenson to discuss the matter. The venue was a hotel outside Drogheda, about thirty miles north of Dublin. O'Reilly and three others were waiting for Steenson to arrive when he burst in disguised in a wig and, along with another gunman, opened fire on the delegation. O'Reilly and Thomas Power (an INLA activist from Belfast) were killed, and a third man was wounded. A fourth, Hugh "Cueball" Torney, escaped and later became chief of staff. There followed a series of revenge killings that ceased only when Steenson himself was gunned down in west Belfast on March 15, at age twenty-nine.

12. Kevin Toolis, *Rebel Hearts.*

13. Interview with Billy McKee, 1998.

14. Interview with Danny Morrison, 1988.

15. Marley's funeral produced a tense standoff between the Provisionals, who wanted a paramilitary display, and the RUC, who wanted to prevent it. The funeral was postponed twice, and clashes broke out between the police and the mourners. The result was a public relations disaster for the RUC, according to Jack Hermon, the chief constable.

16. David McKittrick and Jack Holland, *The Assassins: A History of the Ulster Defense Association.* Unpublished.

17. David McKittrick, *Dispatches from Belfast.* Belfast: Blackstaff Press, 1989.

18. Ibid.

19. Payne was sentenced to nineteen years in prison on November 1, 1988.

20. McKittrick, *Dispatches from Belfast.*

21. John Hume, *A New Ireland: Politics, Peace, and Reconciliation.* Boulder, Colo.: Roberts Rinehart, 1996.

22. Forty-one people were later charged in connection with the soldiers' deaths. Three were convicted under a law based on South African legislation that allowed serious charges, including murder, to be brought against the accused even though he or she might not have been present when the crime was committed, as long as "common purpose" could be established. Patrick Kane, Michael Timmons, and Sean Kelly were not even present when the soldiers met their deaths but nonetheless were found guilty of murder and other, lesser charges. The case gave rise to controversy, especially after it was revealed that Kane was mentally retarded and had not fully comprehended the charges brought against him. The convictions were eventually overturned. Another of those convicted in connection with the killings was Alex Murphy, an IRA gunman who had been involved in the plot to murder Judge Kelly in 1983.

23. Anthony McIntyre, *Modern Irish Republicanism: The Product of British State Strategies.* Queen's University, Belfast. Unpublished.

24. Paul Bew and Gordon Gillespie, *Northern Ireland: A Chronology of the Troubles, 1968–1993*. London: Serif, 1996.

25. *The London Sunday Times,* September 20, 1998. Douglas Hurd was home secretary at the time and, according to Mark Stewart, was ashamed of the measures he had introduced that barred Sinn Fein from the media.

26. It had taken a year for the security services to realize the size of Qaddafi's contribution to the Provisionals' war chest. When they did, a British official described their failure to detect the shipments as Britain's biggest intelligence failure since World War II.

27. *Irish Echo,* December 31, 1988.

28. In the same election the Workers' Party, which descended from Official Sinn Fein, won seven seats in the Dail. The Official IRA had left behind the armed struggle by the late 1970s when its political wing changed its name to the Workers' Party. To Sinn Fein, the example of the Workers' Party was both a temptation and a dire warning. It was achieving political success, but the cost (as Sinn Fein saw it) was the complete dilution of its republicanism to the point of becoming one of the Provisionals' harshest critics.

29. Interview with an IRA member, 1998. An IRA source came forward with this information in order to refute claims made by Sean O'Callaghan, a former member of the Provisionals who became a police agent. O'Callaghan attracted a lot of publicity in 1997 with claims that he was involved in an IRA plot to murder Princess Diana, which he says he deliberately botched in order to save her life. According to the IRA source, who was active in Britain in the 1980s and early 1990s, the Royal family was not considered a "legitimate target," and no such plot was ever hatched.

30. Professor Wilkinson had also earned the Provisionals' enmity when he testified in an extradition hearing against Joe Doherty in New York in December 1984. Doherty, who escaped from a Belfast jail in 1981, was wanted in connection with the murder of an SAS captain. The attempt on Wilkinson's life did not deter the terrorism expert. After the conference he went to Germany to testify at the extradition hearing of Donna Maguire, an IRA member believed to have been involved in a series of attacks on British targets in Europe.

Initial reports about the Green Park incident said that a minister in the Thatcher cabinet, William Waldegrave, was the target. These were incorrect and seem to have been part of a deliberate IRA plan to mislead.

31. Danny Morrison was arrested on January 7, 1990, next door to a house where the Provisionals were interrogating a suspected informer, Sandy Lynch. The RUC believed that Morrison was a prominent member of the so-called Civil Administration Team, the IRA's informer-hunting unit. He was later sentenced to eight years on charges in connection with the incident. Lynch had

been a member of the INLA and was involved in many crimes, including the murder of Gerard Steenson during the feud of early 1987. At the Special Branch's request he infiltrated the Provisionals after some INLA members became suspicious of him. They kept their suspicions to themselves and did not warn the IRA.

32. Sinn Fein, *Setting the Record Straight: A Record of Communications Between Sinn Fein and the British Government, October 1990–November 1993.*

CHAPTER 7
THE TWILIGHT OF THE ARMED CAMPAIGN: 1990–1994

1. Interview with activist, 1995.

2. For instance, Frank Ryan, twenty-five, and Patricia Black, eighteen, who blew themselves up while carrying out a Provisional bombing operation in St. Albans, England, on November 15, 1991, were described by the police as "lily white," without any previously known links to the republican movement. But the Special Branch later identified Black, who was buried on her nineteenth birthday, as perhaps having been the unknown female involved in an assassination attempt in south Belfast in August 1991.

3. He was quoted as saying, "The IRA terrorists are better equipped, better resourced, better led, bolder and more secure against our penetration than at any time before. . . . If we don't intern, it's a long haul." *The Independent on Sunday,* November 17, 1991.

4. Henry Patterson, *The Politics of Illusion: A Political History of the IRA.* London: Serif, 1997.

5. In 1992 the Provisional IRA killed almost as many of its own members (six) who were suspected informers as it did soldiers and policemen.

6. The Stevens inquiry led to the arrest and conviction of three UDR members on serious charges. Seventeen others had minor charges brought against them, some of which resulted in convictions. In his report, published in 1990, Stevens said he found no evidence of institutionalized collusion within the RUC or the UDR. By then, however, the UDR had long been disgraced in the eyes of Ulster nationalists. By 1975, five years after it was formed, over eighty of its members or ex-members were charged with terrorist offenses. This figure increased to almost two hundred in 1990, prompting an Irish government minister to say that the UDR had "no role to play in Northern Ireland." Between 1970 and 1992, 197 UDR members were murdered.

7. The two other Catholics who died as a result of the alleged failure to act on Nelson's information were Terence McDaid, whose brother, Declan, a known republican, had been the target, and Gerard Slane, who had no paramilitary links. According to Nelson's handler, who appeared as a witness for him in court, he had uncovered threats to the lives of 217 people, only 4 of

whom died violently, including the 3 the UDA murdered. The fourth was Belfast IRA's explosive expert Daniel McCann, who seems to have been saved by the RUC only to be left to the SAS. There were UDA threats against the life of two other prominent Nationalist lawyers, Patrick McGrory and Mary McAleese, head of the Legal Institute at Queen's University, who became president of Ireland in 1997.

8. *Irish Echo,* October 30, 1991.

9. *Irish Echo,* February 12, 1992.

10. *The Independent,* August 11, 1992.

11. Henry Patterson, *The Politics of Illusion.*

12. Sinn Fein, *Setting the Record Straight: A Record of Communications Between Sinn Fein and the British Government, October 1990–November 1993.*

13. Ibid.

14. Ibid.

15. Ibid.

16. Ibid.

17. The IRA had called shorter cessations every Christmas since 1990, which was the first in fifteen years.

18. Sinn Fein, *Setting the Record Straight.*

19. Ibid.

20. In November 1993, leaks to the press about negotiations between Sinn Fein and the British government prompted the Northern Ireland secretary of state, Sir Patrick Mayhew, to categorically deny such meetings had taken place. On BBC television he stated, "There has been no negotiating with Sinn Fein; no official, as I see it, is alleged to have been talking to Sinn Fein on behalf of the British government." Subsequently, the prime minister's office also denied that there had been "protracted contact and dialogue" with the republican movement. These denials were repeated, and on November 20, John Major told the House of Commons that the prospect of talks with Gerry Adams would "turn his stomach." A week later Mayhew was forced to recant and admit there were contacts with Sinn Fein, but even then he attempted to limit the damage by claiming they had only begun in February 1993. In order to refute what it described as lies, Sinn Fein published some of the documents relating to its contacts with the government in December and a fuller account in January 1994. A number of documents were withheld, the party said, due to their "sensitivity." Some of these related to the so-called Irish peace process involving Hume, Adams, and others.

21. Mansergh's contacts with Adams, Mitchel McLaughlin, and Martin McGuinness came through a Catholic priest in west Belfast, Father Alec Reid. When Reynolds became taoiseach, they were subsumed into the general Irish peace initiative.

22. Interview with Pat Hume, 1998.

23. *Irish Echo,* April 15–21, 1992.

24. This was apparently because during the talks Hume allegedly avoided condemning recent IRA bomb attacks, enhancing the easy familiarity that seemed to exist between the SDLP leader and Sinn Fein officials such as McLaughlin. Among the subjects they discussed was the IRA's choice of targets and the shift of Northern Ireland's Protestant population to such areas as north Down.

25. Paul Bew and Gordon Gillespie, *Northern Ireland: A Chronology, 1968–1993.*

26. Paul Bew and Gordon Gillespie, *The Northern Ireland Peace Process, 1993–1996: A Chronology.* London: Serif, 1996.

27. Ibid.

28. Ibid.

29. Ibid.

30. Anthony McIntyre, *Modern Irish Republicanism: The Product of British State Strategies.* Queen's University, Belfast. Unpublished.

31. In fact, the RUC Special Branch was kept fully informed as to what transpired and was provided with Lynch's arguments in favor of lifting the ban in advance of the meeting with Holl.

32. *The Sunday Life,* July 26, 1992.

33. The last was twenty-one-year-old Alexander Bannister, who died on August 8, 1988, after being shot by a sniper three weeks earlier while on foot patrol in Ballymurphy, west Belfast.

34. Coffee-jar bombs claimed the lives of one soldier in May 1991 and a civilian the following August. A soldier wounded in the May attack lost both his legs and pleaded to his colleagues, "Shoot me, shoot me." He survived.

35. *The Independent,* November 11, 1992.

36. Joe Doherty and two other IRA men were also arrested and charged with the murder. Doherty escaped along with Magee, Angelo Fusco, and Robert Campbell, and later made his way to New York where he became the center of a long-running extradition case. He was finally deported to Belfast in February 1992 to serve a murder sentence.

37. In murals around the Shankill Road, "C" company's exploits are celebrated under the slogan "Simply the Best," taken from a famous song by the American rock singer Tina Turner. The song is played whenever its members appear on political platforms. No doubt Ms. Turner would be surprised at the use to which her lyrics have been put.

38. Phoenix, along with twenty-four other leading intelligence officers and four crew members, died in a helicopter crash in Scotland on June 2, 1994.

39. McIntyre, *Modern Irish Republicanism.*

40. Ibid.

41. On July 29 an ASU murdered UDA activists Joe Bratty and Ray Elder on the Ormeau Road in south Belfast, not far from the betting shop where two years before five Catholics were shot dead in an attack that the IRA blamed on Bratty and Elder.

42. August 31, 1994, was the twenty-first anniversary of the death of Provisional IRA volunteer Paddy Mulvenna, who was married to one of Gerry Adams's sisters. Mulvenna was shot dead along with Jim Bryson in Ballymurphy after an encounter with British troops. It has been suggested that it was not a coincidence that the cease-fire was announced on that date. But Adams claims he was only reminded of it on the day itself when he was speaking before a crowd on the Falls Road.

43. This figure includes the 3 UVF murders in 1966 as well as 101 deaths in the Irish republic, 117 in Britain, and 18 on mainland Europe. However, the estimate is not exact. It does not include a number of people who died at the hands of the IRA or other paramilitary groups after being kidnapped and whose bodies have never been recovered.

CHAPTER 8
TO FORSAKE ARMS: 1994–1998

1. *Irish Echo,* November 1, 1994.

2. *Irish Echo,* March 1, 1995.

3. Quoted in Paul Bew and Gordon Gillespie, *The Northern Ireland Peace Process, 1993–1996: A Chronology.* London: Serif, 1996.

4. In December 1994 the Democratic Left, a breakaway from the Workers' Party, entered into a coalition government in the south with the Irish Labour Party and Fine Gael, their links to the violent past all but forgotten. The party merged with the Labour Party in 1999.

5. When told of Clinton's intention to shake hands with Adams, Sir Patrick Mayhew said that "50,000,000 British people would not be pleased." The point was that among the fifty million British people there was not one vote for Clinton, but among the twenty million Irish Americans, there was.

6. Clinton liked nothing more than to recount the story of his first trip to Ireland, as he did to this author at a White House party in June 1998. He must be one of the few people for whom the mention of Belfast evokes a broad smile.

7. Trevor Birney and Julian O'Neill, *When the President Calls.* Derry: Guildhall Press, 1997.

8. *Irish Echo,* February 7, 1996.

9. Arrested in the same sweep was Rose McLaughlin, a twenty-six-year-old schoolteacher who lived in Bangor, in north Down. When the police placed her picture in several police stations in the area seeking information about her,

a number of different RUC officers came forward. Each said he was having an affair with her. It appears she was on an intelligence-gathering operation. Also part of the same unit was Charles Tumelty, a thirty-five-year-old law graduate who worked in a legal firm and had access to information on leading judges and police officers. Storey, who had slipped through the fingers of the RUC on many occasions before, did so again in 1998, when he was acquitted.

10. Quoted by Anthony McIntyre in *The Sunday Tribune*, January 25, 1998.

11. *The Guardian,* May 22, 1998.

12. Until the feud, INLA had been quiet since 1994. Its last significant action was the assassination of three loyalists on the Shankill Road on June 16 that year. Two of the dead were leading members of the UVF. Hugh Torney was INLA chief of staff until 1995, when he and three others were arrested with an arms consignment near Dublin. After he was jailed, he was replaced by Gino Gallagher. Released on bail, Torney ordered Gallagher's murder, which sparked the feud. Torney, a republican since 1970, had survived at least two other assassination attempts. Fate caught up with him on September 3, 1996, in Lurgan, County Armagh, where he was gunned down on the street.

13. *Irish Echo,* November 12, 1997.

14. *Irish Echo,* March 18, 1998.

15. Both governments argued that it was linked to a organization which was still using violence, and therefore the party was in violation of the Mitchell principles. The Ulster Democratic Party suffered a similar suspension because the UDA had been connected to several murders in January.

16. Locked in the negotiations were the Ulster Unionist Party, still the most powerful Protestant party, and the paramilitary-linked Ulster Democratic Party and Progressive Unionist Party. On the nationalist side were the SDLP and Sinn Fein. The remaining three parties were the Alliance Party, the tiny Northern Ireland Labour Party, and a newcomer on the Ulster political scene, the Northern Ireland Women's Coalition. In fact, they were as much a cultural phenomenon as a political one. The Women's Coalition was formed in 1996. A handful of women, Protestant and Catholic, middle class and working class, decided they were sick of the male-dominated sectarian biases that molded Ulster's political life into intractable positions. Paisley's DUP and a smaller fragment of the Unionist block, the United Kingdom Unionist Party, remained on the outside braying their warnings of treachery and betrayal.

17. *Irish Echo,* April 8, 1998.

18. *Irish Echo,* September 16, 1998.

19. However, Orange protesters continued to occupy fields near the march site into 1999, threatening "no surrender" until they got permission to march.

CHAPTER 9
IN CONCLUSION: TIME PAST AND TIME PRESENT

1. Sonia Orwell and Ian Angus, eds., *The Collected Essays, Journalism and Letters of George Orwell. Volume 4: In Front of Your Nose.* London: Penguin Books, 1970.

2. Andy Pollak, ed., *A Citizens' Inquiry: The Opsahl Report on Northern Ireland.* Dublin: Lilliput Press, 1993.

3. In his acceptance speech, Trimble—the first Unionist and Orangeman ever awarded the Nobel Prize—seemed at times just as uncomfortable as many of his fellow Protestants with this honor that put the spotlight of world attention on him at a time when he was mired in a stalemate with his Nationalist colleagues in the assembly over the setting up of the new executive. He began by disavowing any attempt to make a "vision" speech, which he condemned for tending to vagueness and utopianism. Instead, he invoked the scientific traditions of the Enlightenment, quoting the eighteenth-century Anglo-Irish political philosopher Edmund Burke's criticism of the French revolution for unleashing dangerous tendencies toward violence and "fascism," as Trimble termed it. This, in turn, he associated with Irish republicanism, using the alleged link as an excuse to attack the IRA and Sinn Fein for not disarming. In other words, the Unionist leader did not rise to the occasion but, with one eye on his constituency back home, let the occasion sink to the level of local politics.

Hume in his speech could just as easily have quoted Burke about the need for magnanimity in politics and gone on to point out that the Orange Order, of which Trimble was a member, was still threatening to defy the forces of law and order in Portadown and march there where Catholic neighbors did not want them. Had local political concerns dictated his remarks, he might have been tempted to suggest that his fellow Nobel laureate address his words about the enlightenment to his Orange brethren in Portadown. Hume's speech was about his vision of how divisions can be overcome when allegiances are in conflict. Even his supporters acknowledged it was the one he had been making without many variations for thirty years. It was just that the Nobel committee had finally caught up with him.

GLOSSARY

PARAMILITARY AND MILITARY

1. Republican

Continuity IRA: Formed in 1986 by hard-line republicans who disagreed with the Provisional IRA's decision to recognize the Irish parliament. Outlawed in 1997.

Irish National Liberation Army: Formed from a split within the Official IRA mainly because of the refusal of the leadership to end its cease-fire.

Irish People's Liberation Organization: Formed in 1986 when a faction within the INLA decided the leadership had become corrupted. Banned in 1990.

Official IRA: Formed in 1969 when the IRA split. Supported left-wing strategies of the then leadership. On cease-fire since May 1972.

Provisional IRA: Formed in 1969 by those within the IRA who wanted a more aggressive military posture and who were uneasy about the political strategies of the leadership. The biggest and most powerful of the republican organizations.

Real IRA: Formed in late 1997 by dissidents within the Provisional IRA who rejected the organization's peace strategies.

2. Loyalist

Combined Loyalist Military Command: Coordinating group for all the loyalist paramilitary organizations.

Loyalist Volunteer Force: Formed in 1996 by disaffected members of the

Ulster Volunteer Force who were opposed to the peace process. Outlawed in 1997. After a brief assassination campaign, it called a cease-fire in 1998.

Red Hand Commandos: Formed in 1971. The smallest of the loyalist groups, it was involved in a brief assassination campaign before disappearing to reemerge in 1991.

Ulster Defense Association: The largest of the Protestant paramilitary groups. Formed in 1971 from bands of vigilantes in Belfast. Behind a series of assassinations and bombings, it could claim twenty thousand members in 1974. It remained legal until 1992.

Ulster Freedom Fighters: Created in 1973 in order to claim responsibility for assassinations carried out by the Ulster Defense Association. Banned in 1973.

Ulster Volunteer Force: Named after the Protestant militia that at the turn of the century opposed Home Rule. It was formed in 1966 and declared illegal that same year. It became involved in widespread sectarian violence in the early 1970s.

3. Security Forces

B-Specials: A part-time paramilitary police force set up shortly after the creation of Northern Ireland to combat the IRA. It was disbanded in 1970.

MI5: Otherwise known as BOX, Britain's internal intelligence-gathering unit. Involved in Northern Ireland in mainly bugging and wiretapping operations since the 1970s, working with the police and army. Took over control of all wiretapping operations in 1994.

Royal Irish Regiment: Formed in 1992 following the disbandment of the Ulster Defense Regiment as a mainly Ulster-based unit within the British army.

Royal Ulster Constabulary: Northern Ireland's police force, created in 1922. Mainly Protestant. Reformed in 1970. Plans to introduce further reforms were part of the overall peace settlement in 1998.

Special Air Service: Crack antiterrorist undercover British army force, known also as the Troop. Introduced into Northern Ireland in 1976.

Ulster Defense Regiment: Replaced the B-Specials in 1970. Locally recruited militia under the British army. In 1992 was amalgamated with the Royal Irish Rangers to form the Royal Irish Regiment.

4. Political

Alliance Party: Formed in 1970 in an attempt to attract the support of moderates in both communities.

Democratic Left: Formed from a split within the Workers' Party in 1992. Moderate leftist. Merged with Irish Labour Party in 1999.

Democratic Unionist Party: Formed in 1971 by the Reverend Ian Paisley to promote uncompromising unionist policies.

Fianna Fail: The largest party in the Irish republic. Founded in 1926 from republicans who left Sinn Fein.

Fine Gael: The second largest party in the Irish republic. Founded in 1933 from various right-wing groups.

Friends of Sinn Fein: Set up in Washington, D.C., after the first IRA cease-fire in 1994 to lobby for and raise money on behalf of Sinn Fein in America.

Irish Northern Aid: Established by the Provisional IRA in New York in 1970 to raise money for republican prisoners and propagandize on behalf of republican issues in the United States.

Irish Republican Socialist Party: Formed in 1974, a left-wing republican group that split from the Official IRA and is linked to the INLA.

Nationalist Party: For many years the main political opposition to partition in Northern Ireland. Became defunct in the early 1970s.

Northern Ireland Civil Rights Association: Formed in 1967 to draw attention to discrimination against Catholics in jobs and housing.

Northern Ireland Women's Coalition: Formed in 1996 to fight women's exclusion from local politics, it campaigns for human rights and cross-community initiatives.

Orange Order: The largest Protestant organization in Northern Ireland. Formed in 1795 during a period of faction fighting between Catholics and Protestants, it now has branches worldwide. Holds marches every summer throughout Northern Ireland.

People's Democracy: Radical students' group formed in 1968 in Queen's University, Belfast.

Progressive Unionist Party: The political wing of the Ulster Volunteer Force.

Sinn Fein: The political wing of the IRA. Formed originally in 1905 to campaign for Home Rule. Has gone through many transformations. Now espouses moderate left-wing policies and a united Ireland.

Social Democratic and Labor Party: The largest nationalist party in Northern Ireland. Founded in 1970 to promote a constitutional solution to the crisis based on winning the consent of Protestants to reforming the state and building closer ties to the Irish republic with the ultimate aim of a united Ireland.

Ulster Unionist Party: From the nineteenth century, the largest party in Ulster. After partition, its chief aim was maintaining Northern Ireland as a part of the United Kingdom.

Workers' Party: Originally Official Sinn Fein, the political wing of the Official IRA. Became the Workers' Party in 1982. Heavily influenced at one time by Soviet model of communism.

INDEX

28 ~~14~~ DAYS

DATE DUE			
SEP 1 7	1999		
OCT 1 6	1999		
DEC 1 3	1999		
JAN 4	2000		
JAN 3 0	2000		
JUN 2 1	2003		

WITHDRAWN

DA 990 .U46 H63 1999
Holland, Jack, 1947-
Hope against history

REDWOOD LIBRARY & ATHENAEUM
50 Bellevue Ave.
Newport, RI 02840-3292

GAYLORD M2